W. M. Bertholds

Connor D'Arcy's struggles

W. M. Bertholds

Connor D'Arcy's struggles

ISBN/EAN: 9783741188015

Manufactured in Europe, USA, Canada, Australia, Japa

Cover: Foto ©Andreas Hilbeck / pixelio.de

Manufactured and distributed by brebook publishing software (www.brebook.com)

W. M. Bertholds

Connor D'Arcy's struggles

CONNOR D'ARCY'S STRUGGLES.

Connor D'Arcy's Struggles.

BY

Mrs. W. M. BERTHOLDS,

AUTHOR OF "ONE IN A CROWD," "UNCLE JOHN'S JEWELS,"
"A GOLDEN HAND," ETC., ETC.

New York, Cincinnati, Chicago:
BENZIGER BROTHERS,
Printers to the Holy Apostolic See.

COPYRIGHT, 1893, BY BENZIGER BROTHERS.

CONTENTS.

		PAGE
Chapter I.,	. . . .	7
Chapter II.,	. . . .	15
Chapter III.,	. . . .	24
Chapter IV.,	. . . .	33
Chapter V.,	. . . .	44
Chapter VI.,	. . . .	56
Chapter VII.,	. . . .	66
Chapter VIII.,	. . . .	75
Chapter IX.,	. . . .	87
Chapter X.,	. . . .	97
Chapter XI.,	. . . .	107
Chapter XII.,	. . . .	118
Chapter XIII.,	. . . .	128
Chapter XIV.,	. . . .	141
Chapter XV.,	. . . .	153

CHAPTER XVI., ...

CHAPTER XVII., ...

CHAPTER XVIII., ...

CHAPTER XIX., ...

CHAPTER XX., ...

CHAPTER XXI., ...

CHAPTER XXII., ...

CHAPTER XXIII., ...

CHAPTER XXIV., ...

CHAPTER XXV., ...

CHAPTER XXVI., ...

CHAPTER XXVII., ...

CHAPTER XXVIII., ...

CHAPTER XXIX., ...

CONNOR D'ARCY'S STRUGGLES.

Chapter I.

"Like April morning clouds, that pass
With varying shadows o'er the grass,
And imitate on field and furrow
Life's chequered game of joy and sorrow."
—Sir Walter Scott.

"HOW the rain keeps pattering on the window! I wish it would stop. It's so cold, such a wretched, pitiless day, and we have such a tiny fire. Don't you think, Denise, that you could contrive to make it burn brighter? Do try."

"I wish I could, dear, for mamma's sake and yours. Are you so very cold, Eva?"

"Cold! I'm starved with cold and famishing with hunger," said the girl piteously.

"I am so sorry, dear," responded Denise D'Arcy, touching her sister's bright hair caressingly; "but do not let mamma hear you, she is so weak and ill. Try to bear it a little longer. In another hour Teddy will be home, and then we shall have a nice cup of tea and a little more fire."

"Another hour! I think I shall certainly die before then. I wish I were like you," Eva cried, in a tone of self-pity. "You never seem to feel anything, while I am such a miserable creature I feel everything. I am always hungry and cold, except when the weather is hot; and then this nasty garret smothers me—it is such a wretched thing not to have nice clothes to wear, and large, handsome rooms to live in, as we used to have long ago. When I go with Aunt Kate to the park and see the ladies so richly dressed, and driving in such handsome carriages, I feel just hateful about being poor, like this, and I so long to be one of them. Now you needn't look at me like that, Denise; I know you're going to preach me a sermon on patience, but all the same it won't make me feel one bit better."

"No, my darling, I am not going to inflict a sermon on you," Denise said, tenderly folding an old faded shawl round her sister's shoulders and kissing the pretty, soft cheek. "What is the good, dear, in preaching patience to a poor little girl who is a victim to cold and hunger? But who knows, dear?—perhaps Connor may bring back a letter, and the sun may come from behind the clouds; then we will forget that the rain is pattering pitilessly against the window, and all our other little troubles. You are not so very cold now, are you?"

"You are always so hopeful, Denise," ignoring her sister's question, "but I don't see any room for hope. I quite believe that mamma will never get another letter from papa; it's years and years since he sent the last one, and if he had wanted to write we would have had a letter long ago; and it's awfully cruel of papa to desert mamma and us like that."

"Oh, do not say that, Eva," Denise cried, in low, shocked tones; "papa has not deserted mamma and us; things have gone wrong with him, you know, dear."

"Well, you must admit, Denise, they've taken a precious long time in coming all right again."

"It will all come right in God's good time, Eva, and

you know, dear mother says all good things come to those who can wait with patience."

"That's one of your many virtues, Denise; you've been endowed with so many there were none left for poor me."

"Do not talk such nonsense, Eva. Is not Aunt Kate very long? I am glad dear mamma continues to sleep so soundly."

"Poor auntie," Eva answered, with a little, low musical laugh, "has faith that should move mountains; surely her prayers will be answered some time and your patience rewarded; but I must be very wicked, for, like Thomas, I can only believe when I see."

"Hush, Eva! do not say such wicked things; prayer is a subject too sacred to jest upon. You know it does auntie good; she always returns from church so much brighter and happier; she seems to bring the sunshine with her into these dull attics when she has been to Mass or Benediction or steals away for an hour to pray as she has done now."

"An hour! Why, she has been two hours if she has been a minute. Perhaps she feels it warmer in church than in this wretched place," glancing with an expressive shiver around the poor, scantily furnished, but exceedingly clean attic-room; "but if she were as cold and hungry as I, she would not have strength. I never feel like praying when I am hungry."

"My poor Eva! I am so sorry that I cannot give you something to eat; but Teddy will soon be here now, and then——"

"Yes, I wish he would come. I wonder," she added, brightening perceptibly, "if Lottchen will come up. I wish she would ask me to tea; I do like to take tea with Lottchen; you are so proud you wouldn't go, just because we are poor and couldn't return it, but I think false pride is a foolish thing, and I wouldn't hurt Lottchen's feelings by always refusing to go in time for tea, and only going for the music. Of course I know music is very nice, and I like it dearly, and it's very kind of the Herr to let us practise on their beautiful piano; it has perfected our musical education, and I do so enjoy our weekly *soirée musicale*."

"Yes, dear, we owe a real debt of gratitude to the good Herr for spending so much of his precious time in instructing us, and our weekly *soirée musicale*, as you call it, with only the Herr for audience and director."

"He says we are splendid in our parts; but, Denise, do you know I quite envy Lottchen? She has everything she can desire. Her papa takes her away from London every summer, wherever she likes to go; she has been all over the Continent, and he buys her such beautiful clothes, and she has real jewels and lots of pretty things, and they have the drawing-room and two lovely bedrooms, and she doesn't need to work, but do just what she likes all day. Now don't regard me with that dreadfully shocked look. I can see that you think me mean and wicked, but I don't see why the artist man should have the dining room flat, and Herr von Rosenberg and Lottchen the drawing-room flat, with lots of room and air and everything they desire, while six of us are compelled to exist in these two poor attic-rooms, with dear, dear mamma an invalid, and Connor thankful to get twelve shillings weekly for copying, and he works so hard too, and poor Teddy glad to earn five shillings weekly from the grocer, and he has been off so early every morning this week, poor boy; and just think of him being degraded in that way—and papa a gentleman and mamma a lady—when he should be at college completing his education, and we should live in a handsome house, with servants and carriages, and should wear costly clothes and have everything."

"Hush, Eva, dear; it is all the will of God; we have no right to rebel or question His decrees. Just think, dear, how thankful we should be that we have dear mamma, Aunt Kate, Connor, and dear Teddy. See how much richer we are than Lottchen, who has only her father; and has not our good God shown His mercy to us in many ways, more especially by leaving to Aunt Kate out of her money, which might have been all lost, you know, sufficient to pay for even this shelter? But here is Connor——"

The words died away on her lips as a young man entered the room, on whose handsome, weary face were plainly written disappointment and bitterness.

"Come here, Connor!" came in a weak voice from a curtained recess where a bed was concealed. The invalid had not been asleep as the two girls had imagined, but had been intently listening for the opening of the door.

The young man, who had paused to shake the rain from his thin clothes before entering the room, on hearing his mother's voice flung down his hat, and with an effort at cheerfulness approached the bed.

"You have not been successful, Connor. Never mind, dear, it is sure to come some of these days. I know your father is alive and only waiting to get money to send to us. Poor father, I fear he may be far worse off than we are," said the invalid gently. "He thinks your aunt's money is quite safe, and he knows she would share her last farthing with us, as she promised to do, and, Heaven bless her, as she has done and is doing."

The young man bent down and kissed the pale, sweet face of his mother.

"I regret," he said, his face clouding momentarily, "that I did not call upon Mr. Philipson earlier; three weeks ago he joined some other scientific gentlemen and sailed for Egypt. There is only an elderly woman in charge of the house; she said that she thought her master would have liked to see you before going away, for he spoke of you, expressing considerable regret at not having had our address."

Mrs. D'Arcy sighed softly.

"I fear, Connor, that was mistaken pride on our part; but never mind, dear, our good God, who is so merciful, will bring light out of darkness and let my dear children be once more blessed with a father's protecting care. Do you think there would be any good in—in leaving our address now with the servant?"

"Once I thought of doing so, but the woman said her master intended being absent for two or three years, so I concluded to get your advice before taking any steps in the matter."

"Don't you think you might write to Mr. Philipson, and ask if any letters had come for mamma before he went away?" suggested Eva. "You would get an answer much quicker that way, I should think; perhaps, if you did leave the address with the woman, she might neglect to send it to her master."

Mrs. D'Arcy turned with a fond smile to the speaker.

"You are always so clever, Eveline; I think, Connor, dear, that is a very good suggestion. Of course the servant will have received instructions about forwarding any letters that may arrive for her master during his absence."

"Yes, she said Mr. Philipson was going to Alexandria, where he intended staying for some time, and she will forward his letters there until she receives further orders."

"Oh, Aunt Kate!" cried Denise, as the door opened and Miss D'Arcy, followed by Teddy, entered.

"Teddy and I met quite promiscuously, and went shopping on our own account, you see."

The rich, full, musical tones, unmistakably those of a

gentlewoman, dispelled the clouds, and every face, even that of the invalid, lighted up with pleasure, as all eyes were turned toward the speaker, whose ineffably shabby garments, betokening so positively the poverty of the wearer, could not conceal a certain elegance and grace which imparted a dignity that robbed shabbiness of its dinginess. She was young and very pretty, but the great charm of her face consisted more in the ever-changing expression, the fascination of the smiling blue eyes, the flitting dimples, and the delicacy of coloring than in perfection of features. A woman formed to gladden and brighten a home; cheerful, hopeful, prayerful, ever ready to soothe and comfort; but as unfit to fight the battle of life or to face all the shifts and struggles of poverty as a little child.

Kate D'Arcy could smile and suffer, making no sign; strong in her power of cheerful endurance, she could sit down, if needs be, and die of want; but she could not go out into the world and struggle for bread, as thousands in the great city of London were daily doing around her.

She could cheer others with pleasant words while her own heart was torn and bleeding; but she could not do as the girl by whose side she was now standing would do for those she loved one day not far distant.

Teddy, a delicate boy of fourteen, approached the fireside and deposited an armful of fagots on the hearthstone; then throwing aside his wet cap he joined the others, and kissing his mother, said a little shyly but with a bright smile:

"Mr. Brown gave me two shillings over my wages, mother, because I went to the shop an hour earlier every day this week and did two or three little odd things, and he says after next month he will give me seven shillings every week."

Mrs. D'Arcy smothered a sigh and touched caressingly the bright, animated face of the boy with her slender white hand.

"God bless my dear Teddy," she said gently.

While Denise coaxed the few embers with the addition of some more fuel into a cheerful blaze, Miss D'Arcy displayed her purchases.

"Now, my dear," she said, addressing her sister-in-law, "you must sharpen up your appetite; see what a delightful chop we have brought you; Denise will prepare it for you—she always cooks your chops so appetizingly; and you will take this biscuit and a nice cup of tea, after which you will feel quite refreshed."

"You always consider me first, Kate; what have you for yourself and the children, my dear?"

"What have I for myself and the children?" Kate repeated, turning her smiling face to the invalid. "Well, my dear, I have some of the most beautiful red herring. I think we shall all enjoy our tea this evening; and see, our clever Denise has got the kettle to boil already."

What a change this sunbeam of a woman and Teddy's seven shillings had wrought in that poor attic-room.

By common consent, Connor's late disappointment was not alluded to until after tea and the invalid had fallen into a refreshing slumber.

Chapter II.

"We make the world we live in, and we weave
About us webs of good or ill, which leave
Their impress on our souls."

CONNOR was soon busy cutting bread and otherwise assisting Denise in preparing the evening meal, which served for tea and supper. Miss D'Arcy, seated beside the invalid, talked brightly, in the full, rich tones which filled the room with a pleasant music.

Eva, still wrapped in the old shawl, was seated cozily beside the now cheerily burning fire, smiling and chattering gayly to Teddy while she contentedly consumed a slice of bread-and-butter which Connor had thoughtfully handed her.

Somehow, every one considered Eveline, from the invalid mother down to Teddy, Eva's junior by two years.

No one ever seemed to think she could either work or want.

When food was brought in, after the invalid she was first considered; the most delicate morsels were selected and given to Eva. She was the pet and darling of the family.

No one ever thought of sending her on a message or of letting her go unaccompanied into the streets of London.

Occasionally Denise succeeded in obtaining needlework from a warehouse in the city; but of late this work had entirely failed, and they had all been obliged to subsist on the pittance earned by Connor and Teddy.

Day after day brave Denise had gone forth in search of work, each morning with renewed hope and courage, cheerful and expectant, but only to return exhausted and dispirited, yet meeting with her brightest smile the loving mother's eyes, that read the pain and disappointment which Denise could not succeed in hiding from them.

They were all seated near the bright little fire. Mrs. D'Arcy was fast asleep; Connor, his elbows resting on the table, his hands thrust through his thick, dark hair, was reading by the light of a shaded lamp a "Treatise on Mental Power." Miss D'Arcy, at the opposite side of the table, was working a piece of beautiful lace.

This had been her favorite in-door employment in the days when her youth held only bright hopes and pleasant anticipations; when the birds sang sweetly and the sun shone brightly on her dear old home on the banks of the lovely Shannon, and life seemed one long dream of happiness.

In her wildest fancies—and in those by-gone days, like other girls of her age, she had had dreams and fancies, and very vivid ones too—Kate D'Arcy could never have imagined anything like the present scene in connection with herself and her brother's children.

The making of this lace had been suggested to her by Denise, who hoped to dispose of it at some of the West End emporiums; but it progressed slowly, the daylight was so short and a clear light so necessary, yet she worked on indefatigably, the soft, white fingers moving incessantly. The blue eyes now bent upon her work were frequently turned toward Connor's bowed head.

Was she thinking of the happy days fled forever, that the handsome eyes held such a sad, wistful expression? An expression which one other pair of eyes were quick to perceive; those other eyes belonged to Denise, who, seated on a low stool, was employed in mending an old frock belonging to Eva.

The most profound silence had reigned for some time, broken only by the scratch, scratch of Teddy's pencil on his slate. Poor Teddy was never idle; when released from his day's duty at the shop he would take his books and slate, and, seated in the corner beside Eva, study till bedtime; sometimes making extracts, at others writing short essays on his slate, which he submitted for criticism to Connor and Aunt Kate before committing to paper; while Eva contentedly sat and read, occasionally favoring Teddy with a suggestion.

Suddenly Connor looked up, glancing toward the curtained recess, and Denise, answering that glance, said softly: "Yes, mother is sleeping quite soundly; I have just come from looking at her."

With a quick gesture Connor thrust aside the book he had been reading and clasped his hands at the back of his head, while the earnest gray eyes, with a new light in them, slowly travelled over the little family circle.

Kate D'Arcy and Denise read that glance; and with woman's ready instinct each knew that he was about to give utterance to something which she would rather he should leave unsaid.

"I was twenty-two last week, Aunt Kate. Am I not right?" he said, in low, slow tones.

"Yes, my dear!" Kate answered, moving her lace-work nervously. Not wishing to show any uneasiness, she folded her white hands lightly together and smilingly met her nephew's intent regards.

Denise dropped her work into her lap and lifted her dark eyes with a troubled, anxious look to her brother's face, into which was fast creeping a rebellious, dissatisfied expression.

"Yes," he said, with inexpressible self-scorn in his tone, in the curl of the well-cut lips, and in the glance of the clear gray eyes, now turned toward the two anxious upturned faces. "Yes, I was twenty-two last week. I am a man, endowed with three glorious gifts, youth, health, and education; and to what use am I putting all three? My mother is dying of inanition—do not interrupt me, please—and you, dear Aunt Kate—dear, self-sacrificing Aunt Kate—deny yourself the common necessities of life in order to keep a roof over our heads——"

"You forget, Connor," Miss D'Arcy interrupted hastily, "that I am sharing with you the shelter of that roof; and if I were deprived of the society of my brother's children and their mother, who is to me as a very dear sister, I should be the most desolate woman on the face of the earth. You wound me deeply by such words, and I beg that you will never allude to this subject again."

There were tears in the eloquent eyes and in the musical voice as she concluded; and Connor looked away uneasily, but after an instant resumed:

"I do not desire to distress you, and in future shall respect your wishes on that point; but let me beg you will listen to what I have to say, for no words can convince me that I am doing my duty. Look at that poor boy Teddy, toiling for twelve—nay, sometimes fourteen—hours daily for a weekly pittance of five shillings; struggling to acquire learning when he should be sleeping, to gain strength for his next day's work; and our poor Denise breaking her heart because she cannot get work to do; while I am nobly spending my strength, manhood, and education in earning the princely sum of twelve shillings weekly. Now, aunt, you must feel that things cannot go on like this. I must look for something else to do."

"But what can you do, Connor? You know you had

tried everywhere, and we were all thankful when poor Mr. Nesbit, just before he died, got you the copying. Try to be patient, dear; in a month or two, you know, things may look brighter, and you are sure to obtain more remunerative employment."

With a swift movement he withdrew his hands from behind his head, and springing to his feet stood his full height before them. Tall, handsome, with flushed face and flashing eyes, he towered above them.

"Patient!" he repeated with a bitter laugh, but speaking in low, intense tones, even in his excitement remembering his sleeping mother. "Have I not been patient? The pity is that I am not at all *Micawberish*. Do my surroundings justify me in folding my hands and waiting in supine indifference for the end, content or, what is much the same, weakly submitting to see you all starve and die in this garret, consoling myself with the reflection that I am doing all I can, while my conscience cries out, God has given you understanding, power, the will to——"

"But, my dear boy, we are not dying," interrupted Kate D'Arcy, "and indeed I am convinced that the uncertainty of your father's fate is the sole cause of your mother's illness."

A dusky flush crept into Connor's face; his straight black brows met in a frown.

"We will not discuss my father, if you please," he said chillingly. "If he is dead, that is an additional argument in favor of my plea; I cannot imagine that he has willingly deserted my mother and us; therefore I am bound to take his place and strive to provide for those who, in losing him, have been deprived of their lawful protector. I must and *shall* change all this."

"But, Connor, dear, what can you do?" Miss D'Arcy asked.

"What can I do?" he repeated impetuously; "my birth and education have unfitted me for manual labor; but I would not despise even that, if I could obtain such. But those to whom I have applied for such employment regarded me with a smile and politely declined my services. Do not look so horrified—I have no false pride; I would do any honest work, remembering that the end ennobles the labor. I have looked at our position from every point: it is difficult to get taken on in an office without interest and friends; I have concluded to try and get as supercargo in some outgoing vessel. I think Mr. Mansel would recommend me; I could leave my pay for mother and you, and——"

He had broached the subject which for months past had occupied his thoughts, speaking with eyes averted, shrinking from reading the horror which he knew was looking out of the eyes of his listeners; but he paused abruptly as his aunt said in low, gasping tones, "Oh, Connor, would you break your poor mother's heart?"

"No," he answered, more quietly. "I would save her life! I would take her where she would enjoy God's glorious sunshine, free from the fogs, the smoke, and dust of this great Babylon, to where the sweet spring flowers would gladden her eyes, to where the songs of the birds would come to her, borne on air fragrant with the scent of the clover meadows and fresh green woods; to where she would regain health and strength, which will never return to her cooped up in this garret. I have resolved to do it, and I shall."

Denise had hitherto remained silent, her great, dark eyes fixed in mute terror on her brother's excited face; she knew there were times when nothing would turn him from his purpose except the dear voice of the mother who was now sleeping so quietly, and whom she feared to awake. Inwardly trembling she quitted her seat, and approaching Connor took one of his hands in hers and pressed it against her pale cheek.

"Connor, darling, do not talk about going away just now; it would kill dear mamma. I am sure that she will get better in the spring. When Father Everard called last Tuesday he said the cold weather was against her recovery, but that he was quite convinced she would rally with the sunshine. Wait till then, Connor; your prospects may be brighter."

Connor looked down with gloomy eyes into the agitated face of his sister, but the firm lines about his mouth did not relax.

"Promise me, Connor, dear, for poor mamma's sake, that you will not speak of going away from us until she is better."

"You do not know what you are asking, Denise," he responded coldly, withdrawing his hand from the clasp of the girl's soft, clinging fingers, and studiously avoiding the haggard eyes so piteously regarding him. "I will say no more about it *now*, but I tell you once for all that our poor mother will *never* recover if she is to remain here, and Father Everard knows that it is so."

He turned to leave the room, but stopped short as a low tap sounded on the door.

Eva looked up with a little gasp of delight.

"Oh, dear, there is Lottchen!" she whispered.

Denise opened the door and a young girl entered the room, carrying in her hand a little basket, which she gave to Denise with the whispered remark:

"For the dear mother. They will be nice and cooling."

Then she joined the little group near the fire, leaving Denise with tear-dimmed eyes that could not see the fresh, delicious grapes, with all the soft beauty of their delicate bloom intact, nestling so temptingly among their green leaves.

Connor, the flush which her entrance had brought there still upon his usually pale face, placed a chair for the visitor, and was repaid with a smile and a word of thanks. As she stood for an instant in the lamp-light one got a good view of Lotta—or, as her father and Eva called her, Lottchen—von Rosenberg.

She wore a gown of wine-colored cashmere and velvet, the long train of which imparted a certain dignity to the graceful, girlish figure, with ruffles of soft lace at her throat and wrists; a band of wine-colored velvet, to which was attached a pretty gold cross, was fastened round her slender white throat; her face was beautiful, with dainty, high-bred features, full of tenderness and power, with a wistful sadness in perfect harmony with the delicate creamy whiteness of her complexion.

The clear hazel eyes were filled with a childlike innocence; her golden brown hair, fastened at the top of her shapely head by an arrow, was cut in a smooth fringe across her broad brow. There was that about the girl which bespoke good birth.

Her mother, the daughter of an English baronet, had secretly married Herr von Rosenberg, her music-master, and in consequence of which rash act she had been disowned by her family. Upon discovering that the marriage ceremony had been performed by a Catholic priest, her enraged father had driven her forth from the stately home in which she had been born.

The Herr was too proud to make overtures of peace; he never sought to be reconciled to his wife's family—though poor he was equally well born; so he took her away to a more humble home than any she had ever dreamed of possessing; but she was happy in his perfect love and in the grand old Faith which she shared with him, and without which she had often declared "life could never have been the same to her; in embracing it, she had found all that was beautiful on earth and perfect in heaven."

But the loving wife and gentle mother, with four little tender blossoms, were all laid quietly to rest in a London cemetery, and Lotta was left to the care of a father who doted upon his motherless girl.

Chapter III.

> "And from the latticed gallery came a chant
> Of psalms, most saintlike, most angelical,
> Verse after verse, sung out how holily,
> The strain returning, and still, still returning."
> —ROGERS.

"YOU are late this evening, my dear! I hope the Herr is well?" Miss D'Arcy said, looking up with a welcoming smile.

"Yes, thanks, father is quite well. I have been practising some new music since he went out, and oh!" with her rare smile which gave such fascination to her perfect face, "I have something to tell you: you know that Father Brady wants to get a new altar and that his funds are very low. He thinks that a charity sermon might do something toward it; that is, you know, a Grand High Mass and a charity sermon, but in order to achieve the desired end it would require to be done as inexpensively as possible. Father Wilmot, the great Jesuit, will preach—that must be the only item of expense—and as Father Brady's choir is more remarkable for strength than harmony, he is at a loss for good singers. My father has consented to play and direct if we promise to sing; he knows that he will be able to get Signor Zavertal from the Italian Opera to assist. There would be then the Signor, Connor, and Teddy, Denise, Eva, and myself, with two of the best singers from Father Brady's choir; you know we are all so accustomed to sing together, and my father will compose a new offertory piece for the occasion. I have half promised for you, for I feel sure that none of you will refuse, and, dear Miss D'Arcy," very coaxingly, "you have such a beautiful contralto voice, if only I dare ask you to join us."

"No, my dear, you dare not. Now do not put on that overpowering look, it is quite thrown away upon me, I assure you. Seriously, Lotta, my dear, we could not all leave Mrs. D'Arcy, but I will go to an early Mass on that day, and we will do what we can. While you are in church singing we will be here praying for your success; and I am sure that the children will be happy to aid in the good work."

In the midst of the whispered consultation the invalid awoke, and Denise went to the recess and, drawing aside the curtains, lifted the basket of grapes from the little table upon which she had laid them, saying with a smile:

"See what Lotta has brought you. Are they not just beautiful, mamma?"

"How kind of Lotta," a faint glow rising to the delicate face. "Is she here now? I thought I heard her voice."

At a word from Denise she was joined by the others, and Mrs. D'Arcy, wrapped in a large shawl, raised herself in bed and talked the projected ceremony over with surprising animation.

An hour later Connor and Teddy withdrew to their little attic-room, no larger than a good-sized closet, where beneath the closely slanting roof, so cold in winter and so suffocating in summer, stood the bed they jointly occupied.

When they entered their sanctum, Teddy, in boyish fashion, talked volubly on all the occurrences of the day, the promised addition to his wages, how much good the extra two shillings would do, what he intended doing in a year or two, and, waxing confidential, "Would it not be nice, in the warm summer days, to take mother and the rest for a day to Epping Forest or Greenwich?"

Then Lotta was discussed, her beauty, her unfailing kindness to the sick mother; Father Brady, the music for the Grand High Mass, and the part allotted to each, until, utterly worn out, he fell asleep, unconscious that he had done all the talking, and that, but for an occasional word of assent, Connor had been silent and moody.

In the drawing-room, on the second floor, Lotta was seated at a little table. From time to time she glanced at the clock on the mantel-shelf, counting the minutes, for it was now close upon the hour at which her father returned from the Italian Opera House, where he was director.

For his child's sake the Herr never supped out, refusing all invitations, contenting himself with occasionally bringing one or two old friends to partake of a pleasant little repast at his lodgings; but very rarely indeed, and these friends, like the occasions, were exceptional.

For the next fortnight our amateurs met in Herr von Rosenberg's drawing-room to practise Mozart's No. 12 Mass and a very beautiful offertory composed especially for the occasion by the Herr von Rosenberg. They were joined each evening by Signor Zavertal, the great baritone of the Italian Opera, who was always willing to oblige his leader.

Those were pleasant evenings, during which Connor's moodiness in a measure disappeared.

It was the evening of the last rehearsal; they were talking over the coming event, when Father Brady, who with his curate, Father Everard, was present, said, with a profound sigh and one of his comical smiles:

"My dear friends, I feel that I am a man to be pitied."

"Do you fear for our success, Father?" Denise asked timidly, a soft blush stealing into the sweet young face.

"My dear child, that is just what troubles me, the *knowledge* that your success will fall far short of your merits. Imagine, if you can, my mortification," with a merry twinkle in his blue eyes, " when Montague told me this morning that all the tickets were sold; and that he could have sold a hundred more."

"Then why not have more tickets struck off, Father?" Connor suggested, smiling at Father Brady's mock distress.

"Because, my dear boy, it would be no use unless we could enlarge the building; we have issued tickets to the extent of our accommodations. You see how much I am to be pitied, for the present at least, in having such a small church; with such singers I might reasonably hope that Sunday would see me favored with a congregation sufficient to fill the largest church in London."

"I think, Father," Signor Zavertal remarked with a laugh, "that if we, in conjunction with Father Wilmot, succeed in finding you a good benefit you need not envy others the possession of a large church."

"Ah, but with such talent, my dear Signor, who will blame me if I plead guilty to the pardonable desire that, for the time being at least, I had the use of a handsome West End church."

"Oh, wouldn't it be nice," Eva cried, delightedly, clapping her slender white hands, " to see lots of beautifully dressed people, and to——"

Father Brady's pleasant laugh sounded through the room.

"My dear child, I did not think of the people's dress, but of the money for my new altar; do not let me be instrumental in filling your mind with visions of fashion and folly, Miss Eva."

"I am afraid, Father, that Eva is a very worldly-minded

young person," Connor said, with an indulgent smile and glance at his beautiful young sister.

"A face so fair might obtain pardon for a greater fault," the Signor said gallantly.

"Eva likes all things bright and beautiful," Denise put in shyly.

Father Brady turned his now grave eyes with a kind smile in their depths on the youthful speaker.

His seventy years of life had taught him many lessons. Accustomed to read faces, he read the face into which he was looking as he would have read the pages of an open book, and he said gently:

"Human natures are like flowers, my dear child; it takes such varieties to make a perfect garden, and even the same culture bestowed impartially on all will not produce the same results." Then turning to the others:

"I will not utter one word of thanks, but there is one thing of which I am convinced, that is, no such singing has ever been heard within the walls of my poor little church; and if Father Wilmot acquits himself as satisfactorily as our talented choir, our Grand High Mass will be a grand success."

And it proved a success. The church was crowded to suffocation. The fame of the preacher and the singers had gone far abroad; every spot within the edifice was made available; people who could not hear the words of the preacher spoke long after of the music; the singing, they declared, seemed to carry them straight to heaven.

That winter was a very hard one to thousands in the great city. After a few weeks' struggling, Denise had again succeeded in procuring warehouse work, and as the days began slowly to lengthen Mrs. D'Arcy seemed to revive, rising each morning about ten o'clock and not again retiring until darkness set in.

The sight of her returning health brought joy once more into the little family circle, although there still came no word from the long-absent husband and father.

The Signor Zavertal, who had taken a sudden liking to Connor, had striven to persuade him to join their troupe; he knew that he could get him an engagement.

It would be a little slow at first, but in a few years, with his (Connor's) voice, talents, and appearance, he might command a fortune.

But that was not the career which Connor had marked out for himself. The prospect so alluringly painted by the Signor possessed no charm for him. He loved music as an art, but not as a profession; and the Signor was not the sort of man of whom Connor would choose to make a friend. Among the very few Signor Zavertal was known to be a Catholic, but that he held on by the "hem of the garment" was about as much as could truly be said in that gentleman's favor; while Connor, with his steadfast and loyal nature, his ambition and proud contempt of this Janus-like policy, would not bestow his friendship where he could not give respect, and had already sketched out for himself a future in which the musical profession had no part—a future which, had he but known it, was never to be realized.

The improvement in Mrs. D'Arcy's health made Connor more hopeful; he assured himself that he should soon be able to convince her how necessary it had become for their future well-being that he should strive to make a home for them somewhere out of London. He knew how hard it would be to overcome her horror of a separation from any of her children; but Connor had faith in his powers of persuasion over his mother, and concluded to wait until she should be strong enough to be reasoned out of her objections.

The winter sunshine struggling through the haze and fog of a cloudy London sky faintly penetrated their attic window, touching the bent heads of Kate D'Arcy and Denise as they sat at work, glinting on the needles flying swiftly through their busy fingers, or flashed back an answering smile to the low, rippling laugh now so often heard from Denise's lips.

She was happy, for Connor had ceased to talk of going away, her mother's health was improving, Teddy was getting on wonderfully well, and she and Aunt Kate were busy.

Little snatches of hymns and songs intermingled went up from her glad young heart as she worked, Kate's full, rich voice taking the refrain; sometimes Eva's fresh, clear treble would chime in, while the gentle invalid listened and smiled, never looking more happy than when Lotta would run up for a little chat, begging leave to help them to sew, just a little, declaring with her sweet, rare smile that she quite envied them.

And when Connor and Teddy joined the family circle in the evening and the former read aloud or prepared Teddy's Latin lessons, all seemed happy, and for the time Connor forgot his longing.

Sometimes their evenings were spent with Lotta and her father. Those were red-letter evenings that would live in their memories in the years to come, when the genial though sad-eyed Herr von Rosenberg would no longer with gentle kindness correct a false note, or with a fatherly little pat on her shoulder and a quiet smile say, "*Ach!* Denise, *mein Kind*, that is one note above the lark," and Denise with pretty confusion would cease to soar.

Nature had bestowed upon Denise one of her most glorious gifts, and the kind German had done his best to perfect the work of nature, feeling an intense interest in

Mrs. D'Arcy and her family. At first attracted to them by the mystic cord of faith, that attraction became a sincere friendship.

The Herr formed few friendships, but these were true and lasting.

He knew that Denise could make a fortune as a public singer, but he had a deeply rooted horror of the stage as a career for a pretty, innocent girl; he would rather have seen his own dear Lottchen dead and laid to rest beside the dear, dead wife who had followed their four little innocent ones than know her, with all her gifts and her beauty, win fortune and fame on the stage.

He had promised his dying wife that he should save their little Lottchen from that fate, and while God gave him life he would keep that promise.

His one great trouble was what would become of his little girl when he should be called away. Many a bitter pang the thought brought to his heart, knowing as he did that at any hour the fatal summons might come which would leave her fatherless and alone in this vast unknown world. But he never told her this; he could not bring himself to darken her young life and fill her mind with the dread anticipation of a calamity which might be delayed but could not be averted.

The Signor Zavertal had proposed for her hand, speaking eloquently of his love for her; but the Signor was not the man on whom he would bestow his one great treasure.

He thought of the brother whom he had not seen since both were young; that brother in the far-off land, with the broad Atlantic rolling between them.

Was he much changed, this brother? Would he be a father to his beautiful Lottchen when the father who loved her was called away?

Nothing more beautiful could well be imagined than the

affection of father and daughter for each other; he consulted her on all things, and listened, well pleased, wondering at the sweet, grave wisdom of her advice; he gratified her slightest wish, shielding her from all contact with the outer world, its trials and temptations.

It might be injudicious training, but it had the merit of keeping her innocent, and no shadow could dim the future if her father was by her side—that father who was to her the embodiment of all that was grandest and noblest in man.

Chapter IV.

> "Work—work—work,
>   From weary chime to chime!
> Work—work—work,
>   With never a resting time!
> Hem, and stitch, and hem,
>   With weary aching hand,
> Till the heart is sick and the brain benumbed
>   But none will understand."
>
> —"Song of the Shirt"—Hood.

"MISS DENISE, Miss Denise! just wait a minute, will you?"

Denise paused in the act of ascending the stairs to their humble rooms at the top of the house, and turned a pale, listless face, very unlike the face of three weeks before, to meet the sharp but kindly eyes of Mrs. Norris, as she came up from the cellar-kitchen, her own especial region, which with the exception of a little, neatly furnished back room on the first floor—by courtesy designated a parlor—was the only part of the house which she occupied, the rest being given over to lodgers.

She came toward the girl with a pleasant smile.

"I knew your ring, Miss Denise, and when I heard you speak to Susan, I just thought I might as well say what I had to say to you, which it would save me going up them long stairs; I'm not as supple as I was twenty years ago, Miss Denise, and my legs is soon tired."

Mrs. Norris' grammar was somewhat faulty, but Denise did not think of that.

"You just came in the nick of time. I have something to say to Miss D'Arcy, but you'll do as well. Just step into the parlor, if you please; we can talk there."

With heightened color and startled eyes Denise followed Mrs. Norris into her little parlor, where everything was the perfection of neatness and order.

A bright fire in the low, well-polished grate imparted an air of home comfort to the little room.

On either side of the fireplace was a low American rocking-chair, into one of which at Mrs. Norris' invitation Denise thankfully sank.

She was wearied with her long walk, but no bodily exertion could have taken the power from her youthful limbs as did the words of Mrs. Norris.

She turned deathly cold; her warm blood seemed suddenly frozen; and, despite the glow of the bright fire, her teeth began to chatter as she sank into the comfortable chair. She was not a coward, this gentle, graceful girl with the weary young face and tender mouth, but the brave, earnest gray eyes have a troubled, hunted look in their depths as they turn toward the fire.

"What can Mrs. Norris want?" she thought. "Is she about to speak of the rent, which has fallen due one week since? Surely she must know that Aunt Kate will not get her money for another three days."

She had always been so civil hitherto, waiting without demur until Miss D'Arcy's money came to hand, that had Denise been less miserable she might not have felt that sudden sinking at her heart, even at so unprecedented an occurrence as the present. Although when any member of the D'Arcy family came in contact with their landlady she had always a kind inquiry or a pleasant remark to make, this was the first time that she had ever—unmistakably—waylaid any of them; and Denise with a fast-beating heart waited, dreading to hear Mrs. Norris speak, lest it might be to tell her that they cannot have the attics any longer, as she had found lodgers who would pay more strictly up to time. But the subject of her thoughts broke the silence by observing cheerily:

"Desperately cold outside, but one don't feel it in here. Quite cozy, this little parlor, when a fire's on, isn't it? I always likes to keep one on in cold weather, for fear of any visitors or friends dropping in. One can never tell when they'll come; they're always flying about."

"Yes, it is a very comfortable little room, Mrs. Norris."

And something like a sigh escaped the girl as her thoughts flew to the attics, where Teddy lay ill and feverish and her poor mother was wasting away for want of the necessities of life.

"Well, yes, it's comfortable; but I likes it best when the fire's got to be burned in it; you see it keeps folks from looking out of the window, which the view from it isn't very inviting."

"No, not very," Denise assented mechanically, wondering if it was for the purpose of expatiating on the comfort of a fire-warmed room that Mrs. Norris had brought her hither.

"I am rather stiff and breathless, and if you don't mind I'll sit down, Miss Denise?"

"Oh, certainly, Mrs. Norris, do not stand, please."

With a sigh of relief that good lady sank into the vacant seat, and after a short pause said:

"I know you'll wonder why I brought you here, Miss Denise. I want to ask you or Miss D'Arcy if you could do some fine needlework for a young lady; it is wanted very soon, and there will be a good deal of it. There is going to be a marriage; I think it will come off in less than two months, and the young lady won't allow any of her *lingerie* to be done on a machine; so you see you wouldn't need to have anything else on hand; the payment will be good; you can charge your own price, and I wouldn't stint it, if I was you. Fine sewing isn't like machining, it's hard work; I always say the money earned that way is blood-money; besides they're very rich people. The young lady is the granddaughter of Sir Arthur Cardlyon; she is going to marry a great lord. I suppose you heard of Sir Arthur?" with a quick glance from the bright, sharp eyes.

"No, I do not think that I have ever heard the name before."

"Not heard of Sir Arthur Cardlyon!" in a tone of incredulous astonishment. "Well, I never, and you such good friends with Miss von Rosenberg too; isn't it strange that she should never tell you that Sir Arthur is her grandfather?"

"Sir Arthur Cardlyon Miss von Rosenberg's grandfather! Surely you are mistaken, Mrs. Norris."

"Mistaken? I'm about the last person to be mistaken, I assure you, Miss Denise! I lived in the baronet's family for many years, and was upper housemaid at the time that Miss von Rosenberg's mamma was put away and disowned for marrying Herr Rosenberg. Oh, but Miss Verra was a beauty! just like Miss von Rosenberg. The Cardlyons are all handsome, men and women of them; but though she had three sisters, Miss Verra was the flower of the flock. It was a terrible time when it was discovered that she had privately married the Herr—begging your pardon, miss; but you see, it was worse of all his being a Catholic, and she told Sir Arthur and my lady that she was going to become one herself; and as she was of age they couldn't hinder her to do as she liked. So she was thrust out of the hall, a splendid old place it is; and she went away to her husband, poor young thing; and after a time my lady found out where they were staying and sent all her clothes and jewelry after her, telling her she need never hope for forgiveness from them. Shortly after I got married, and came to London, which my husband he was in the leather business, and we took this house, and we always got in genteel lodgers. One day my young lady she found me out by chance; she was so glad to see me that she begged I would let them have the drawing-room flat when it was vacant. They had three pretty baby boys, when they came to my rooms; Miss Lottchen and another little baby girl was born in this house, and her beautiful mother and little brothers and sister died when she was quite a little girl. The Herr has never been the same man since, and though I says it, he's as much of a real gentleman as if he was a born duke, and quite as proud as the Cardlyons; he never tried to be reconciled to any of them; to be sure I don't think myself it would have been any use. And though Miss Lottchen is a perfect angel, she has all the pride of the Cardlyons and her father to boot. My daughter is own maid to Miss Cardlyon, the daughter of Sir Arthur's eldest son; and Bella—that's my daughter—came to me in a great way about an hour ago, to know if I could recommend any one who could take in hand some fine needlework for her young lady, and I thought of Miss D'Arcy and you, and promised to speak to you and let her know what you said."

"You are very kind, Mrs. Norris, and—and will you say that we shall be very pleased to do it?"

With a feeling of infinite relief and thankfulness, Denise quitted her cozy seat by the fire, and as her eyes fell on the pleasant, smiling face, such intense gratitude filled her heart that she felt like taking the ample form of Mrs. Norris in her arms and kissing the plump, rosy cheek.

As she ascended to their rooms, no longer pale and listless, but with flying feet and eager, smiling face, Denise did a very girlish act. She was on the landing, close to their rooms, out of sight of any of the other lodgers, when she paused, and with a face glowing with gratitude she sank upon her knees, and, stretching her hands heavenward, she cried in low, intense tones:

"O my God, Thou art so kind and loving to us, ever coming to our aid, and I have been so doubting, so ungrateful; pardon me, pardon me, all my rebellion, and believe, dear Lord, that I thank Thee for this great mercy with all my heart and soul."

Then devoutly making the sign of the cross, she rose to her feet and went into her mother's presence looking bright and cheerful.

All week Teddy had been ill, the effects of a hurt received while helping to load a light van with goods. He now lay tossing feverish and restless on his confined bed, with the roof slanting closely down upon him, too ill to rise, and retarding his recovery by his anxiety to get back to the shop, lest his place should be given to another. His poor little earnings were so sadly needed, more especially so since, for the last fortnight, there had been no employment for the willing hands of Aunt Kate and Denise.

"I think it's just getting free of one trouble to make ready for another; if the sun ever seems inclined to come from behind the clouds and shine down benignly on us, the wind is always sure to rise and send them drifting over it blacker and more opaque than ever before; our sky is never unclouded."

Eva enunciated this remark with a pathetic little sigh and an expressive shiver, as she glanced toward the cheerless grate in which a few embers were struggling to live— or die.

"My dear Eva," Miss D'Arcy remonstrated brightly, "try to think that the sun will soon be shining again. In a day or two at furthest we will have all this work done; and just think what a lot of money we shall have earned in the last three weeks; we shall soon be able to procure some strengthening food for our two invalids, and in another week or two Teddy will be able to resume his duties at the shop."

"And then something else is sure to happen; I always see that it is so. I don't know how we are to live for a day or two longer; and really, auntie, I think you don't care one bit. I wonder what you and Denise are made of; you never seem to feel cold or hunger; just look at my fingers, I cannot hold the needle any longer," holding up the slender, childish-looking hands, which were blue with cold.

"You poor little thing," Denise said pityingly, dropping her work and going to Eva's side, "don't mind working any more, darling; just wrap your hands in this, and auntie and I will work hard to get done. The time will soon pass, then we shall have a nice large fire for poor mamma and you."

Connor reached over, and took the two little blue hands in his.

"You poor little grumbler, always imagining that others cannot feel because they are not overwhelmed with self-pity at every turn, and are not ready to cry out when they are hurt. You were never formed for enduring privations. Let me rub your hands, friction is good for producing heat."

"Then I do wish, Connor, that you would try it on the fire, and never mind wasting your energy in lecturing me; the benefit might be more general, you know."

Every one laughed at Eva's answer, and Connor smoothed her golden hair caressingly, as he said:

"Clever little girl; take courage! If Heaven will help me you will not always be in want of fire and food."

Eva looked up with a bright smile.

"I do hope you'll soon get something better to do, Connor," with a quaint little sigh, folding her hands together, into which Connor had succeeded in bringing warmth.

"It seems so hard that we should be so especially unfortunate; just as things were beginning to look bright, the warehouse failed; Denise couldn't get any work to do, because she hadn't a large deposit to leave. Teddy got hurt and has been lying ill for four weeks, and we can't get a good doctor; poor mamma has been nearly as ill as ever before; and the man from whom you got the copying had to die."

"Why, child, that was more the man's misfortune than his fault; depend upon it, had his wishes on that—to him—important event been consulted, he would have declined taking that last step, and I should have still been copying for him," Connor said, with a slight laugh.

"And it would have been better for us, Connor, as well as for the man, for you would still have been paid weekly; and now this man who has taken you in the place of his sick clerk won't give any money till the end of the month, and if the sick clerk gets better you'll have nothing to do."

"My dear Eveline, what a chapter of misfortunes," Mrs. D'Arcy said, very gently. "Why do you not enumerate our blessings: Teddy is recovering, and Mr. Brown has kindly promised to keep his place vacant; Connor will get more money at the end of the month than he would have earned at his late employment; and there is all this work which God has mercifully sent in place of the warehouse work, and which will be so much better paid."

"Oh, yes, mamma," Eva responded sagely; "the money will be very good when it comes; but how we are to survive this cold and starvation, I cannot imagine. Must all good be bought with pain and suffering? How is it that Catholics are so much more unfortunate than others? There are people, lots of them, who are not of the faith, and they are rich and happy."

"But the rich are not always happy, child; every state in life has its cross."

"If I were rich I should be happy, Aunt Kate, I know. I should not have a single cross, not even a shadow of one. Mrs. Norris says there are people who never go to any church, who do not even believe in God, that are wealthy and prosperous—isn't that very terrible while others who are good Christians are wretchedly poor and afflicted? Of course I don't mean those low people who are born to want and misery; they could never be expected to rise out of their surroundings, they don't want anything better; they enjoy their misery and couldn't be happy apart from it; but then *we* don't belong to those people, and I dare say we are worse off than the lowest of them, and *we* should be so different; and there is poor Lottchen, her father brought home dying to her, and if he dies—which the doctor says he is sure to do—she will be all alone in the world; she cannot even go to her rich old grandfather because she is a Catholic. Why is it that being of the faith entails so much suffering?"

Her listeners looked with surprise at the childish speaker, and Mrs. D'Arcy answered in a tone of kind reproof:

"My dear Eveline, we have no right to question the dispensations of Providence. Our Heavenly Father knows what is best for us. Wealth is not always a guarantee of happiness, nor is poverty a sign of acceptance; to submit cheerfully and unquestioningly is the true Christian spirit, and to bear meekly the cross laid upon us, because it is the will of our Father. See how patiently Lotta bears the heavy cross that has come to her, and try to emulate her example. We are very poor, but I think I may promise that Lotta will never want a true friend while God spares any one of us."

Connor stooped, and kissed his mother's cheek, and she smiled up into his agitated face.

"Then, mamma, dear, I alone am wanting in the true Christian spirit," Eva responded. "I do not submit patiently, and I cannot be cheerful and sing and pray when I am cold and hungry. Of course, I should be ashamed of myself, but I cannot help it; even Teddy says it will all come right some day soon, and 'God knows best.' I know He does, but it would be so easy for Him to make everything bright and beautiful for us."

"O Eva! Eva!" Kate D'Arcy cried, with a gasp of horror.

"Foolish little Eva," Connor said, with a grave smile, "have you yet to learn the meaning of '*Quem Deus amat castigat*'?"

She looked at him earnestly for a moment. "That is, 'Whom God loves, He chastises.'"

"Very clever. I think I shall make something of you yet. If we bear it patiently, this chastisement is sent to us for a blessing. In order to be worthy of heaven we must endure suffering. If we had all the good things of this earth we would never wish to quit it, and heaven would be no more to us than the ancient fables of the heathens."

"Perhaps some rich people may feel like that," very thoughtfully; "but I'm sure if I were rich I should be so grateful; I would want to be very good, and go straight to heaven when I died."

"Yours would be a very exceptional case, Eva," Kate D'Arcy said, with a bright smile; "you would want two heavens. Do you think such a state of things would be reasonable, going straight from a terrestrial to a celestial heaven? Would not purgatory be a wholesome intermediate?"

"But if I were very good, why should I go to purgatory at all, Aunt Kate?"

"Ah, my dear, such Utopian sentiments are pleasant but untenable," Kate D'Arcy answered, with grave emphasis, as she rose and collected a quantity of work.

"Are you going down to sit with Lottchen now, auntie?"

"Yes, dear; I should have gone long ago, but listening to your talk has made me forget my promise to our poor Lotta."

"May I go too, mamma, please?"

Mrs. D'Arcy looked at her sister-in-law before answering. "Yes, dear, but be sure to return with your aunt."

Eva kissed her mother hastily and followed her aunt.

Chapter V.

"Cauld and weary, sad and dreary,
  Toiling on through London town."—OLD SONG.

"O gleaming lamps of London that gem the city's crown,
  What fortunes lie within you, O lights of London town!"

"THE work is very prettily done; I am very well pleased with it."

A soft glow of pleasure stole into Denise's pale face at these words. She was standing in a Mayfair drawing-room. Before her was seated a girl, perhaps a year or two older than herself, a girl with a high-bred, patrician face and cold, proud hazel eyes, with golden hair crowning the haughtily poised head—a girl dressed with the most faultless taste; looking so like, yet so unlike, Lotta von Rosenberg.

At first glance Denise had been struck by the resemblance, but a second showed her that Miss Cardlyon's beauty was by no means as perfect as her cousin's.

The bride-elect, as she sat idly swinging her fan, never imagined that this girl in the shabby, well-brushed serge dress would presume to criticise her or for a moment question her claims to perfect beauty.

"It was very nice of you to get all these things done in such good time," she continued, in cold, clear, metallic tones; "I think Norris could find something more for you to do. I am quite sure you have not done all that I shall require, Miss—a—a—I did not quite catch your name, I think?"

"Denise D'Arcy, madam."

"What a very pretty name! You are young, not any older than myself, I should think."

"I am eighteen, madam."

"Do you like sewing? But I suppose you do. Persons brought up to that sort of thing always do. No doubt it is best to be content with one's state in life, don't you think so?"

Denise merely bowed to this insolent speech; she was too exhausted by close sitting, late hours, and want of food to fully realize all the contemptuous scorn of Miss Cardlyon's remarks and tone. Since the previous day she had not tasted food, added to which she had been sewing since an hour after midnight.

No wonder, then, if her pulses were throbbing and her brain burning, or if a strange sensation began to steal over her.

Ever since her entrance some one had been playing and singing in an inner room; and the words of the song kept repeating themselves and beating on her brain. She had heard Lotta sing it so often. When was it that Lotta last sang that song?

Was it yesterday or a month ago, or was it years and years since she last heard it? What was the matter with Lotta that she sang so oddly? Surely it was Lotta, and yet—no, no—that voice could not belong to Lotta.

She could hear nothing, think of nothing but the voice of the singer. With a sudden feeling of terror she tried to move; the walls of the room appeared to sway and totter, a *jardinière* near which Miss Cardlyon was seated seemed walking toward her.

Pictures, statues, and furniture all appeared hurrying forward to crush her, the tall palm ferns waved their stately fronds threateningly, but above all the voice of the singer rang in her ears:

> "She stood within her childhood's home,
> Despair was on her brow,
> Beneath the weight of agony
> Her spirit seemed to bow.
> She stood there pale and desolate,
> The sun no longer shone;
> Alas! alas! what is this earth
> When those we love are gone?"

There came a sudden lull, a velvet *portière* was drawn aside, and—

"What is the matter? Are you ill?" in cold, clear, startled tones, recalled Denise to a knowledge of where she was, just in time to save her from fainting.

She saw standing by her side a young lady, tall, slender, dressed in black, with a pretty, bright face and dark eyes—a little anxious now—regarding her with a look of compassion.

"Are you not well?" the new-comer inquired kindly. "Sit down until you are better," drawing forward a chair and with gentle authority compelling Denise to be seated.

Miss Cardlyon pressed the knob of the electric bell, and a servant appeared to whom she gave a whispered order.

Denise scarcely noticed the incident, and was not a little surprised when wine was presented to her by a tall footman.

She hesitated, fearing its probable effects upon her in her present exhausted state, and at a word from the young lady the man placed the wine on a small gypsy-table beside her and retired.

"Pray do take the wine," the young lady said kindly; "you look so pale it will do you good, I assure you. Have you been ill?"

Wishing to avoid further importuning, Denise raised the glass to her lips and sipped a little. The faintness had fled, but there was a wild fear tugging at her heart; she could not remain here, in a few minutes she must take her departure—must she go without money?

Would Miss Cardlyon not pay her?

She had requested Denise to bring her bill; but such a trifling matter as a seamstress' bill had quite escaped the mind of the proud heiress.

What was she to do? How return to the cold, dreary attic, where there was neither food nor fire, and where the dear ones were eagerly awaiting her return with means to procure both? And while she quietly answered the questions put to her by the two young ladies, her brain seemed on fire and a wild despair had seized upon her.

"I hope you feel quite better?" Miss Cardlyon said, as Denise rose to go, and gracefully thanked both ladies for their kindness; "if not, do not go away just yet; I will ring for Norris to take you to her room and you can rest there until you are quite recovered."

"Thanks, very much, Miss Cardlyon; but I am quite better now, and would much prefer returning home."

Even as she spoke, she was mentally repeating:

"What shall I do? what shall I do?"

It was her last resource—for the sake of the dear ones at home she must do it. She paused and took from a little morocco pocket-book an envelope, and with a deep blush placed it on a table close to Miss Cardlyon.

"Your maid said that you wished me to bring this bill. Have I done right?"

There came into the creamy whiteness of Miss Cardlyon's haughty face the faintest accession of color, and the clear eyes were opened with a look of cold displeasure.

Perhaps had the spoiled beauty known all the pain and humiliation it had cost the poor girl to speak the words, her displeasure would have given place to sympathy; but she only saw in it an act of impertinence, and answered with freezing hauteur:

"Certainly! you have merely *obeyed* my wishes; I shall send Norris in the course of the week to pay you."

She pressed the knob of the electric bell, and a footman appeared to conduct Denise to the door.

How she got into the street she never knew. She was all unconscious that a light snow was falling, or that a bitter north wind was blowing the falling particles into her face. She could only think of her mother and Teddy at home starving for want of food and fire.

Within the last four weeks they had parted with *everything* to keep them all in life, and they had toiled so hard, so unremittingly, Aunt Kate and she, to get this work done, this work which when finished was to bring such comforts and blessings.

She gave no thought to cold or hunger when she set forth bright and hopeful; she was going to return with plenty of money, and all would be well again. Connor would get paid in another fortnight, and there would be an end to their misery—and now there was only the blackest despair before her.

She wandered on, not knowing whither she went. She took no heed of time; the snow continued to fall more heavily, the dull gray afternoon was giving place to evening; it would soon be dark, but she did not heed, she thought only of her mother and Teddy. Two days before Lotta had begged that Eva might be allowed to remain with her, so Eva was still with Lotta.

Strange enough, as she wandered on the strains of the music and the words of the song she had so lately listened to in the Mayfair drawing-room kept haunting her.

She felt like singing them aloud.

Then some other words came to her, words they often

sang at home; she paused abruptly and looked around her.

A wild determination seized her, she felt like one impelled on by an invisible power—a power she could not resist.

She did not know where she was; the dusk of evening was closing like a pall around her, lights were flashing through the gloom, "the lights of London town."

At a little distance she saw a great hotel all ablaze with lights; she took a step forward, then paused—she did not know that a blue-coated guardian of the peace had been favoring her with his regards for the last few minutes.

One thought possessed her mind: she could sing, people got money for singing. Mother and Teddy were starving at home; she would *not* return without money.

In a private room of the Albany four gentlemen were seated beside a table, on which were wines and choice cigars.

One, a military-looking man, Captain Seymour, was half-hidden from view behind the *Times*. The Honorable Philip Wortly and his unfailing chum Jack Somers, smoking, while the fourth—Frank Brand—was leaning indolently back in his chair, and for want of something more interesting looked attentively at his shapely hands and well-kept finger-nails.

"I say, Brand," the captain cried, flinging down his *Times* and breaking in upon the silence, "isn't it time that Clifford was back? What the deuce can keep him so long? He promised to be back an hour ago."

"Yes," Brand answered, transferring his attention from his nails to the speaker, "but I wouldn't be surprised if he searched till midnight."

"To-morrow will be a new day; could he not have waited till then? What's the good of going knocking about unknown localities in the dark? It's too bad, by George! keeping us waiting here. I promised Lady Nolans to present him to-night."

"What's Clifford after?" Philip Wortly asked, coming from behind a wreath of smoke, and withdrawing his cigar from his lips with a look of newly-awakened interest.

"Promised a friend in New York to look up his wife and family," Brand answered, stretching his long limbs lazily.

"Where are they?"

"Somewhere in London, I expect."

"Couldn't he have done it better himself?"

"Couldn't, my dear fellow; he has got a broken leg, and was laid up when we came away; Clifford promised to find them for him and bring them out."

"What's his name—the fellow with the broken leg, you know?"

"Gerald D'Arcy, a splendid fellow, you bet."

"A king's son of Ireland, lineally descended from the 'O'Squanders of Castle Squander' that Carleton writes about," Jack Somers said, with a laugh.

Brand slowly pushed back his hair from his forehead and said quietly:

"Gerald D'Arcy *is* a gentleman; my uncle, Sir John Brand, knew the family well; they had a splendid estate near that place he bought in County Limerick. Gerald D'Arcy was a young fellow then—not very old yet, only forty-four—he married a Miss O'Connor, a beauty and an heiress."

"Lucky fellow," Jack remarked, *sotto voce*.

"As regards his marriage, yes. After a time the young couple came to London. He had a friend, a fellow who was crazy on speculations, and who persuaded D'Arcy to join him. For a few years everything went on well. D'Arcy was going to be returned for his native town.

His constituents were enthusiastic; his triumph was sure; but one morning poor D'Arcy woke up to find himself ruined by the man he had thought his friend. Everything was gone; even his wife's fortune had been speculated on and lost. She had some valuable jewels, which she gave him to dispose of. His sister, a pretty young girl of sixteen, was residing with himself and wife when the crash came; she had some money, something over two hundred a year. She promised D'Arcy to share her last shilling with his wife and children. When all demands were met, he found himself possessed of the pitiful sum of one hundred pounds. He gave fifty pounds to his wife, and with the other fifty sailed to America in search of fortune. That was eight years ago, and for the last four he has not had a letter from his wife or sister. Now he is in despair. I have tried to show him that his letters must have miscarried. He has led such a nomadic existence the last four years, here, there, everywhere, as it is with most of us fellows who leave the Old for the New World in search of fortune."

"And has this D'Arcy been successful?"

"Successful? Well, I think so. After the most bitter battle with fortune, in one day he became a millionaire."

"But how? Tell us all about it."

"When D'Arcy went to America he meant to succeed. He tried everything he could get to do. I don't think any of you can understand what *that* comprises on the other side of the Atlantic; but I won't bother trying to instruct you. He vowed to make a home for his wife and children before he should see them again, and in some measure atone for all his folly had lost them. At length fortune smiled upon him: he had a prospect of realizing all his hopes; he was negotiating the purchase of a very fine farm; he would soon have his wife and family beside him.

He wrote to his wife in high spirits, but wishing to give them a pleasant surprise, made no mention of his intended purchase, merely observing that he would not write again until he had a home to bring them all to. The answer to that letter was the last he got from his wife. He was anxious to get things settled and would give himself no rest. He worked too hard, in consequence of which he took fever. For months he was unable to do anything. He would not let the people with whom he boarded write home for fear of alarming his wife. He came back to life to find that another man had bought the farm and that his means were fast disappearing. Unable to work, he knocked about as best he could for some time, ashamed to write home and tell of his failure. As soon as he was sufficiently recovered he went further west and recommenced the battle with fortune, with ever-varying results. About nine months ago he met Clifford in Nevada County. They became fast friends; he saved Clifford's life. Two months after, D'Arcy was fortunate enough to secure a handsome farm which he purchased with some money he had saved. Clifford wanted him to take a loan, but he wouldn't hear of it. The house on the farm was not a very suitable residence for ladies; so D'Arcy set about choosing a site, and put men on to dig a foundation for a handsome brown-stone house. It was just as pretty a spot as could be imagined; he asked Clifford and me one day to go over and see the place. We were standing watching the men, when suddenly there arose a wild shout. They had struck an oil-well. The news soon spread, offers of assistance came crowding in, and so D'Arcy's fortune was made. He got a clever Yankee fellow to take charge, and as Clifford and I were coming to England, he determined to join us. We wrote and secured berths in the ——, and the day previous to her departure for England we arrived in New York. We all put up at the same hotel, and feeling rather knocked up after our long journey we agreed to retire early. In the middle of the night I was aroused by cries of 'Fire!' Starting up, I dressed hastily and rushed out of my room; in the corridor I encountered my two companions, who, like myself, had been awakened by the shouts. We found that the next block of buildings was in flames.

"Poor D'Arcy, in saving the life of a woman, had his leg broken and got pretty generally smashed up; as you may guess, he did not sail with us. His disappointment and anxiety threatened to bring on fever, so Clifford promised to search up the wife and family and bring them back with him."

"Confounded hard lines for a fellow! It seems to me, his fortune hasn't brought him much luck," Jack Somers remarked sympathetically.

"Nonsense, Jack, don't be sentimental; he'll soon get a broken leg mended, and the weather's pretty cool just now, that will keep the fever down. But I say, Brand, isn't your friend Clifford awfully rich?"

"Rich as Crœsus; owns no end of silver and coal mines; a splendid old place in Virginia, and——"

The further enumeration of his friend's possessions was here cut short by the captain exclaiming:

"By George, what a voice!"

A breathless hush followed the exclamation. One of the gentlemen softly quitted his seat and opened a window, admitting a rush of cold air and snow-flakes, and a flood of melody and words were borne to their listening ears—words that sounded strangely out of place when sung on a London street:

> " Hark! I hear the organ peals,
> O'er the tide its music steals,

O'er the waters, soft and clear,
Louder as our bark draws near.
Gondolier, ah, rest awhile—
Hark! from yonder sainted isle
Through the woods now darkly fair
Softly comes the Vesper prayer.
 Hark! I hear the organ peals,
 O'er the tide its music steals—
 Ave! Ave! Mother bright,
 Guard us through the coming night.

Fainter now, as on we glide,
Comes the music o'er the tide;
Darker shadows o'er us fall—
Ave! Mother, guard us all.
Hark! upon the wind it steals!
Hark! the solemn organ peals
Still along the silent way,
Fainter till it dies away.
 Hark! the solemn organ peals,
 O'er the tide its music steals—
 Ave! Ave! Mother bright,
 Guard us through the coming night."

As the first notes sounded on the chill evening air, a hansom cab was driven rapidly in the direction of the Albany, but came to a sudden stop, and a gentleman alighted, pausing and listening with rapt attention until the last notes had died away in a long, low, pleading wail, like the prayer of a soul in utter desolation. He had heard the most famous public singers, this stranger who had paused to listen, but the soul, the pathos which breathed in every throbbing note of this pure young voice stirred his proud heart to its very core. Drawing a deep breath, he advanced and dropped a glittering coin into the hand of the shrinking girl, whose timid air and snow-clad garments appealed strongly to all the chivalry in the man's nature.

With a glance of compassion at the girlish figure he

turned and ran lightly up the steps of the Albany, humming the last two lines softly:

> "'Ave! Ave! Mother bright,
> Guard us through the coming night.'

"Ah, poor child! alone in the streets of London, and with such a voice! how much you need the protecting care of that sweet Mother whose aid you implore," he soliloquized, moved by a strange feeling of pity; but Marmaduke Clifford never dreamed that the voice whose music would haunt him in all the years to come, or that the little bare hand so timidly extended for *his* charity, were the voice and hand of Denise D'Arcy, the daughter of Gerald D'Arcy *the millionaire*.

Chapter VI.

> "All heads must come
> To the cold tomb;
> Only the actions of the just
> Smell sweet and blossom in the dust."
> —Shirley.

THE cold, gray dreariness of the bleak February afternoon had given place to the dusk of evening; snow was falling thickly without, and misty shadows were filling the cheerless attic in Charlotte Street; but Denise had not returned. In vain Kate had striven to comfort the anxious mother with assurances of her child's safety.

"Miss Cardlyon may have detained her—some slight alterations perhaps," she suggested. But for once the rich voice and winning smile were powerless to soothe the alarmed mother. Connor returning from his office and finding Denise still absent, had started off in search of her.

Lotta, who, despite her own bitter suffering, never forgot her friends, had twice run up to bring some little delicacies to Mrs. D'Arcy and Teddy; remarking with a faint attempt at a smile on the worn, haggard young face:

"As Denise may be detained, you know, and Miss D'Arcy is unused to cooking, you must really take something from me, dear Mrs. D'Arcy, and for the time being just try to imagine that I am Denise. Eva is reading to the dear father. She has been such a comfort to me; it is so good of you to let her stay with me."

How her listeners understood and appreciated the tender

delicacy which prompted her words! Underneath all her efforts at cheerfulness, Kate D'Arcy's heart was a prey to the most terrible fear.

What if some mischance had befallen Denise! Such dreadful things happen daily in the streets of London. Her very soul stood appalled before the picture which her vivid fancy conjured.

She could not pray—only pitiful little ejaculations went up from the tortured heart to the throne of mercy; again and again she asked herself with bitter self-accusing: "Why had she not accompanied Denise to Mayfair? Why had she permitted the poor child to go such a distance, alone, through the streets of London? True, she had gone alone before, and no harm had come to her, but now something *must* have happened."

She was glad of an excuse to steal out and hurry away to the church, which she knew would be open for confessions at that hour; she could not pray in any set form of words, but she could fling herself at the feet of her dear Lord in the Holy Sacrament. *He* could read her heart, *He* could give her peace and send their brave, innocent, darling Denise safely back to them.

Animated by this hope, she hurried out into the gloom and snow, heedless of her thin, worn shoes, and indifferent to the pitiless wind that sent the snow drifting mercilessly into her face, feeling a great sense of gratitude to Lotta for remaining with the invalids.

Meantime Lotta, thankful for the opportunity thus afforded her, hastened to take advantage of Kate's absence. After whispering a few seconds with Teddy, whom she presently left blowing vigorously at the few expiring embers in the dreary-looking grate, she hurried from the room, and soon returned, dragging between the two little white hands a large scuttle of coals.

Half an hour later, when Kate returned, brightness and warmth had chased away the coldness and shadows; the lamp was lighted, a large coal-fire was blazing and flashing in the grate, close to which Mrs. D'Arcy's chair was drawn; the kettle was boiling cheerily, and the table, drawn up to the fire, was spread for tea; while Lotta, her pale face glowing with the haste she had made, was buttering muffins, which Teddy was employed in toasting.

What a change was here!

A great joy flashed into Kate's face, an ineffable sense of gratitude surged through her heart. One swift glance she cast around the now cheerful room; then, as if an icy breath had blown over her, all the color and gladness faded, leaving her ashen pale, and the clear blue eyes were turned upon Lotta with a mute, questioning horror in their depths.

"She has not come yet, dear, but she will be here soon," Lotta said, answering that look.

"See! We are quite ready, Teddy and I. We knew that Denise would be lost with cold, and as we saw that you were unnerved, we decided to save you all trouble."

For Mrs. D'Arcy's sake Kate struggled to appear calm; but tears of gratitude filled her handsome eyes as she looked around her, and without a word she took Lotta in her arms and kissed her smooth cheek.

"Ah, here they are, thank Heaven!" Lotta suddenly cried, disengaging herself from Kate's embrace, and a glad cry rang through the room as Connor, loaded with parcels, and Denise, clinging to his arm, entered. In another moment the latter was kneeling by her mother's side, kissing the thin white hands and sobbing and laughing by turns.

"I missed my way," she tried to explain between her sobs. "My head felt so strange, the noise confused me, but oh, I was so glad when I saw Connor, and—and I am quite safe now, mamma, dearest, and Aunt Kate," as the latter bent down and tenderly kissed her.

"Now, Denise," Lotta said, gently drawing the kneeling girl to her feet, "just see how wet you are. You will give the dear mother cold; let me take off your jacket. Here is Teddy with a hot cup of tea and a warm muffin; sit down and take them just at once; the tea will keep you from taking a chill."

Denise, still dazed by her late experience, mechanically obeyed; then glancing around her in utter bewilderment for the first time since her entrance perceived the glowing fire, the temptingly spread table, and the look of home comfort which pervaded the room, and that Teddy, his pale, thin face glowing with delight, his dark eyes unnaturally large, the combined effects of his late illness and inanition, was standing before her, holding in one hand a cup of tea, in the other a plate of muffins.

At that instant Connor entered from the little room, where he had gone to change his wet coat lest the damp arising from it might injure his mother.

"How is this?" he said, glancing around in surprise. "I thought that—that——"

"That we had neither food nor money; it was so until Lotta brought light out of darkness," Kate answered softly, a great light shining in her eyes. A dusky flush mounted to Connor's brow; he turned to look for Lotta, but Lotta had quietly escaped.

No one dreamed that Denise had not been paid for the work which she had taken away that morning; or that the money which she blushingly dropped into her mother's lap had been earned by singing on the streets of London. Not until a week later, when one day Bella Norris came to pay Miss Cardlyon's bill, did Kate come to know the truth. Then with tears and blushes Denise confessed to her aunt what she had done for the sake of her mother and Teddy.

"It must remain a secret between you and me," Kate said, kissing away Denise's tears. "Your dear mother must be spared the knowledge of that which would prove the last drop of bitterness in her most bitter cup."

Days and weeks passed, and although Marmaduke Clifford in his unceasing search for the D'Arcys had twice encountered Connor—had even on one occasion paused to apologize for running up against him—each went on his way unconscious of what the other held for him, or that the mention of a name would have brought the most intense happiness to so many—a happiness which at least one faithful heart was never to know in this life.

Truly the ways of Heaven are inscrutable.

Lotta seldom visited the D'Arcys now; she could not leave her dying father. Night and day she sat by his bed, sometimes reading to him, sometimes talking in her low, sweet tones; but always watching for every change on the beloved face.

"Lottchen, *Herzliebchen* [heart's dearest love], I do not fear to leave you now, since he has promised to be to you a father," Herr von Rosenberg said, touching Lotta's bowed head with his thin, almost transparent fingers. "Franz was always good and true; there will be no one to come between you and his love; you will always remember that he is your uncle, the brother of the father who in life loved you as a precious gift from Heaven, and who in death blesses you with his last breath. For my sake, *mein Herz* [mine heart], you will love him, but do not forget thy poor father, Lottchen," a yearning, wistful pathos in the dying eyes, bent so tenderly on the drooping figure kneeling by the bedside, the face hidden from view, and only an occasional smothered moan telling of the storm of despair and anguish which threatens to rend the soul from the slender, girlish body.

Lotta had knelt thus for over an hour, ever since Father Brady had departed, after bestowing the last blessing upon the soul so soon to render an account of its stewardship. At the last words she raised her head and with a sudden passionate gesture kissed his cold hand.

"*O mein Vater, ich habe dich so unendlich lieb!*" [O my father, I love thee so intensely!] she cried. "I shall never forget thee, never, never!"

"I know thou wilt not, *mein liebes Kind.*"

She flung out her hands with a passionate cry.

"Why will not our good God leave thee to me, or in taking thee take me also? In all the world I have but thee!"

In her weeks of bitter anguish and suffering these were Lotta's first words of rebellion.

How altered the young face had become during those weeks of watching! The cheeks were thin and pallid, the beautiful eyes were sunken and haggard, with heavy blue waves beneath; every feature bore the impress of the agony which wrung her soul.

All through this illness which had struck down her beloved father with such appalling suddenness, she had bravely fought against any outward display of emotion; she had listened silently, and even called a smile to her lips, when he spoke of leaving her for that other world, and of meeting the dear ones who had gone before. She had written, at his request, a letter to the brother with whom her father had parted when both hearts were filled with the glowing hopes and aspirations of early manhood, when to each young and sanguine mind the world appeared an enchanted land—a land of fairest promise, which to willing hands and determined wills must yield a golden harvest and the fruition of their desires. So to this uncle, whom she had never seen, Lotta had written—her father dictating, begging his brother for the love of the old days to be a father to his little Lottchen when he was gone.

Franz von Rosenberg had written back gladly accepting the charge; he was alone and childless, and she would be to him as his own daughter.

Poor Lotta had hoped against hope, she had prayed unceasingly that her father might be spared to her, but all in vain were her prayers. Slowly the conviction of this dawned upon her soul.

She would not add to *his* suffering by any display of her anguish, but now that the hour had come when she must part with him for all time, never more in this life to hear the dear voice, never more to look upon the dear face so fast fading from her sight, never more to know his protecting care, her lips refused to be longer silent, and her heart cried out in fierce rebellion. Why should he who is so good be taken, while others so unworthy were left to cumber the earth? What had she to live for?

"Lottchen, *mein Herz*, it cannot be," said the dying man, and the sound of that voice quenched the last spark of rebellion in the young and hitherto untried heart.

"We must submit. Who knows for what the good God is reserving thee? Be faithful to Him, to our holy faith, and to all I have striven to teach thee! Do thy duty faithfully, unswervingly, and as I bless thee, so shall Heaven bless thee with its choicest blessings. Our good God is giving *mein liebes Kind* a father in place of the father He is calling away."

"Oh, forgive me—forgive me!" the poor girl moaned. "I have troubled thee, *mein Herz;* I am so cruelly selfish."

"Selfish! *Ach, nein*, that *mein Lottchen* could never be.

The tender heart is sore, but the loving mother who suffered so cruelly here on earth will comfort thee when I am gone. Then write to thy uncle, go to him at once. Do not linger here. Avoid the Signor Zavertal. Connor and our friends will see thee safely on board; and—and tell Franz for my sake to love thee—and be kind to—to——"

She sprang to her feet, and caught him in her outstretched arms as he sank back, a smile of ineffable peace on the noble face, where the shadow of death already rested.

Hearing the suppressed cry of agony that escaped from Lotta's sorely tried heart, Kate and Denise came quickly from the adjoining apartment.

But although the warm-hearted composer had spoken his last words on earth, the end had not yet come. In silent prayer all three watched by his side, until a low sigh told them that the soul had passed to the eternal shore.

The continued strain on heart and brain could no longer be borne. Lotta sank down insensible.

With gentle tenderness loving hands raised the lifeless girl, and carried her from the chamber of death.

In this her hour of bereavement Lotta received many kind offers of assistance from those who had been her father's friends; offers whose sincerity was all the more reliable coming as they did from the *Bohemian* side of "society." She was deeply touched, and, while gratefully declining their offers, assured those friends that her dear father had left her sufficient money for all her wants, and that she was going to the best of protectors, her uncle in the Western States of America.

All save the Signor Zavertal thought the arrangement a good one for the lonely girl; he was angry and disappointed, for he had looked upon this as his opportunity.

He assiduously sought to dissuade her from her purpose, using every argument at his command, and picturing in forcible language the uncongenial life before her.

"You are very good, Signor, and I thank you for the interest you express in my welfare," Lotta said coldly, almost haughtily, feeling somewhat irritated by his persistence. "But I should go, were it to a Siberian desert, since my dear father wished it so."

There was no appeal against that decision, yet he would not relinquish all hope until she decidedly refused to see him.

Lotta's preparations were all completed; Mrs. Norris, assisted by Denise, had packed her boxes, and during the operation the good soul had never ceased weeping.

"Don't leave us for another month, Miss von Rosenberg; don't, my dear young lady," she pleaded in a choked voice. "You ain't fit to go upon the ocean, which they do say is the *stormyest* of 'em all, no more you ain't. Haven't Miss D'Arcy just been a-telling you what the doctor said? Why, you haven't any more strength than a day-old infant, that's what you haven't. You'll be ill, my dear, and what's to become of you then, all alone on the wild stormy ocean? You want time to recover from your trouble; you want to sleep and eat, and——"

"There is no use trying to frighten me, Mrs. Norris," Lotta interrupted gently; "I am not going to be ill as you predict. There will be plenty of people on the vessel and I shall not be alone. I promised the dear father that I should go as soon as I had had a letter from my uncle, and that letter has come—such a kind letter. He will meet me at New York. I could not disappoint him, you know; so I shall sail on the *Teutonic*."

Mrs. Norris shook her head dolefully, and heaved a profound sigh as she looked at the slender, graceful form in its trailing crape gown, and the pathetic wistfulness of the perfect face. Denise, a great sympathy and tenderness in her eloquent face, a troubled light in her clear gray eyes, stood by her side, the fingers of both hands interlaced and resting on the shoulder of her friend.

"If you would write to your uncle, Lotta, darling, and say you are too ill to take a long sea voyage for another week or two," Denise urged tenderly.

"But I am not too ill, Denise. Why should I put off the inevitable? Every hour I stay makes it harder for me to go. I promised the——" she swayed suddenly as if about to fall, and Mrs. Norris caught the fainting girl in her motherly arms and laid her on a couch.

Lotta did not sail on the appointed day, and the breath of May was wafting sweet odors over the land when she took her last look of the weeping friends who had come to see her off, her last look of the shores of England—the land of "her home and her dead."

Chapter VII.

> "God of my sires! o'er ocean's brim
>   Yon beauteous land appears at last;
> Raise, comrades! raise your holiest hymn,
>   For now your toils are past.
> See o'er the bosom of the deep
>   She gayly lifts her summer charms,
> As if at last she long'd to leap
>   From dark Oblivion's arms."
>
> —D. Moore.

NEW YORK at last! But not as Columbus hailed the first glimpse of that fair land—not as the poor immigrant, to whom that bounteous land seems a veritable "Land of Promise"—did Lotta greet the first sight of the land which held her future home. She was oppressed by a sense of loneliness, of desolation, as she stood apart from her fellow-passengers and gazed wistfully out toward the green fields and villages on Staten Island, as the stately ship sailed up through the Narrows, and on the tall roofs and spires of the Empire City.

Like one in a dream, she saw the animated faces around her—little groups talking, laughing, bantering each other gayly; but amidst the general excitement she felt strangely alone.

"You will soon be released from the monotony of life on shipboard, Miss von Rosenberg," said a bluff, cheery voice at her elbow. "I have no doubt you will be thankful to get away from us."

"Indeed I shall not, Captain Hunter," Lotta said, greeting the speaker with a smile. "It has been very pleasant, and you have been so kind to me that I feel like losing friends when I think of going away from you and good Mrs. Mullins; and I must not forget to include the doctor."

"I am very glad that you have had a pleasant time, Miss von Rosenberg; but as for the doctor," with a good-humored laugh, "the weather has been so fine that he has had very little chance of practising his healing art, and I am afraid that the sight of your pale face had led him to imagine that he would find a patient in you. Mullins is a good soul; she has been stewardess aboard this ship ever since her husband, Jack Mullins, was lost in a storm on the Irish coast. Her mother, a decent old body, lives in New York, and Mullins makes her home with the old lady."

"It must be a great comfort to have a mother," Lotta said wistfully.

"Ah, yes, Miss von Rosenberg, a good mother's a safe anchor in time of storm," the captain answered, with real feeling. "In a few minutes we will pass quarantine," he added, "and you will soon see your uncle." With a word of kindly encouragement he hurried away as the quarantine yacht steamed across the bay to the steamer.

There was a rush upon deck and a good deal of lively talk among the passengers; and soon the great ship was steaming proudly up the bay to the city.

It was all so novel to Lotta, who soon became interested in the immigrants. She had never imagined such a scene, and watched with fascinated eyes the eager, hurrying throng, in which man in every stage of life was represented, from the unconscious babe of a few weeks old to the aged and weary who had crossed the ocean to their children or their children's children and to new homes in the New World.

They were for the most part Irish, and one in faith with her, those immigrants; and as she gazed her heart went out to them, moved by a great pity for their misfortunes. They had suffered—yes; but— "Would they ever forget their own old land, though wealth should gladden the new?" she wondered sadly.

People were running hither and thither about her decks as the steamer swung into her berth at the Bremen pier, and a general rush was made for the gang-plank.

The noise and bustle, the running up and down of porters, the confusion and jostling, the babel of voices and rattle of vehicles, the yelling of newsboys, their mocking laughter and smart, sarcastic remarks, mingled in one wild, ear-splitting tumult. With a little shiver of newly awakened alarm Lotta closed her weary eyes to shut out the hurrying, seething crowd, and asked herself, would her uncle never come? As if in answer to her unspoken question the captain and stewardess came to her side.

"Your uncle is not here, Miss von Rosenberg," Captain Hunter said, with evident concern, "nor any message from him. I have communicated with the principal hotels and boarding-houses. So far as I can learn he is not in the city. There may have been some delay. It often happens that parties coming from a distance are not up to time for us; but you must not distress yourself, your uncle will be sure to turn up all right some time to-day or to-morrow."

"Not arrived yet? What shall I do?" Lotta cried, in deep distress; the lonely young heart yearning for the dear father who in life had shielded her from every care, from every harm.

For the first time in her life she found herself alone in the midst of strangers, in a strange land. No wonder that she shrank from descending that gang-plank and turning her back upon the great ship, which now seemed to her an ark of refuge, and going forth into an unknown world—no wonder that she raised her startled eyes, with the old, childish wistfulness in their clear depths, to those two kind faces, and repeated in a tone of dire dismay: "What shall I do?"

"Now, don't distress yourself, miss, dear," Mrs. Mullins said, in her kind, motherly way; "sure it often happens, as the captain says, that when they've a long journey to come, as your uncle has to do, there's a mistake in the trains, or something that delays them; but it'll all come right, never fear. With the help of God, you'll be seeing him to-morrow or the next day; so keep up your heart, my dear young lady, and just say what you'd like to do till he comes."

"Do? Oh, I really do not know, Mrs. Mullins. What can I do, captain?"

"Do!" repeated the captain, meeting the innocent, appealing glance with a smile of kind encouragement. "Why, make yourself as happy as possible. I will place you safely in any hotel you may choose to go to, and we will make it all straight for your uncle when he goes to the office. You know Mullins and I promised to see you taken care of, and we are bound to see our ship safely into port."

"You are very, very kind, Captain Hunter. I do not know in what words to thank you. I am afraid you will think me very foolish, but I must tell you, even if you do laugh at me. I am a shocking coward, and shrink from the thought of going to stay by myself in one of those great hotels. Now, dear Mrs. Mullins, Captain Hunter has told me that your mother lives in New York. Don't you think that I could stay with her until my uncle comes? I am accustomed to you, and I am sure I should like her."

"Well, indeed, miss, we're very plain, homely people,"

responded the good woman, confused and flattered. "If me poor mother's house was a palace, let alone the kind it is, sure and 'tis proud I'd be to take you to it; but it's not a house fit for the likes of you, at all, at all!"

"But I am sure I should be very comfortable with your mother," Lotta urged. "Do help me to convince her, Captain Hunter."

"I can vouch for the old lady's respectability. Her house is not large, but she lives alone, and if you can put up with her accommodations, I am quite sure, my dear young lady, she will do her level best to insure your comfort."

So the captain's answer turned the balance, and the stewardess' objections were soon overruled, to Lotta's intense satisfaction.

No. 24 Rose-Myrtle Street was one of a long block of red brick houses; the street itself was a quiet little street, turned off from one of the city's great thoroughfares. The door, which was reached by a short flight of steps, was painted a dull brown, as were also the sashes of the not too large windows, which were shaded by pretty, clear muslin curtains, behind a row of bright red flower-pots, in which bloomed pink and crimson roses, fragrant musk and glowing geraniums; while in a cage of wonderful foreign workmanship a little fluffy ball of gold poured forth a strain of sweetest melody.

Strangers passing through Rose-Myrtle Street usually paused to bestow a second glance on the neat window and its cheery inhabitants, the beautiful blooming flowers and the sweet singing bird.

As the cab dashed up to the house the small door was flung open from within, and a little elderly woman, in a dark calico gown, large white apron, and snowy cap, stood on the top step.

In an instant Mrs. Mullins had the little figure in her arms, and was kissing and whispering at one and the same time.

In Lotta's troubled heart the dreary sense of desolation seemed redoubled when, from her seat in the cab, she witnessed that tender meeting.

In all that great city, with its thousands of joyful or sadly throbbing hearts, there was not one to bid her welcome to that new land.

> "Alone she sat—alone! that worn-out word,
> So idly spoken and so coldly heard;
> Yet all that poets sing, and grief hath known,
> Of hope laid waste, knells in that word—alone!"

A small chirping voice—like the cheerful noise of birds —speaking words of welcome; two little hard brown hands grasping hers, and Lotta was drawn from the cab into the house.

"A thousand welcomes, dear; shure yer jist smothered with the hate and the dust. Micky agra," to the driver, "will ye jist carry the young lady's trunks upstairs to the first bedroom, and put that bag on the wee table in the kitchen? This way, miss, dear; it's sich a bit strip of a lobby that they do be tellin' me that it's only fit for a wee cratur like meself to be passin' in an' out av. Now here we are; sit down, plaze, in that chair beside the winder, and we'll have a cup of tay in five minutes. That's right, Mary, dear, take off her things an' put them in the bedroom, while I see about the tay; the kettle's been singing the 'Groves of Blarney' this last hour."

With a merry little laugh she hurried away, followed by her daughter carrying Lotta's wraps.

Not alone! Thank Heaven, not alone!—with these two warm-hearted women attending upon her. If her present surroundings were humble, she would at least be comfortable and less lonely with the mother and daughter than in any of the great hotels.

The quiet of the little house was strangely soothing after the hurry and tumult of the last few hours. It was so good to be once more on *terra firma*. A feeling of peaceful serenity stole into her troubled mind. Letting her head rest against the back of her chair, she slowly rocked herself and listened to the little feathered songster overhead.

Presently Mrs. Mullins made her appearance carrying a well-filled tray.

"As you are my mother's guest, Miss von Rosenberg, she hopes you'll not feel offended at her treating you like one of her own children," she said, as she proceeded to cover a table with snowy damask and deftly arrange a tempting tea.

"You'll not mind, now, will you, my dear?"

"But, indeed, I will mind very much, Mrs. Mullins, for I cannot find words in which to thank your kind mother and yourself for the welcome you have given to me—a stranger!" Lotta answered, tears filling her beautiful sad eyes.

"Now don't say that, miss, dear. Do you think we don't know the honor you've done us? Now you won't be offended if I tell you what my mother has been saying about you, will you?"

"I think I may safely promise that I will not," Lotta responded, with a smile.

"Now mind you promised. She says, you look like a beautiful young princess, come to visit a poor little woman in her cabin," Mrs. Mullins said, with a good-natured little laugh, anxious to amuse Lotta.

"Have you made the acquaintance of Bob yet, Miss

von Rosenberg? Now mind, Bob, you must make great friends with this young lady."

Bob set his little yellow head on one side, fixed a black eye on the new claimant for favor, coolly considered the matter, polished his beak vigorously, then hopped round to the sun-flooded window, flirted out one wing defiantly, and burst into song.

The little room was dark and shadowy when the trio separated for the night. Bob had folded his soft wings over his little golden head, the atmosphere was heavy with the breath of the sleeping flowers, and Lotta had heard the simple story of her entertainers.

Good-nights were exchanged, and Mrs. Wood preceded her young lodger up the narrow staircase to a tiny room, very little larger than a closet, by courtesy called a bedroom.

Simply furnished, but spotlessly clean, a small iron bedstead, a little washstand, a table covered by a snowy cloth, on which stood a cherry-framed looking-glass, a miniature bureau, and one splint chair, completed the furniture of the room, in one corner of which Lotta's boxes were carefully piled—the furniture, but not the adornments.

At the head of the bed, within easy reach, hung a white-and-gold font; a branch of palm behind the gold cross. Above the little washstand was a neatly framed picture of "Our Lady of Perpetual Succor," and on top of the bureau was a plaster cast of the "Mother of Sorrows." This last appeared to be an object of special veneration, for it was covered by a glass shade and rested on the preserved skin of a once gay-feathered denizen of the Australian woods. On either side the sweet, mournful figure stood—sentinel-like—a curious little vase filled with white feather flowers.

"It's not what ye're used to, miss, but it's clane and

nate," said Mrs. Wood, placing the light she carried on the bureau and drawing down the blind. "'Tis meself wishes it wus finer for yer sake, me dear."

"Oh, thank you, Mrs. Wood, I shall be very comfortable."

"Och, thin, if ye're plased that's everything. Jist say yer prayers there, *mavourneen*," pointing to the statuette, "and the blissed Mother of God'll help ye, niver fear. Isn't she the mother of the orphan and the comfort of the widdy? She'll change yer dhread to joy, blessed be her name foriver and iver, amen!" with which pious valediction the old woman disappeared.

Long and fervently Lotta prayed, and when she rose from her knees a great peace filled her heart. She could not retire until she had written to the D'Arcys, telling them of her safe arrival and temporary disappointment in the non-appearance of her uncle, and promising to write full particulars of her voyage in a day or two.

Having sealed and addressed her letter, she raised the blind, opened the little window, and leaned out.

A cool, refreshing breeze stole up from the Hudson, bearing on its wings a sweet greeting from the distant wooded heights, bringing a loving message of welcome to the stranger from the simple flowers that bloomed in the heart of the primeval woods, and from the silver streamlets that murmur so gently in their dreams.

Chapter VIII.

> "Shone the white stars through the lattice—
> Sighed the night wind low and sweet—
> Rolled the river through the lindens,
> Like the rush of many feet;
> But the dead face answered only
> With the same look strange and far,
> With that mouth set white and smiling,
> Fixed and changeless, like a star."

IN a handsomely furnished apartment at the Albany—where the two young men had chambers—Marmaduke Clifford and Frank Brand were conversing earnestly. The latter gentleman was standing, leisurely smoking a cigar, while from behind the gracefully curling wreaths of smoke he thoughtfully watched his friend, as he lay back in the depths of an easy-chair, with a look upon his face which went far to say that Marmaduke Clifford was not in a mood to enjoy the luxuries by which he was surrounded; yet though by no means a Sybarite he was fastidious to a degree.

"You are still unsuccessful, then?" Frank Brand inquired, lightly filliping the ash from his cigar.

"Still!" with an impatient movement of his shapely hand. "It seems to me that I am as far off gaining a clew to their whereabouts as I was on my first arrival in this land of fogs and rain."

"Don't abuse the old land, Clifford, if we have had little but rain, snow, and fogs, since we landed; it's not fair."

"Perhaps not," with serene indifference; "the land is

nothing to me; never has been, you know. The present object of interest and of real importance is the finding of the D'Arcys, and the fact that I *must* return home at once. What will poor D'Arcy think? It is most surprising that none of those advertisements have been answered; surely some member of the family must read the newspapers."

"Has it ever occurred to you, Duke, that they may have left the city?"

"Yes, I did imagine such a possibility, and in one of my letters to D'Arcy I suggested a doubt of their being in London; but in his answer he assured me that his wife had promised they should remain here until he should come, or send for them. It might have been all well if that Mr. Philipson had not been smitten by the travelling mania, or if the old woman he left in charge had not taken a notion to visit her daughter at Chelsea. Maternal feelings are so strong in the bosoms of some old women, you see, in order to prove her affection she foolishly appropriated the malady from which her daughter was suffering, and—died."

"And the daughter still lives, I presume."

"My dear Brand, your presumption is most undeniably correct; worse luck; if the old woman had not been so affectionate, she might have been alive yet to answer my questions."

"Are you quite sure she could have told you anything likely to help you?"

"Yes, I know that she could have helped me very materially. The people in the next house were very civil, indeed, took quite an interest in my success, and procured me Mr. Philipson's address from a friend in Curzon Street; their footman had seen young D'Arcy talking to Mr. Philipson's housekeeper. He had been struck by the expression on the young man's face as he turned from the door, and had passed some remark upon it to the woman, who explained that the young gentleman was disappointed at not finding her master at home, and that there was something about letters which his mother was expecting. You see there could be no mistake, as she also informed the footman that the young gentleman's name was Mr. Connor D'Arcy. As soon as I got his address I wrote to Mr. Philipson begging him to let me have the address of the D'Arcys, which I knew he must have, as Connor had called a second time at the house, and left a letter to be forwarded to him. It is quite two months since I dispatched that letter, to which, as yet, I have had no answer. Now you see this letter"—pointing to one on a table beside him—"compels my immediate return home; and to return with my promise to D'Arcy unfulfilled distresses me deeply."

"Yes, I know how you feel about it, old man. But why not engage a detective?" Mr. Brand suggested, lighting a fresh cigar, and watching his friend.

"A detective! Heavens above, man! To what end?"

"There, my dear Duke, don't look so horrified; there is nothing in my suggestion to appal your refined sensibilities."

"But they are not criminals, Frank."

"Certainly not! But a detective will ferret them out quietly for you. There need be no *exposé*. I advise you to engage the services of some clever fellow at once. Had you done so at first, it would have saved you all this worry, and Mrs. D'Arcy would now be with her husband."

Clifford meditated deeply for several seconds.

"I wish, Frank," he said, drawing up his tall figure and sitting erect, "that you had made this suggestion sooner. As you say, it would have saved a heap of trouble, and hastened the reunion of D'Arcy and his wife."

"Never too late to mend, old man. I'll tell you what I will do. You must return at once, you say; then why not engage a detective within the hour? Then leave the rest in my hands, as I may be detained here a month or two longer, and I promise with his help to work it up for you."

"Will you?—will you really, old man?" eagerly.

"Yes, really!"

"Thanks! it's a bargain, then. Poor D'Arcy insists upon coming over to prosecute the search himself. He has not the strength, and yet I can't bear to go away and let them have no news of him."

"But they shall have news, Duke, I promise you."

"And if I can get this confounded business, that takes me away just now, settled in time, you may expect to see me back by the end of next month."

"I shall have found them before that."

"Perhaps," rather dubiously.

"Well, we shall see," Brand rejoined, confidently. He was resolved to prove to his friend what he could do.

> "'Ave! Ave! Mother bright,
> Guard us through the coming night,'"

Clifford hummed softly as he rang for his man.

Frank Brand had not been far astray when he suggested the possibility of the D'Arcys having left London; at least all but Connor and Teddy had left. They were in the city every day, but after office hours they joined the others in the new home to which Mrs. D'Arcy had been removed. She had yielded—ah, how unwillingly!—to their united entreaties and Connor's promise that he should call daily at Charlotte Street, until an answer to the letter he had had forwarded to Mr. Philipson should come.

It was a pretty, unpretending cottage to which the

gentle invalid had been removed, standing in the midst of a rambling old flower-garden with fragrant-smelling honeysuckle and jasmine clustering around the windows and climbing over and around the rustic porch before the door, from which a narrow gravelled path led to a little green gate, shaded on either side by a beautiful laburnum, whose golden tassels drooped gracefully above the low hawthorn hedge and the white road beyond.

All day long the song of the birds mingled sweetly with the dreamy murmur of a little brook that ran down one side of the garden close to the hedge, where, under the shade of a tall lime tree, was a rude seat formed of roots and moss. On the balmy air came sweet odors from blossoming orchards and smiling gardens.

A lovely spot, close to London, but looking in its quiet rural beauty as if hundreds of miles lay between it and the great city.

It is June now—fair, smiling June.

A month had passed since Lotta, standing on the deck of the stately ship which was to bear her from her native land, bade farewell to her friends, and in this month a change had come to the D'Arcys.

Connor, through the recommendation of his then employer, had obtained the situation of managing clerk in a branch office in the city, and had secured for Teddy a junior clerkship in the same office.

True to his resolve, Connor had sought for and found this little peaceful retreat, to which he had had his mother conveyed.

To the delight of the loving hearts around her, Mrs. D'Arcy had rallied and brightened up wonderfully after the fatigue consequent on her removal had passed away; it was but the last flash of the expiring taper, and was succeeded by a sudden and startling change.

Very gently, very kindly, the doctor who had been hastily summoned broke the sad tidings to Kate and Denise.

Oh, the anguish unutterable that that dread announcement brought to the hearts of those who loved the dying woman so tenderly!

It was terrible to witness Connor's silent despair. Teddy, utterly stunned by the blow, went about with white, stricken face and great sorrowful eyes. Eva wept unrestrainedly and with a passionate disregard of the feelings of others; and fearing the effects of such an outburst of grief upon the dying woman, Kate for once forgot to be patient with her pet and forcibly removed the weeping girl from the room.

The western sky was ablaze with the gold and crimson and amethyst of the setting sun, which sent long shafts of light into the little bedroom, bathing as if in loving benediction the face of Honoria D'Arcy in its golden splendor, and lighting up its sweet beauty with a glory not of this world.

"Denise!" said the low, sweet voice.

"Yes, mamma, darling."

"There is something I must say to you while we are alone for the last time, my child. I will soon be gone; but you must not grieve that Heaven sees fit to call me. I know all that is in your brave young heart, my Denise, and I also know that you will remember the words I am about to speak—my dying words to you."

"Yes, mamma, darling!" the poor girl responded, struggling, oh, so hard, to keep from crying aloud in the intensity of her anguish; and bending down she passionately kissed the thin white hand of her mother.

"It is the will of God that I shall not live to see your dear father; but you will see him soon, my darling, I feel that you will, and I want *you*, my Denise, to tell him that I never doubted, never blamed him. I know that it has not been his fault. Give him my love; tell him that to the last I prayed for and blessed him."

She paused, and gazed with a wistful pathos in the beautiful gray eyes, now dark and intense with approaching dissolution—out on the sun-flooded garden, on the golden laburnums, and on the blue sky, with its crimson and gold and soft amethyst clouds. Lingeringly the eyes of the dying woman turned from contemplating the tranquil beauty of the scene to look at Denise.

"There is something else I want you to promise," she continued, in faint, clear tones.

"You know that although you are so much younger than Connor, he will yield to you as he would not yield to the wishes of any other but myself. My noble Connor, Heaven bless him! He is so good, and generous, and affectionate; but, ah! he is proud, and passionate, and—and I fear just a little headstrong; but you, my Denise, can stay the storm of his wrath, you can influence him. He will listen to you when I am gone. Will you promise me?"

"I promise, dear, that I shall do my utmost to fulfil your wishes in all things."

"Heaven bless you! Your aunt could not have the heart to be firm with him; she is only a girl after all, just two years older than Connor, you know; and she always lets him have his own way in everything; poor Kate is so large-hearted.

"Connor does not understand your father. He judges him from his own standpoint and blames him accordingly. But that is all wrong. No child has a shadow of a right to arraign and condemn a parent. Your poor father may have failed in his endeavor, but I want you to remember *always* that he has never been guilty of wrong or injustice to us. When they meet you will remember this."

Oh, the loyal, faithful heart that will not doubt! Oh, the love which years of separation and apparent neglect cannot alter!

"Yes, darling mamma, I shall remember always."

"Something tells me that at no distant day you will meet Lotta. Give her my love and blessing, and tell her I thought of her, as of one of my children, to the last. Heaven could not bestow a greater boon upon my Connor than the boon of Lotta's love; she is the one in all the world I should desire to see his wife."

She leaned back among her pillows faint and exhausted, and pouring out some wine and water, Denise tenderly moistened the parched lips.

At that moment the door was softly opened by Kate, who noiselessly ushered in Father Brady, and soon after they were joined by Connor and Teddy.

.   .   .   .   .   .

The laburnums were pierced with shafts and arrows of sunlight, and dewdrops, glittering like rarest gems, still hung on the blades of grass and sparkled in the lily-cups. The birds sang their sweetest, golden shadows flickered and trembled across the little brook, as it wimpled and gurgled, like baby laughter, over its pebbly bed.

All nature seemed to rejoice on this fair June morning when Honoria D'Arcy lay cold and still in death within the little cottage.

How beautiful looked the face of the dead woman, with that mystic seal upon it, that subtle, inscrutable smile on the still, pale lips—a smile such as living lips never wore, a light, like the silver gleam shed by the moon, resting on the serene, white brow!

The slender hands, clasping a silver crucifix, were folded

above the pulseless heart, which would never again be moved by earthly joys or sorrows.

Kate and Denise still knelt and prayed by the silent form; the darkened room was lighted by tall wax-candles, and the air was heavy with the fragrance of sweet white flowers gathered by loving hands from the pretty garden without.

It wanted an hour of noon, when a gentleman opened the little green gate and walked quickly up the narrow path. Suddenly he paused, struck by the strange, oppressive stillness which pervaded the place, and, glancing toward the cottage, perceived that the blinds were all down.

He stood there an instant perplexed, irresolute, glancing from the windows, with their closely drawn blinds, to the closed door.

As nothing could be learned by standing staring at the house, he advanced and knocked softly, fearing he knew not what. But not until he had knocked a third time was there any response.

Then the door was noiselessly opened, and he drew back a step and raised his hat courteously to the graceful, dark-robed girl who stood before him, with fair face, pale and tear-stained, and blue eyes red with much weeping.

"I—I beg pardon, madam," he stammered, "but I have been informed that Mrs. D'Arcy and her family reside here. I hope my informant was correct, as I am acting in the interest of a friend who has been searching for the lady or her family for some months; and I am the bearer of a letter from Mr. D'Arcy."

"A letter—at last! And—ah! merciful Heaven, you are too late!"

Frank Brand would never forget the look that leaped into the blue eyes, or the hopeless, regretful misery in the soft, musical voice, as two little white hands went out in a gesture of wordless despair.

She seemed on the point of fainting, and with ready courtesy he put out his hand to save her from falling; but she recovered instantly, and with a faint smile offered an apology.

"This is so unexpected. I think you said that you bring a letter for Mrs. D'Arcy from her husband? I regret to say that Mrs. D'Arcy expired at half-past one o'clock this morning, without the consolation of even seeing that letter."

Her listener's face showed that he was startled and deeply shocked by this announcement.

Kate saw that his words of sympathy were sincere.

"I have the pleasure of being personally acquainted with your father, Miss D'Arcy," he continued, secretly wondering that she expressed no interest in the letter of which he was the bearer, "and I know it will prove a very severe blow to him when he learns that your mother is dead."

She bowed with quiet dignity.

"Permit me to thank you for the words of sympathy you have so kindly and, I feel, sincerely spoken. But allow me, sir, to set you right. I am Miss D'Arcy, the *sister*, not the *daughter* of Gerald D'Arcy."

For once in many years Mr. Brand crimsoned over face and temples. He had made a mistake, but a very natural mistake notwithstanding.

Despite the traces of bitter grief and unrestrained weeping, Kate D'Arcy looked very young and girlish in face and form; as she stood in the open doorway, framed in by its vine-wreathed porch, the most severe critic could not imagine that twenty-four summers had passed over her head. Her gown is plain and shabby, but scrupulously clean—a dark prune-colored cashmere, which she had worn religiously for the past fifteen months, with frillings of thin white muslin, neatly crimped, at throat and wrists. She looked pale and exhausted after her night's vigil; but usually her complexion was a blending of the rose and the lily; hers was a bright, tender, truthful face, with a certain touch of pride in the curve of the lips, in the glance of the handsome blue eyes, in the poise of the shapely white throat, and in the erect, graceful carriage.

Strictly speaking she was not beautiful, but she was exceedingly pretty and winsome, and notwithstanding the undeniable shabbiness of her attire, in every gesture, in every inflection of the soft, musical voice, Kate D'Arcy was a gentlewoman.

For an instant, as her visitor realized all this, he paused, but only for an instant, so brief that Kate, though perceiving that swift flush, scarcely noticed his silence.

"Pray accept my apologies, Miss D'Arcy," he said, with pleasing frankness, "although a more clever man than myself might have made a similar mistake, and permit me to introduce myself: I am Frank Brand, very much at your service, Miss D'Arcy. If there is anything I can do for you or any of your brother's family, I beg you will not hesitate to call upon me. I shall not return to the States for a week or two, and meantime command me in all things.

"I believe you will find every instruction in your brother's letter, which I shall now give you—since I have unfortunately been denied the pleasure of delivering it to the lady for whom it was written; and shall no longer intrude upon your grief."

These words, so gently spoken, brought a swift blush to Kate's fair face, as she suddenly remembered that all this time she had been keeping this messenger from her long-absent brother standing on the doorstep. The shock of this letter, coming at such a time, had for the moment stunned her into forgetfulness.

"The loss we have just sustained must be my apology for keeping you so long standing here, Mr. Brand," she said, with quiet dignity; "let me hope that you will kindly overlook my neglect and favor me by entering the house."

He bowed, and she led the way into a small room.

"This is my present address, Miss D'Arcy," he said, presenting his card, in one corner of which he had hastily scribbled "The Albany."

She took it with a word of thanks and gracefully indicated a chair to her visitor.

Chapter IX.

"The voice of thy streams in my spirit I hear.
    Farewell! and a blessing be with thee, dear land!
On thy halls, on thy hearths, on thy pure mountain air;
    On the strings of the harp and the minstrel's free hand!
From the love of my soul with my tears it is shed,
    Whilst I leave thee, O land of my home and my dead!"
                                    —Mrs. Hemans.

"Bright spells are on the soothèd sea,
    And Hope, the child, is gone to dream
Of pleasures—which may never be!"
                            —Barry Cornwall.

"I SHALL most certainly decline to go! The husband and father who could so utterly neglect his wife and children—for four years never writing to them—leaving his wife to die of want and a broken heart, cannot be surprised if I, his son, refuse to accept his money or go to him. I am of age, and I shall never be a dependent on the bounty of a man who has proved himself so utterly heartless."

"Connor D'Arcy, I beg you will remember that you are speaking of your father, and that although you *are* of age, that time never comes to any one of us when we cease to owe obedience and respect to our parents."

Under the lime-tree, by the wimpling brook, a little group was gathered. Connor, with pale, set face and gleaming eyes, his dark hair swept back from his handsome, massive brow, where the great blue veins stood out like knotted cords, his tall figure drawn up to its full height, determination and defiance in every line of his clear-cut features.

Before him stood Denise, with white, stricken face and pleading eyes, and beside her Kate, with a new look upon her face, a look of anger and command.

"Then I *decidedly* prefer evincing my respect for my remaining parent at a distance."

"But, Connor, you forget what the gentleman told Aunt Kate; indeed, dear, you must see that papa was not to blame; his letters to dear mamma had miscarried; you know she always said there was some mistake about them, and that it was a pity we had not left our address with Mr. Philipson when the bank failed and we were obliged to remove to an attic."

"Of course," Connor responded, with fine sarcasm, "we had no right to the possession of a spark of self-respect; and because, forsooth, we attempted to exercise a little reticence, in the vain hope of hiding from the world the state of utter destitution to which we had been reduced, you possibly consider that all the misery and suffering which the last few months have brought us just retribution. What do you think the world would say of the matter? I will tell you: the world would say that our father, after having spent his own and his wife's fortune on speculations, had fled, leaving his wife and children destitute, penniless, dependents upon the bounty of his girl sister, whose warm, generous heart would——"

"Connor, I insist that you respect my feelings and cease speaking in such terms of your father and my brother!" Kate said severely. She could not conscientiously allow Connor to cast a reproach upon his absent father, although she had long secretly blamed her brother for his neglect of his wife and children, whose welfare, by the laws of God and man, was his first duty; but she could not encourage Connor in rebelling against his father.

She had brought Connor and Denise here, away from the presence of their unburied dead, to tell them of Mr. Brand's visit and to give Connor his father's letter, which at first sight he had positively refused to open, until moved by Denise's tears and entreaties. As, with frowning brow, he cut the envelope and drew forth the inclosure, a folded paper fluttered to the ground. Denise stooped and picked up a draft for three hundred pounds, which she placed in her aunt's hand.

It was a tender, loving letter—that letter to the dead wife, whose eyes in life had so ached to see it, but would now never look upon it.

Who can say for what mysterious reason this pleasure had been denied the poor longing heart?

It gave a slight *résumé* of his life and struggles during the last few years. He hinted at his disappointment in not having received an answer to any of his letters, and mentioned the accident which had prevented him coming in person to find his beloved ones.

If the inclosed would be insufficient for present expenses the bearer of the letter, Mr. Clifford, would be their banker to any amount. He would wish them to prepare and come to him at once; and he promised to have a fitting home prepared for them. His friend Mr. Clifford, in whom he had all faith, had promised to take charge of them on the passage. It concluded with loving messages to all.

But Connor's heart was hardened against his father and the sight of the money only served to further embitter him. As Denise listened to the hot, angry words that fell from his lips, she shivered and inwardly murmured:

"Thank Heaven! he will never know that to save our dear mother's life I once sang on the streets of London."

Prayers and entreaties were alike thrown away upon Connor, who was inflexibly bent on carrying out his resolution of remaining in his present situation.

He was young and strong, he asserted, and it behooved every man to fight the battle of life alone and unaided.

Finding that she could not shake his resolves, Kate left him alone with Denise and went into the cottage to write a letter to her brother.

For a few seconds after Kate had left them, only the sweet music of the brook and the song of the birds broke the stillness; Denise leaned against the bole of the lime-tree, her slender hands locked tightly together, her beautiful eyes fixed with a look of hopeless misery upon Connor's stern, set face; she was inwardly praying for strength to combat his resolution.

"Connor!" she was standing by his side now, her cheek against his shoulder, her trembling hands clasping his arm. He did not look at her, but he touched her clinging hands gently with his fingers, and said in kind tones:

"My poor Denise! you have suffered so much lately, but no amount of grieving will restore our dear mother to us; go to your room and try to sleep for an hour or two. Sleep is the best restorative, and you are trembling."

"O Connor, darling brother! do not be vexed with me, it will break my heart if you remain in England and refuse to go to papa," she pleaded.

He forcibly withdrew the clinging fingers from his arm, and with darkening brows thrust her from him.

"There is no use, Denise, I shall not be moved from my resolution. Do you think I am a child to be led hither and thither at the will of those around me? Had you been left to my care, Heaven knows how willingly I should have worked to keep you all from want; that duty has been claimed by one possessed of a better right; but, once for all, I distinctly refuse to profit by his sudden accession to fortune. I could never forget that his neglect killed our mother—let this be the last we shall ever say about it."

He turned and went toward the cottage, leaving her to follow, with bowed head and cruelly aching heart. In all her young life Connor had never before treated her so harshly; but she did not think of that, she thought only of her promise to her dying mother.

It was the evening of the second day after the funeral. Denise stood alone at the little green gate, gazing out along the dusty road, where long purple shadows were beginning to fall.

There was an eager light in the girl's eyes, a soft glow on the pale cheeks; she looked so fair, and sweet, and pretty in her deep mourning dress, which contrasted so well with the fresh young face and pure complexion, as she stood there, all unconscious and unheeding what a picture she made with the golden laburnums drooping from their sweet green leaves above her. In her hands, which were folded at her back, she held a letter.

She had stood thus for the last half-hour watching— watching for the coming of Connor and Teddy from the city.

At last she saw them coming; they had evidently caught a glimpse of her, for they quickened their footsteps, and she quitted her post and went to meet them, one hand holding up her train, the other, in which she held the letter, still at her back.

"Were you watching for us?" Connor asked, smiling into her eager, upturned face, as she passed her hand through his arm. "Did you think we were not coming? This is Teddy's last day at the office, you know, and we were detained."

"Yes, you are late, but it is not quite that; there is a

letter for you, at last, from Mr. Philipson. Connor, dear, it went to Charlotte Street, and Mrs. Norris sent Sarah here with it. Was it not kind and thoughtful of her?"

"Very! Mrs. Norris is a good, motherly soul."

"Is it an answer to the letter you sent away long ago, Connor?" Teddy asked eagerly. He was looking thin, pale, and anxious-eyed.

"I suppose so," Connor responded carelessly, as they entered the gate and Denise gave him the letter, which he received without comment of any kind, and taking the little path leading to the brook, left Teddy and Denise to enter the cottage alone. As they went slowly up the path she told Teddy that Mr. Brand had called to tell them that he had also had a letter from Mr. Philipson in answer to the one sent by Mr. Clifford.

Connor's letter had been sent to quite a number of places after Mr. Philipson, and had only just reached him at the same time as Mr. Clifford's.

"And Teddy, dear," she said, clasping her brother's arm eagerly, "just think what a dreadful mistake we have all made. Mr. Philipson has had three letters from papa for dear mamma: two are lying at his house in London, and should have been given to Connor when he called, but the stupid woman must have forgotten; and the third arrived after Mr. Philipson's departure for Egypt, and was sent after him; but he did not know our address until he got Connor's letter. O Teddy, if we had only got these letters in time mamma might still have been alive, and we should all have been so happy."

"Yes," Teddy answered, with a profound sigh, as they entered the house.

His mother's death had been a severe blow to quiet, undemonstrative Teddy, and now that Connor had decided to remain in England the poor boy felt utterly heart-broken.

In a little while Denise stole out to the garden to where Connor was seated under the lime-tree, his face hidden in his hands, and on the ground at his feet two letters were lying. She went softly up to him, and sinking on her knees beside him stole her arm around his neck.

"Connor, darling, come in to tea; Aunt Kate is waiting." He looked up with pale face and haggard eyes, trying to smile.

"Then we must not keep her waiting," he said gently.

He stooped and picked up the letters.

"This letter was sent after Mr. Philipson, and he inclosed it with his own to me; it contained a bill for fifty pounds; if it had but reached us in time our poor mother might have been alive to-day. Here it is, Denise; since she is dead the money is yours."

He put a folded paper into her hand.

"Connor, dear, think it all over. You see papa has not been to blame after all; do come with us! Poor Teddy is breaking his heart, and oh, darling, just think what poor dear mother would feel if she knew you would not go to papa. You *will* come, Connor, won't you, and make us all happy?"

She saw that he was softened, and now that they were alone was her time; she knew he would not brook being talked to before others.

He looked up, meeting her eyes fully, and answering slowly:

"I confess that in a measure I have done our father an injustice, yet you must admit that his letters have been few and far between. He mentions having sent several others; Mr. Philipson writes that he received two more, which he left on his desk at home to be delivered to me if I called. But allowing that others have gone astray, what are six or eight letters from a husband to his wife in the space of four years?"

"But you see, Connor, papa never got an answer to any of these letters, and might he not quite as reasonably blame dear mamma for not writing? He did not know that these letters never reached her, and you know, dear, it is wrong for us to sit in judgment upon our parents."

Half an hour later they entered the little sitting-room, where Kate, Teddy, and Eva were patiently awaiting their coming. Denise, with a glad light shining through tears in her beautiful eyes, a smile dimpling round her pretty mouth, advanced to the table.

"Connor is coming with us, Aunt Kate," she said.

Kate's blue eyes were raised with an answering smile.

"Ah, now indeed you are my own Connor."

"And you are no longer angry with me, Aunt Kate?"

"Angry! I have never been so long angry with you before, my dear boy; but it is all past now, thank Heaven. Ah, how happy it would make your dear mother if she could know this!"

"Denise conquered," Connor answered, as he took his seat.

"Won't it be splendid, going all together, and won't Lottchen be surprised when we meet her! But then, of course, papa being so very rich, we'll not have much chance of meeting her, as her uncle is only a farmer, and we are sure to live in a large house in the city," said Eva grandly.

Connor frowned, and Kate said, a little severely, as she poured out the tea:

"I should hope, Eva, that no change of fortune would ever cause us to neglect Lotta, whose unvarying kindness to us in our time of poverty has given her a strong hold upon our lasting friendship; and, setting all that aside,

Lotta von Rosenberg is the noblest girl I have ever known; and it will be an unspeakable pleasure to me when we meet again."

"O auntie, I did not mean that we should forget Lottchen, as you seem to think," Eva cried, with a little pout. "I am sure I should like to see her very much; and I shall ask papa to invite her to some of our parties, it will be so nice to have her come."

"You are early beginning to patronize," Connor remarked scornfully.

"Don't put on airs, Eva; I wouldn't if I were you," Teddy said indignantly. "Lotta is not a girl to be patronized."

. . . .

The passage had not been quite so pleasant as had been anticipated; the good ship had encountered more than one stiff gale, but to-day the Atlantic is smooth and glassy, the blue sky cloudless.

Every one had come on deck to look at the blue hills of Neversink. They were nearing land now, and Denise, as she stood gazing sadly toward the land which she had once so longed to visit, thought of the dear mother lying peacefully at rest in the little English churchyard so far away, and wondered if she knew they were so soon to see the father who for so many years had been a stranger to them.

She glanced at Eva, who was laughing and chattering gayly with Mr. Brand and quite a little knot of passengers, and a sharp pang came to her heart.

"How soon Eva has forgotten!" she thought sadly.

She looked away from the gay party and softly repeated Tennyson's beautiful lines:

"——the stately ships go on,
　To their haven under the hill;

> But oh, for the touch of a vanished hand,
> And the sound of a voice that is still!"

She saw that Connor was thoughtfully watching the track made by the prow of the stately ship as she gracefully cut her way through the blue waters, and knew that he shared her feelings. Then she found herself wondering, with vague uneasiness, how Connor would meet their father.

Chapter X.

"We look before and after,
  And sigh for what is not;
And our sincerest laughter
  With some pain is fraught.
Our sweetest songs are those
  That tell of saddest thoughts."
—SHELLEY.

WHEN Lotta descended next morning, the sun was shining brightly and Bob was flooding the little house with music. With the glad morning sunshine the brave young heart had cast aside much of the previous day's misgivings, and she smilingly greeted the two women, who anxiously inquired how she had rested.

"Thanks, I was very comfortable; but have you really waited breakfast, Mrs. Woods? It is quite too bad to have kept you waiting so long," she said as she took a seat at the neatly spread table.

"I think of going out after breakfast; might I ask you, Mrs. Mullins—if you have no other engagement—to accompany me to the post-office? I should like this letter posted at once. I promised to write home and tell my friends of my safe arrival."

It would be long before Lotta would cease to look upon the old land and the drawing-room flat in Charlotte Street as home.

"Well, surely you haven't lost much time in keeping your promise, Miss von Rosenberg, and indeed I'll have much pleasure in going with you to the post-office, or, for the matter of that, taking you all over the city if you'll let me."

"Thanks, but——"

The little knocker on the front door gave out a loud peremptory summons, startling all three and causing Lotta to pause abruptly.

"Never mind, mother, I'll open the door—I know you'll excuse me, Miss von Rosenberg," Mrs. Mullins said as she hurried from the room.

The sound of a man's voice—a hasty step in the narrow lobby—and Lotta is standing in the centre of the little room, looking at the door with wide, startled eyes, her beautiful face flushing and paling alternately. She uttered a little cry as the door was flung open, and advanced a step, both hands outstretched to a tall, broad-shouldered man standing framed in the open doorway.

"*Lottchen, mein liebes Kind!*"

"Uncle!"

He placed his hands on her shoulders and kissed her on either cheek, then pushed her gently away and looked at her long and earnestly.

"It is *mein* little Lottchen, who has come from over the sea to brighten her old uncle's home and make him happy. Is it not so, *mein Herz?*"

"It is so, my uncle. I am Lottchen, and, if you will let me, I will try to make your home happy."

"*Ach Himmel!* that is good," he said, with a profound sigh. He laid his hand upon her shoulder and looked her steadily in the face. For a few seconds there was silence between them; neither noticed that the two women had quietly slipped from the room.

"Carl's daughter," he said sadly, tears standing in the still clear blue eyes. "Poor Carl! You are all that is left to care for the old man, Lottchen. I will be a father to you, and you will try to care a little for me?"

"I will care very much for you, uncle, if you will let me."

"*Ach!* That is what I have been wanting for the last eight years—some one to care for me. I felt it very bitterly when they were all taken from me and I was left alone. But you have been sent to take their place, *mein Kind*, and I will grieve no longer. But will you be content on a Western farm, Lottchen?"

"I will be content, uncle, so long as I am with you."

Something like a smile twinkled in the blue eyes so earnestly regarding her.

"*Ach, mein Herz*, you will look like a beautiful white lily all alone in a garden filled with nettles and dandelions. But you will not need to soil your white hands, Lottchen; there are helps to do the work, and you shall have everything that money can buy to make you happy."

"But indeed, uncle," Lotta answered, a tremor in her sweet young voice, "money could not purchase that which alone could make me happy."

"*Ach! mein bestes Lottchen*, it is a very powerful agent; but what is the essential which money cannot purchase?"

She lifted her beautiful eyes filled with tears to his face.

"The dear father loved me!" she answered tremulously, "and I was so happy."

"Then you shall be happy! Carl's daughter shall be to me as my own."

She lifted his strong, sunburnt hand and pressed it to her cheek. "Then I shall be very happy, *mein bester Onkel.*"

"Now that is settled," he said, smiling down upon her. "I will take you away from here." But glancing at the breakfast-table, "As you have not breakfasted and I am in the same condition, I will join you; then I will take you away. We will not go home for a week or two, and you will see all the sights. But why did you come here, Lottchen? Why did you not go to a hotel?"

"I was so lonely, uncle. I have never gone anywhere unaccompanied by my dear father; when he was engaged I remained at home. When the London seasons were over and his patrons out of town, we always went somewhere for a holiday, to Italy or the South of France, but more frequently we went to dear old *Vaterland*—but I have never before travelled a mile without my dear father by my side. If I had not been so unhappy I would have been dreadfully frightened to have undertaken this journey alone. But when the ship came up to her pier and I beheld the confusion and strange faces around me, and for the first time realized that I was alone in a strange land and that you did not come, I grew sick at heart, a great terror seized me, and I begged the stewardess to take me to her home. The captain promised that you should not be kept in suspense about me, and they have been very kind to me, uncle."

"Then, *mein Lottchen*, they shall have no cause to repent having been kind to thee."

If Lotta could have ceased to mourn the loss of a father who had loved her so truly, she might have been happy, for her uncle seemed determined to make up in affection for the loss she had sustained; she was grateful to him for all his care and attention, and made an effort to appear bright and cheerful.

During the next fortnight they visited every place of interest in or about the city.

Mr. von Rosenberg seemed never tired of buying Lotta costly presents. At first she remonstrated, but seeing that the bestowal of these gifts afforded him pleasure she desisted.

"We live so far away from everything," he would say, with a laugh, "and when you go home you will be wishing you had bought these things when you had the chance."

They were staying at one of the principal hotels. Mr. von Rosenberg was very proud of the beauty and grace of his niece, but although it pleased him that every one should admire her, he preferred that it should be at a distance; she had come to fill the void in his lonely heart, and already he looked upon her as his child.

They were coming out of "Delmonico's" when a pleasant voice, with the least possible drawl, close beside them said:

"Hadn't the most remote notion I should see you here, Mr. von Rosenberg; going to stay long?"

The speaker, a very fair specimen of a handsome young American, dressed in a light summer suit, was regarding Lotta with evident surprise and a very strong mingling of respectful admiration.

"I thought I had left you out West," Mr. von Rosenberg said, shaking hands with the young man; then turning proudly to his niece: "Lottchen, this is Mr. Herbert Haviland, the son of a neighbor; Mr. Haviland, this young lady is my niece, Miss von Rosenberg."

"I am very happy to make your acquaintance, Miss von Rosenberg," the young man said, returning Lotta's bow with easy grace.

"May I venture to ask what are your impressions of us? But I suppose my question is premature; you have scarcely had time to judge us as a people, and in order to appreciate the beauty of our land, you would require to leave the city."

"I confess to being already pleasantly disappointed, Mr. Haviland," Lotta answered, her slow, rare smile lighting up the beautiful, sad face.

"I am very pleased to hear you say so, Miss von Rosenberg, and I venture to prophesy that you will not be long among us until all your insular prejudices have vanished. But pardon me, you are not English, perhaps?"

"I scarcely know how to answer that question, Mr. Haviland. I was born in England; my dear father was a German, my mother was English. I love both nations very dearly, and feel that both have claims upon my affections."

"Let me hope, Miss von Rosenberg, that you will keep a little place in your regards for the new land."

"I am sure I shall like it very much," she responded.

She felt pleased when her uncle engaged the young man in conversation all about cattle, crops, and farm implements. He accompanied them to their hotel, and after asking and obtaining permission to call upon them next morning, took his leave.

During the remainder of their stay in the city Mr. Haviland called frequently upon them and accompanied them to different places, often bringing or sending bouquets of flowers to Lotta, who did not know how to refuse these delicate attentions, yet felt constrained to do so.

"It is very kind of Mr. Haviland, uncle, but I would much rather he did not send those flowers," she said one morning with a slight shade of annoyance on her beautiful face, holding up an exquisite bouquet which a messenger boy had just brought to their parlor.

Her uncle looked up from his breakfast, a whimsical smile in the shrewd blue eyes.

"Haviland has been to Europe, *mein Kind*, and has picked up a few nonsensical French airs. He is not a bad sort of a fellow, though, and pays these little attentions to the young stranger in a spirit of friendliness; but if they annoy *mein* Lottchen I shall take care he sends no more flowers."

A warm blush tinted the creamy whiteness of Lotta's

face; she regretted having spoken on the subject, and feeling how ridiculous her objections must appear, responded hastily:

"Oh, please do not say anything about the flowers; of course it is very kind of Mr. Haviland, and I am very absurd, uncle."

"We will start for home in a few days, and the young fellow will not be able to leave New York for another fortnight; so unless you like I will say nothing about them, but remember, *mein Herz*, no one will need to annoy my little Lottchen."

It was evident that Mr. von Rosenberg was eager to get back to his home, and Lotta began to tire of the heat and dust of the city. They had visited all the churches, Long Branch, Coney Island, and Lake George, and before starting on their journey she once more wrote to her friends in England.

The heat was becoming overpowering, and Lotta felt thankful to escape from the noise of ever-rolling omnibuses and the sight of valise-laden humanity on the move in search of cooler quarters—thankful to escape from the tumult and confusion at the railroad depots, the bustle and oppressive heat of the city—thankful to catch a glimpse of the fresh, green country as they flew along, and her eyes could rest refreshed on the beauties of nature bathed in the glory of the summer sunshine.

The long and seemingly interminable journey came to an end at last.

"Here we are at last, *mein Kind*," Mr. von Rosenberg said, his face glowing with pleasure, as the train for almost the hundredth time began to slow up, and the conductor, looking in at the door of the coach, shouted in a stentorian voice: "Mooseville!"

"We get off here, Lottchen," her uncle said, giving her

his hand as he spoke, and assisting her to descend the steps to the platform of the little country way-station, where, close to the station-house, a light wagon was drawn up.

The young man standing by the horse hastily flung the reins over the animal's back and advanced, his face beaming with delight.

"Ah, thin, Mr. von Rosenberg, but ye're welcome home," he exclaimed joyfully.

"How are all at home, Dan? Everything getting on well?"

"Niver was betther, sor, an' sure I'm heartily glad to see ye back."

"Thanks. This young lady is Miss von Rosenberg, your future mistress, Dan."

"An' a beautiful young crathur she is, sor, axin' your pardon, ma'am," Dan answered, with a gasp of genuine admiration. "An' indade, miss, ye're as welcome as the flowers in May."

"Thanks, very much!" Lotta returned, with a smile that went straight to the heart of Dan and made him her willing slave ever after.

"Now, Dan, see to Miss von Rosenberg's luggage and all these packages, and let us be off home. Give me the whip—I shall drive."

"Indade an' ye'll be there in a wink, sor," Dan responded, setting about his work with alacrity.

Since her first arrival in the States, Lotta had never enjoyed anything so much as that two miles' drive from the depot to her new home.

The deep azure of the cloudless sky, the golden sunlight all around, broken here and there by the outspreading branches of the grand old oaks, which cast long purple shadows on the soft green grass; lovely, unpretending violets half hidden in cool mosses peeping shyly forth, and in the most unexpected spots beautiful groves starting into view. The slender branches of the tall trees drooping gracefully over the edge of a silvery lake, whose mirror-like surface reflected the emerald tint of their foliage, added a mystic beauty to the dim recesses opening back in the forest.

Suddenly they came upon a different scene, a vast tract of land, cleared and cultivated, reaching to the verge of the distant horizon. Clusters of shanties were scattered here and there in the distance.

Close at hand were great fields of grain, the well-kept fences studded with fruit-trees; to the right, sleek, mild-eyed cattle grazing knee-deep in the rich pasture; facing the south a large, comfortable-looking brown house, with a piazza running along the front and in the rear a large orchard and garden.

No more beautiful or peaceful scene could well be imagined—the emerald billows of the softly swelling pasture, the pleasant low of the cattle, the rich fields of grain, the air of substantial comfort around and about the house. In the distance the grand old forest, closely wooded heights; here a picturesque waterfall, there the shining silver sands bordering a lovely little lake; the brooding stillness of the sweet summer evening, and above all the blue arch of the smiling heavens.

Mr. von Rosenberg brought the horse to a sudden stop, and fixing his eyes eagerly on Lotta's face, with his whip pointed toward the house.

"That is your future home, Lottchen," he said. "Do you like it?"

He read the admiration and pleasure in her face and eyes even before she answered with a deep inspiration of delight:

"It is beautiful!"

A gate leading to the house was laid back, and as they drove up to the entrance a huge dog came bounding from the piazza barking joyfully and leaping upon Mr. von Rosenberg as he alighted from the wagon. It was an instant or two before he could free himself from the animal's caresses and turn to Lotta. Then he assisted her to the ground and, taking her two hands in his, kissed her on either cheek.

"*Willkommen, mein liebes Kind!*" he said warmly. The voice was so like the voice of her beloved father that the blinding tears filled Lotta's eyes, for she felt that that welcome came from the speaker's heart.

Chapter XI.

> "To one a perfect halcyon nest,
>   All calm and balm, and quiet, and rest,
>   And soft as the fur of the coney;
>   To another so restless for body and head,
>   That the bed seemed borrowed from nettlebed,
>   And the pillow from Stratford the stony!"
>   —HOOD'S "*Miss Kilmansegg.*"

> "For the Viking blood within me
>   Tempest stirs my rebel breast,
>   I am wearied of this splendor—
>   Of this perfum'd silken rest."
> —MRS. W. M. BERTHOLD'S "*Lays of the Vikings.*"

"BUT indeed, papa, darling, I don't see why we should go anywhere away from this lovely place. Of course it is awfully hot; and one likes to be cool, you know."

"Therein lies the necessity for change, Eva, and I have written to engage lodgings at a country-house during the heated term; I hope you will all be pleased with the place. We will be quiet and retired, even should our accommodations fall short of what we might desire."

"Oh, how good you are, papa! but"—a little less fervently—"I do hope it will be a nice place—not *quite* so grand as this, perhaps, for no one possessed of such a residence would want to take in lodgers; but indeed, papa," Eva continued naïvely, "I should much prefer remaining here than go to lodge in a poor house, no matter how cool it might be."

Mr. D'Arcy laughed good-naturedly.

"Well, Eva, if you cannot dispense with luxury, I am afraid you must remain where you are," he said. "Still, I venture to think that the prospect of locating for two months at a nice farm-house, in the vicinity of wooded hills, green valleys, and running waters, might compensate for any trifling disadvantage, more especially when I can promise you a plentiful supply of rich milk, fresh eggs, golden butter, luscious honey, and fish fresh from the stream; shady grounds, pine and maple groves; no malaria, no mosquitoes."

"Those who could withstand such inducements must be more or less than mortal. Apart from every other consideration, it is such insufferably hot weather and so debilitating that if we can get to any cool country place for the time being, I think we should be highly reprehensible to cavil with our accommodations," Kate D'Arcy remarked, plying a palm-leaf fan with surprising energy.

"But I do like nice things, Aunt Kate."

"My dear Eva, I do not imagine that your friends can hold two opinions on the subject of your likes," rejoined her aunt pleasantly. "I may add, I think you are just a *little* worldly *au fond*. I wonder where Connor and Teddy can be?"

"I heard them talk about going for a drive to the Central Park with Mr. Brand, Aunt Kate," Denise responded in her clear, bright tones.

"I don't know how they could think of going out again under such a sun. What does the thermometer stand at, papa?"

Gerald D'Arcy was seated in a wicker garden chair upon a shaded piazza; around the balustrade rare plants were ranged, filling the atmosphere with perfume.

He had been conversing in a desultory fashion through

the open door, close to which he was seated, with the occupants of the room beyond; and as Denise addressed him, he withdrew the Havana which he had been enjoying from between his lips, and turned to answer her question as the questioner stepped out from the cool, lofty room and stood by his side.

It was a palatial mansion, this home of the D'Arcys, with its handsome marble front, grand entrance, broad halls, wide sweeping staircases, gleaming statuary, costly paintings, and stately, cheerful rooms.

A home which might satisfy the most ambitious; yet although his by the most indisputable of all rights, that of having toiled for and purchased it, Gerald D'Arcy, as he sat there inhaling the perfume of the flowers and the faint, briny air stealing up from the river, his white summer sack thrown widely open, a far-away look in his handsome blue eyes, did not appear a thoroughly happy man.

He was thinking of the hour in which he had first brought his family to this magnificent home, and he had said to Connor, with a feeling of pardonable pride in the results of his efforts:

"This is your new home, Connor. I hope you will like it."

The look on Connor's face comes back to him now, even as Connor's answer seems ringing in his ears:

"It is a splendid dwelling, sir; but a tithe of this splendor and your presence would have given my mother happiness and saved her from dying."

They were cruel words, although his son did not mean them as such; but they conveyed a reproach and were as a sword-thrust to the warm Irish heart of Mr. D'Arcy.

He resented the words and the look which accompanied them, and although he had answered quietly:

"You cannot mourn your dear mother's death more

truly than I, Connor. Had I known the state to which my beloved ones were reduced, no earthly consideration would have kept me apart from them; but how could I know when my letters remained unanswered? I relied upon your aunt's money being secure, and having all faith in her, believed my wife and family safe from actual want."

Yet the sting remained. A feeling of resentment and disappointment sprang up in Mr. D'Arcy's mind which the ecstasies of Eva or the admiration and surprise of the others could not remove.

It was "the rift within the lute," slight and unseen, but the harmony would never be the same again; perhaps a secret consciousness that he was not blameless made the reproach conveyed in Connor's words more keenly felt. No man likes to have his shortcomings brought vividly before him, and that too by a son whose esteem he values, and at the very moment when he had expected praise and congratulations.

Gerald D'Arcy had said truly, "he mourned his wife's death."

It had been a severe blow to him when the letter containing the sad tidings had reached him; but eight years of separation from wife and family, the whirl and excitement inseparable from his untiring chase after fortune, had somewhat blunted, but certainly had not deadened, his affections. He loved his family and felt justly proud of them; perhaps he was at first a little disappointed that Connor had outgrown his boyish resemblance to himself.

No father and son could be more unlike: Connor with his pale, dark, handsome face, rich black hair and fearless gray eyes, tall, lithe figure and haughty carriage, strong to feel and slow to forget; Mr. D'Arcy fair, blue-eyed, sanguine, warm, impulsive, generous to prodigality, lacking his son's perfection of features, but gay and *débonnaire*, with the easy grace and tone, the unmistakable *je ne sais quoi* which bespeaks the gentleman.

He was changed, less impulsive, less gay, possibly a little less generous, but his wild, nomadic life had not robbed him of the grace of manner which had never failed to win respect and admiration from the rudest.

He looked up now with a smile in his eyes as Denise laid her hand upon his shoulder and said gratefully:

"It is so kind of you, papa, to think so much of our comfort; but why should we desire a change when we have such a splendid home as this?"

Mr. D'Arcy looked intently at the earnest face, so bright and changeful, with the eyes and lips of his early love, the wife whom he had vowed to shelter and protect and whom he had left to die believing herself neglected.

He knew now that he should never have parted from his wife, or, having done so, should have returned years before and sought her out.

A cruel pang pierced his heart as he met the gray eyes looking into his; but Denise never dreamed that the sight of her face was a reproach to him, or that, although his heart yearned toward her with unspeakable tenderness, it was a tenderness always mingled with remorseful regret.

If he could but recall the last few years of his life—but he knew that regrets were worse than useless, and no shadow appeared on his face as he smilingly answered Denise:

"My dear child, you cannot understand this climate; you will find that after the middle of this midsummer month the torrid heat in the city will make you long for a sojourn in a cooler latitude. It is now only the middle of July, but a few days like this one with the mercury in the nineties will make you thankful to get away. I cannot take you to a fashionable resort, for I wish our term of mourning to be passed in retirement; to this end I have selected the place I have just mentioned as being healthy, where you can enjoy the invigorating air without restraint and be quietly secluded. Some of the men will row you all across the river every Sunday morning, to where, close to the bank in a little wooden chapel, the Holy Mass is offered up for the benefit of a number of poor Irish families scattered about the district. When we return home your aunt will engage a resident governess for Eva and you. She will remain with you for two years, at the expiration of which time I design that you shall take your place in 'society,' and I feel sure that I shall have reason to be proud of my daughters."

Eva had come out upon the piazza and now stole her arm around her father's neck.

"O you dear, darling papa," she exclaimed rapturously, "how good you are! It will be just delightful to see our splendid rooms filled with beautifully dressed people, and to give balls and parties, won't it, Denise?"

A look of pain darkened Denise's clear eyes at her sister's thoughtless words, and she answered hastily:

"It will not be for a long time yet, Eva, and papa is telling me that we shall be rowed across the river every Sunday to Mass while we are staying at Beechville. Won't that be splendid, dear?"

Gerald D'Arcy read the aversion with which his eldest daughter shrank from discussing gayeties so soon after the death of her mother, and appreciated the delicacy and affection stronger than girlish vanity in the young heart.

"The glitter and pomp of wealth will never turn *her* brain or make her false to her affections," he thought proudly; aloud he said: "But Eva would rather remain at home than relinquish her precious *lares* and *penates* even for a time. Is it not so, Eva?" with a quizzical laugh.

Eva looked about her and sighed softly.

"Well, it *is* a pity to go away and leave this beautiful house," she admitted regretfully; "and I really don't see why we should, papa."

"Then I suppose you prefer remaining here, Eva? What does Aunt Kate say? She shall decide."

"It is too bad," Kate responded, "to leave the onus of the decision with me; but if I am to decide, then by all means let it be the country. I confess that the prospect of the bracing mountain air, the unrestrained freedom and retirement, the weekly row across the river to the little wooden chapel with its humble worshippers, together with the promise of fresh milk, eggs, and butter, perfect immunity from malaria and mosquitoes, hold a special charm for me. It is always best when we can blend the spiritual with the material, thus attending to the wants of the soul and the body. But perhaps Eva would prefer remaining behind; if so, the servants can look after her personal comforts, and she can go as usual to the cathedral—one of the men can drive her there, you know."

"I'm sure, auntie," Eva said, with a pout, "I'm quite willing to do whatever papa and you think best. I would not remain all by myself with only the servants in this great house for—for—oh, for anything; but surely papa will take some of the servants?"

"Well, my dear, I have not engaged a hotel, simply apartments and boarding in a large farm-house. Denise can take her maid—that is, if your aunt would not prefer taking hers; but, in any case, one maid must attend to all three."

"I can do without an attendant, papa, and Sara can wait upon Aunt Kate and Eva," Denise said quickly, seeing Eva's sudden look of disappointment.

"Very well, my dear, you must arrange among yourselves how it is to be. I regret being obliged to limit you to one attendant, but we will take Cato and Connor's man and— Ah, Teddy, my boy, back again? How did you enjoy your drive? Found it hot, eh?"

"Yes, sir, very hot, but it was just splendid!" Teddy, who, followed by Connor, had just joined them, answered, in a tone of genuine appreciation, as he fanned himself with his hat.

Mr. D'Arcy smiled. He liked to see those around him happy.

"Well, Connor, I hope you have found the heat as enjoyable as Teddy seems to have done? What have you done with Brand?"

"I could have dispensed with the heat, sir, but I certainly enjoyed the park. It is magnificent. Mr. Brand had an appointment, but he will call to-morrow. He regretted being unable to return with us."

"I am sorry that Clifford is not here. I should like you to make his acquaintance, Connor. I know no two men whom I value so highly as Marmaduke Clifford and Frank Brand. Did I tell you that Brand's uncle had a place beside us on the Shannon?"

"Yes, sir."

"Ah, yes. Sir John was one of the fine old English gentlemen fast passing away, generous and hospitable. Clifford is also a gentleman, descended from a fine old stock. You see, Connor, my sojourn in this land of freedom has failed to eradicate the prejudices of birth. Despite my enlarged knowledge of my fellow-men, I cannot accept the doctrine that 'One man is as good as another.' I believe in descent, Connor. In all my wanderings I have invariably found that blood tells."

Eva was telling Teddy of the coming change in a stage whisper, and Mr. D'Arcy, catching the pleased look on Teddy's face, hastened to explain to Connor, adding:

"I think the change will do Teddy good. As your aunt remarks, this heat is very debilitating, and I should like to see him look stronger."

"Yes," Connor answered, glancing toward his brother, "poor Teddy has never quite got over the severe illness he had last spring."

"Illness last spring?" Mr. D'Arcy questioned, with a startled look. "I did not know that. I thought his delicacy of look the result of rapid growth."

In a few words Connor told of Teddy's illness, carefully avoiding any allusion to their poverty in those days; but he noticed that a frown of pain contracted his father's forehead as he listened.

"My poor boy, he must lay aside his books and for the next twelve months relinquish study," Mr. D'Arcy decided firmly. "Something must be done for the promotion of his physical health, and you must assist me, Connor. We cannot afford to lose Teddy."

"I am with you heart and soul, sir, in any scheme for Teddy's welfare, but I fear he will not be willing to give up his books. It was only this morning that he begged me to speak to you about letting him go to school, as he would wish to go at once."

Mr. D'Arcy flushed hotly, and a frown of displeasure darkened his pleasant face.

"And you encouraged him in this notion of going to school, I suppose?" he questioned, speaking calmly.

"No, sir. I told him that he must wait until you made what arrangements you should deem necessary for the completion of his education, which I felt sure you would do in good time. For the present I considered that a little mild amusement—such as is likely to be found in this projected change—would prove more beneficial than study."

"I am glad you said that to him, Connor," Mr. D'Arcy said, his face clearing, "but why should he appeal to you? Great Heaven! can my children not trust me? Will they not believe that I desire only their welfare and happiness?"

The passion and pathos in his voice and eyes went straight to Connor's heart; for the first time he felt that he had been unjust to him.

"My dear father," he said, in a tone of deep emotion, "you must not misunderstand Teddy; you know that even as a child he was shy. Since he left school, four years ago, I have been his teacher and director, and he naturally comes to me in all his little difficulties; trust me, sir, he will soon learn to transfer his troubles to you. I think he is already beginning to overcome his shyness; in time I quite believe it will altogether disappear. Have a little patience with Teddy, father, and all will soon come right."

All coldness and restraint had passed from Connor's tone and manner.

"I will have patience. I suppose I am unreasonable; but I want you to trust me also, Connor, my boy. We have been long separated, but do not let coldness and estrangement come between us, but believe that your father will do all he can to make you happy," Mr. D'Arcy said, grasping his son's hand with much emotion.

Denise, who had been a silent witness to this scene between father and son, with a glow of delight in her eloquent face stole softly into the room beside her aunt.

"Father!" Connor said, his pale face lighting up, "you say that you desire to make me happy. I am going to make a request which I beg you will not refuse; it will be the first since we have met."

"Name it, Connor, and consider your request—whatever it be—already granted."

"Thank you, sir! you give me courage. My request is this: Give me—or let me find—something to do. Idleness does not suit me; the wealth and state by which I am surrounded oppress me; I should like to earn the right to it before sitting quietly down to enjoy it. I feel that I must do something. You employ men in the city—let me help you, father! I could save you many of those long journeys which you are obliged to take. Surely you can give me something to do."

A shade of disappointment came into the elder man's face, but was succeeded by a smile a trifle hard and bitter.

"It is not every young man who is anxious to work with the prospect of wealth and idleness before him. I think it must be your grandmother's Scotch blood asserting itself, Connor, my boy! You were born to wealth and position— yet you are right, a little work will do you no harm; idleness engenders vice; your wish is granted. When we return from the country you shall be put in a position to help me, and shall choose your own work."

"You have made me very happy, sir!" Connor declared gratefully, but the feeling of disappointment remained with his father.

Chapter III.

"Slow rippling in the zephyr's breath,
The murmuring waters flow beneath;
Warm glows the sun—sweet breathes the air."
—MISS SHERIDAN.

"Riches are for spending, and spending for honor and good actions."—BACON.

A BOAT in which three gentlemen were seated was being rapidly impelled across the little river that runs by the village of Beechville. Just at this point the smooth, unruffled surface of the river lay like a sheet of silver under the brilliant August sun, but murmured with a gentle humming sound, like a tender mother lulling her infant to repose, as the boat neared the opposite bank, where, descending precipitously to the very edge of the water, was a grove of maple, cedar, birch, and beech trees, their gracefully drooping branches casting long, cool shadows on the stream at their base.

The rowers paused simultaneously and leaned upon their oars while they gazed silently upon the exquisite scene. The beautiful mountains looking so near to that side of the river they had left behind them, here and there a soft, white cloud floating dreamily, like a white thistle-down blown against the azure background of the smiling heavens, the fantastic windings of the pretty stream, its graceful curves and turnings, here so placidly tranquil, while farther down, where its course became impeded by rocks, it dashed impetuously forward impatient of restraint or obstruction. The air was filled with pleasant sounds and rich odors from the woods, where the trees were in their brightest summer livery.

"Look here, Frank!" cried one of the gentlemen, suddenly seizing his oars, "the boat is heading down stream, while we are off in dreamland. Come, this sun is scorching; let us get into the cool shade of those temptingly inviting trees opposite."

With a laugh, Frank Brand seized his oars.

"Christopher Columbus! you are right, Clifford," he answered. "The heat of those sunbeams is oppressive; but this scene is so beautiful I lost sight of that. Here goes with a will, old boy," and with the long, sweeping strokes of practised rowers, the two young men sent the boat swiftly across the river.

"Come, confess, Brand," Mr. Clifford said, with pleasant malice, "were you not engaged in a mental conjugation of the verb *amare?* The symptoms are loss of appetite, unconscious sighing, absence of mind——"

"A personal experience could alone make you so conversant with all the symptoms," Brand interrupted, flushing hotly, conscious that his companions were smiling at him.

"No, my dear fellow," Clifford responded, with that languid, *difficile* grace so peculiar to him and so provoking to Brand, "I never permit *my* peace of mind to be disturbed in that way. I am a planet many degrees removed from the sun, you know—hold on, or we shall run into the bank," as the boat was sent with a sudden impetus under the outspreading branches of a splendid cedar.

"We will take them by surprise," Mr. D'Arcy observed as they ascended the sloping bank and walked on through the thick grass and rank vegetation. "They are quite unprepared for my coming; they do not expect that I shall return to the farm before evening."

All three paused suddenly and glanced through an opening in the trees as the sound of voices came floating on the summer air and a fresh young laugh, sweet as a chime of silver bells, rang out. It was an idyllic scene.

A natural avenue, formed by a double row of splendid elm trees, led to a rude wooden structure surmounted by a cross, which at once proclaimed the sacred character of the edifice.

The door was laid back, the low, broad windows were all open; a bright, intelligent-looking colored girl was carrying an armful of green boughs up the path. Connor, seated in the branch of a tree, was in the act of fastening up a garland, with which a young colored man mounted upon a ladder was assisting him; a number of garlands were already suspended from tree to tree across the avenue.

On the trunk of a magnificent elm, under the shade of its drooping boughs, sat a girl surrounded by fresh green branches, which she was daintily assisting a youth at her feet to wreathe into garlands. She was dressed in black; a large, wide-brimmed straw hat encircled by a black gossamer scarf rested upon the glittering hair and shaded the dazzling complexion. This was not pretty, disconsolate Eva, wrapped in the old plaid shawl in the poor attic-room in Charlotte Street, but Eva beautiful, bright, joyous, surrounded by what was to her as the breath of life, all the comforts and luxuries which wealth could purchase.

Teddy, too, was looking brighter and stronger as, regardless of the many blisters on his slender, delicate hands, he talked and worked away.

A little distance farther on was another group.

Kate D'Arcy was seated on the thick grass, a heap of snowy muslin and cloudy lace in her lap, the old smile on her lips, but a thoughtful shadow in her handsome eyes; near her Denise was fastening blue and gold tassels to a blue silk banner, which two men, kneeling at her feet, were busily employed securing to gilded poles; a little banneret just completed lay on the grass, which the sun, gleaming through the trees, wove into a shimmering carpet of green and gold.

With his hands clasped behind him, a look of pleased interest on his thin, worn face, stood a priest.

He was talking pleasantly to the little group as he leaned forward, intent on the progress of their work; occasionally, as Eva's laugh rang out, he glanced with a gentle smile at the youthful figures under the opposite elm tree.

A man armed with a long broom was sweeping in front of the little chapel, from within which the sound of vigorous hammering proceeded; an air of cheerful alacrity and pleased anticipation prevailed.

It was a lovely scene, and one which Marmaduke Clifford, with his fine artistic soul and keen appreciation of the beautiful, longed to see transferred to canvas.

"Such a pity it should be lost," he thought.

"I wish, Father Donnatti," came in Denise's fresh, clear voice at this juncture, "that we had dear Lotta here to help; she has such exquisite taste."

"I regret the absence of your young friend, my dear child, if her presence would give you happiness; but I am delighted to think that our festival promises to be a perfect triumph, a festival of nature, a festival of hearts uniting to rejoice in the glorious triumph of the Queen of Angels."

The deep, incisive voice of the priest sounded distinctly in the ears of the three men.

"Ah, but, Father, you do not know what an acquisition

Miss von Rosenberg would be. Her taste is simply perfect," Kate interposed, her needle suspended above her work, her eyes turned with an upward glance to the pale, worn face bent over them.

The answer hovering on the lips of the priest was interrupted by a shrill little cry from Eva, who had just caught sight of her father.

"Papa! papa!"

Springing delightedly to her feet, she scattered leaves and branches as she rushed to meet the trio, who now advanced from their concealment.

Frank Brand flushed like a schoolboy as he shook hands with the ladies. Kate said a few pleasant words as her brother presented Mr. Clifford.

Like Connor, he was tall, dark, and strikingly handsome. His features were of the fine, delicate Roman type; his hair a rich, dark chestnut; his eyes, a deep violet-gray, were long and almond-shaped, surmounted by finely-arched black brows and slightly drooping eyelids; his hands and feet were small and delicately shaped, his complexion pale and slightly olive; the fine curve of his lips and arch of his handsome eyebrows told that he was proud and painfully fastidious. He looked so cool and handsome in his summer suit of white grasscloth, sheer as muslin, as he stood beneath the shade of the trees, his head uncovered, his wide-brimmed hat in his left hand as he bowed to the ladies, then cordially shook hands with Father Donnatti.

Connor, dropping from his perch in the tree, came forward followed by Teddy.

"My sons, Connor and Teddy, Mr. Clifford. My dear boys, this gentleman is my friend Mr. Clifford, of whom you have so often heard me speak and with whom I have much pleasure in making you acquainted."

Connor's clear eyes looked straight into those of this

new acquaintance and encountered an equally searching glance; then the hands of both met in a warm clasp.

Eva had seized upon Frank Brand, who was her special favorite, and with both hands clasped round his arm was drawing him away to the chapel.

"Just come and see! We've got all beautifully done, and the men have swept away the litter; we have got the large statue of Our Lady on the pedestal, and auntie is finishing the drapery. The little statue will be borne in procession under a white silk canopy, and oh, Mr. Brand, don't you think the banners are just beautiful? This is the chapel—only a poor little place, you know, but isn't it pretty?"

With large, expectant eyes fixed upon his face, she waited breathlessly for his answer.

He respectfully uncovered as they entered the little building and looked around. The hammering had ceased. Sara, Denise's maid, a bright, intelligent-looking colored girl, was on her knees arranging something at the altar.

It was only an humble wooden edifice, possibly in point of construction not one degree removed from the stable at Bethlehem; but it looked sweet, cool, and picturesque; everything was immaculately clean, from the well-swept floor to the pure white linen on the altar. The rude walls were hidden by green boughs and tasteful garlands; the rough benches gave evidence of having been well scoured, and were carefully arranged so as to leave a passage-way on either side. A beautiful white statue of Mary Immaculate, the gift of Kate D'Arcy, stood upon a pedestal enthroned in green boughs, with clusters of unlit wax candles glimmering through.

The sanctuary and steps of the little altar were covered with a rich white carpet, dotted here and there with bunches of green moss under white lilies; it had been presented by Denise for feast days. The six tall candlesticks shone like burnished gold against the green branches that formed the background.

The peaceful altar, with long rays of sunlight falling athwart it from the low, broad windows, intensifying the glitter of the candlesticks, the white statue gleaming purely in its green bower, the quiet hush, the silent awe in the faces and attitudes of the two rough-looking men who, having just finished nailing up the last garland, stood quietly gazing around them—all tended to impress Frank Brand as nothing had ever done before.

"Yes," he said, answering Eva's low, eager whisper in the same tones, "it is sweetly beautiful."

"See, this is the little statue that is to be carried in procession to-morrow. We've not brought any flowers yet; we'll bring them to-morrow morning; we want them to be fresh, you know."

"I think it is just perfect."

"Oh! but it will look lovely with the flowers and lighted candles."

"Yes," Frank answered abstractedly as Clifford and Teddy, followed by the others, entered.

Mr. Brand was not a Catholic, but he would have been very indignant if any one had presumed to doubt his claims to be considered a good Christian; but religion had never disturbed his peace of mind. Years ago he used to attend the old parish church every Sunday with his parents and such of his brothers and sisters who, like himself, were home from school.

Being a younger son he had to choose a profession, and when little more than twenty his father purchased for him a junior partnership in a London mercantile house of long standing. After a time, finding him possessed of good business qualities, the elder partners intrusted him with the management of a branch house in New York, which under his care flourished rapidly.

Shrewd and practical, although he invested largely in railway, mining, and other shares, his speculations always proved safe and highly remunerative.

Since coming to America he had had little time—or thought he had had, which was much the same—to devote to the practice of religion, and seldom attended any place of worship; when he did, it mattered little to him where he went if the music was good or the preaching exciting. Somewhere hidden away in his breast was a secret spark of antagonism to Catholicism and all its teachings; but the spark emitted no light on the present occasion, and he was blissfully unconscious of its presence.

His eyes followed Kate and Denise as they approached the statue; Kate carrying across her arms the heap of white muslin which she had fastened to a coronal, and which Connor proceeded to secure above the statue with Clifford's assistance.

The snowy muslin and lace fell in soft, billowy folds around the silent figure, and Kate knelt to carefully arrange the drapery so as not to come in contact with the candles when lighted. Denise stood with hands locked loosely together watching the workers; Mr. D'Arcy with a pleased smile on his face was whispering with Father Donnatti; Teddy was at the altar rail. The banners were carried in by the two men, and everything having been completed, they all silently quitted the little chapel, and having securely locked the door, the priest accompanied them to the river's edge, conversing pleasantly on the way.

"You have reason to be proud of the work of your hands, Miss Denise," Mr. Clifford said as he walked by her side.

"Not my hands alone, Mr. Clifford," Denise answered,

with a shy blush and bright smile; "it is said that many hands make work light, and I think our combined efforts have accomplished something pleasing."

"It is more beautiful, more touching to the soul in its rude simplicity than the fairest cathedral raised by the hands of man; that little altar looks fairer in my eyes than an altar flashing with gold and gems, such as I have seen. What is so acceptable to the Divine Creator as the hearts of His creatures? You have proved the love which animates your heart by dedicating your time to the adornment of that poor little shed, into which Christ condescends to enter for love of His poor creatures; you have offered to Him a tribute of His gifts, thus rendering to God the things that are God's, and to-morrow men and angels will rejoice in the work of your hands."

Denise looked up with a glad light in her eyes.

"You are a Catholic, Mr. Clifford?"

"I am a Catholic, thank God!" he answered, reverently raising his hat.

"I am so glad!" impulsively extending her hand. "It makes things so much more pleasant. Don't you think so, Mr. Clifford?"

He looked down into the eloquent, innocent, upturned face as he took the little gloved hand in his.

"Yes," he answered, "it is pleasant to know that those whose friendship we value are one in faith with us."

"It is such a pity that Mr. Brand is not a Catholic also; he is so nice and agreeable, we all like him so much; he is an especial favorite with Eva."

"Your sister is little more than a beautiful child, but"— with a slight laugh—"I think, Miss Denise, that the conversion of Brand would not prove a sinecure to any friend who might undertake it; he is comfortably unconscious of his spiritual wants, and I believe if once aroused would prove an obstinate subject. It is a pity, for he is a really good fellow and I esteem him highly."

They had reached the others, who were waiting their approach; then all shook hands with Father Donnatti, who stood watching them as they pushed out into the stream.

Connor took an oar, and in his full, rich tenor commenced to sing the "Canadian Boat Song," which was instantly taken up by all the other gentlemen but Mr. D'Arcy, who leaned back and listened.

The words and music floated back pleasantly to Father Donnatti as he stood gazing after them, and unconsciously Frank Brand's eyes were drawn back with a strange fascination to the tall, thin, black-robed figure standing under the cedar tree, with the river softly lapping the bank at his feet.

Chapter XIII.

"Pure fell the beams and meekly bright
 On his gray holy hair,
And touched the book with tenderest light,
 As if its shrine were there!
But oh! that Patriarch's aspect shone
 With something lovelier far—
A radiance all the spirit's own,
 Caught not from sun or star."—MRS. HEMANS.

NO more beautiful day ever dawned than that fifteenth of August, the Feast of the Assumption. At an early hour the little chapel was crowded; door and windows were open to admit the air; the atmosphere was close and heavy with the breath of lovely white lilies and heliotropes; meek little anemones, red columbines, great yellow and purple violets, with pale wildwood geraniums clustered in graceful profusion around the statue of Mary Immaculate, fresh, odorous, and grateful offerings to the Queen of Angels.

But what a tribute of praise, of love, of adoration offered up to the Eternal Throne was the intense devotion, the silent awe, the rapt attention which characterized the demeanor of the poor, rude, but faithful worshippers during the celebration of Holy Mass.

Frank Brand watched the priest, and noticed with surprise the devotion of the people, rude sons and daughters of toil, all but the D'Arcy party.

At the conclusion of the Gospel Father Donnatti preached on the virtues, the sufferings, the triumphs of

Mary; eloquent, glowing, passionate words—words that moved the hearts of his hearers as the waters of a mighty torrent sweep onward in their rapid course the frail objects that float upon its surface.

Women wept, and the hard, weather-browned faces of the men worked with repressed emotion.

Mr. Brand listened with fast-increasing attention, watching in mute astonishment the face of the preacher as he stood in his white alb, the golden sunlight falling on his silvery hair, lighting up his pale, æsthetic face and glowing eyes with a light that never shone on land or sea; and as he listened, carried beyond himself, Frank Brand by his very presence, by his reverent silence, his profound attention, paid all unconsciously a mute tribute to Mary Immaculate and her Divine Son.

The charm of a pair of bright eyes had brought him here, had caused him to beg leave to accompany the D'Arcys and his friend Clifford to that humble little place. Had any one presumed to ask him that morning if that visit was prompted by a desire to become acquainted with the truths of Catholicism he would have resented the inquiry with a burst of angry indignation.

Yet here he was—eyes, heart, brain absorbed in the words which flowed like the stream of a rapid river from the lips of that white-haired priest, whom at one time he would have stigmatized as no better than a priest of Buddha; listening with tingling nerves and rapidly throbbing pulses; the long-sleeping soul, strangely stirred, fluttered into a troubled disquietude; listening, so carried away by the words of the preacher, that he never once glanced at the fair face that had been the sole attraction in bringing him hither, the face that, from the first hour in which he had beheld it, had never ceased to haunt his sleeping and waking dreams.

At the conclusion of the sermon he unconsciously bent his head as the others did when the priest made the sign of the cross in blessing, and mechanically rose to his feet at the Credo. He read the book which Connor had handed to him with an outward appearance of quiet attention; but he was strangely pale.

The words: "*Hoc est enim Corpus Meum,*" "*Take and eat ye all of this, for this is My Body,*" those thrillingly sublime words of Christ to His disciples, arrested his attention, and as he lingered over them, pondering deeply the while, there occurred to him a passage in Hidelbert's "*Oratio Devotissima,*" almost forgotten, but flowing strangely now through his mind, and he found himself mentally repeating:

> "Son of God, Thy Father's equal,
> Of His substance, and arrayed
> In the brightness of His glory.
> Maker! yet like creature made,
> In our garb of flesh Thou camest
> For our rescue from on high.
> Born in time, though everlasting,
> Deathless, thou didst come to die;
> God in man, and man in Godhead,
> God with mortal flesh allied.
> Manhood not with God confounded,
> Godhead not undeified,
> One in Godhead with the Father,
> He has mortal flesh assumed.
> Man is to God's bosom taken,
> And yet man is unconsumed.
> God Most High and Virgin Mother,
> Claim that first begotten Son."

"Bah!" he thought, closing his book as the last blessing was given and Father Donnatti followed his three acolytes from the little altar, passing through an open door on one side into a rudely constructed room, elevated to the dignity of vestry. "Bah! what have *I* to do with such enigmas? Theology is not in my line. To what an absurd length has the preaching of that man carried me! It must be the strength of his convictions which lend such force to his words. If he really believes all he teaches—and he appears to—that is his affair, not mine; why should *I* permit myself to be disturbed by *his* belief? Such a faith no doubt suits the ignorant and uneducated who delight in miracles, but for a man of education in the nineteenth century it is quite too absurd, too nonsensical."

But the feeling would not be crushed out, reason as he might; the small voice that would not be silenced kept whispering in his soul.

He looked around him, and, passing his hand through his bright, ruddy hair, smiled scornfully at his late weakness, but flushed hotly the next instant as he met a pair of handsome eyes turned earnestly on his face; there was no smile in the eyes nor on the fair face turned toward him, but there was a sad wistfulness that somehow irritated him.

A few minutes later Denise, followed by Mr. Clifford and Connor, went into the vestry, and Mr. D'Arcy, leaning toward Frank Brand, whispered:

"The procession will not form for a few minutes; if you find it too hot here we will go out till the signal is given."

Frank gladly acceded, but to his intense disappointment Kate and Eva remained behind.

A number of the poor people followed the example set by the two gentlemen and sought the cool shade of the trees.

Inside the little vestry there was a pretty scene.

Father Donnatti was unvested and was standing in his alb. He was looking pale and exhausted, but he was smiling benignly on the little group by which he was surrounded.

Teddy, in white surplice, was holding a handsome processional cross, the gift of his father; the two young acolytes were preparing the thurifer and incense; Mr. Clifford was looking at a beautiful white silk canopy, while Connor was reverently drawing forth a handsome cope of rich white poplin and gold brocade, which, as the sunlight fell upon it, sent forth a blinding flash.

At that moment Denise entered through a doorway at the far end of the rude apartment.

"You really must come away, Father Donnatti," she said, approaching the priest, "just for a minute, you know. Mary has a lovely cup of tea waiting for you, and you are much too exhausted after that long, exquisite sermon you preached us to fast any longer."

"But the good people are waiting, my dear child!"

"Let them wait, Father," she answered, with her bright smile; "they have each and every one of them had breakfast hours ago, while you have tasted nothing since last night."

Clifford glanced across at the two figures, the figure of the priest in his white alb and the figure of the girl in her black gown. He so worn and aged, even beyond his sixty-eight years of life, aged by the toil, the trials, the vicissitudes of his long missionary labors; she so fresh, so impulsive, so fair, so innocent; he standing so near to the verge of the great unknown land; she—

> "Standing with reluctant feet
> Where the brook and river meet,
> Womanhood and childhood fleet."

He sighed inaudibly and took a step to where they stood.

"Let me beg that you will listen to Miss Denise," he said, with respectful entreaty; "you are utterly exhausted and positively stand in need of a refreshment. You know, Father, that ten minutes will suffice."

With a dubious shake of the head and a pleased smile on the worn face, Father Donnatti allowed Clifford to lead him away.

The ringing of a bell recalled the loiterers, and as they re-entered the chapel they found that the procession was being formed, and each dropped quietly into place, Teddy as cross-bearer going first; everything was perfectly *en règle*.

The silence, the respectful attention, the profound happiness and admiration on every face were good to behold as the humble processionists passed out of the little building—out under the blue sky, under the drooping elms, where the sunlight, mellow and golden, flashed down on the glittering cross, on the acolytes in their white surplices, on the silver hair and shimmering robe of the priest; on the statue of Mary, refuge of sinners, surrounded by green boughs and dainty flowers, borne under a canopy of gleaming white silk fringed with gold; on the handsome banners, on twenty-four girlish figures clad in white, all wearing the badge of "Children of Mary," and on the weather-stained features of sturdy men and women with healthy, sunburnt children clinging to their skirts, sending a brilliant flash as if in loving benediction on all as they turned slowly down the avenue of elms and overhanging garlands. Then up through the elms—up through the blue ether swelled the music of many voices in the beautiful hymn:

"See, to God's high temple above
Mounts amid angel hymns of love
The mystical ark of grace.
See aloft on victory's throne,
Blended in glory both Mother and Son
In one eternal embrace!"

At the conclusion of the last verse they re-entered the chapel and paused in front of the statue of Mary Immaculate, where the lighted tapers gleamed whitely against their green background, and the sweet flowers sent out fragrant odors which mingled with the incense as it rose in soft clouds around the white statue. All stood while the hymn "Immaculate" was being sung; at its conclusion the people returned to their benches, and the priest entered the little sanctuary and ascended the altar steps, where tier after tier of lights and flowers rose upward, reaching above the altar. Amid a hush of profound awe the sacred Host was placed above the tabernacle, and like heavenly music Mozart's "O Salutaris" burst upon eager, listening ears. Four girls and two young men, who had been in training for the past three weeks, a little timidly at first, joined in.

As Denise's splendid voice broke upon the stillness, Clifford turned his eyes upon her with a strange, startled look. The Litany, the Anthem, the "Tantum Ergo" had been sung, the last amen had slowly died away, and every head was bent to receive the benediction of our dear Lord. Only then, when his proud head was bent in deepest humility before the Lord of Hosts, did Clifford turn his gaze from the face of the unconscious girl, who never dreamed that the man who dropped the gold into her shrinking, outstretched hand, as she stood in the shadow, away from the glare of the brilliantly lighted Albany, with the snow falling around her and drifting pitilessly into her face on that cold February evening, now so far away and yet so seldom absent from her mind—the man whose money had for the time being saved her mother's life, was now kneeling within a few feet of her, listening to her voice and thinking of that other voice which he had heard that bitter February evening on the streets of London, and wondering at the strange resemblance between this voice and that other one; wondering and watching the sweet young face as if fascinated.

They were all out, gathered in clusters under the shade of the elms. Father Donnatti was moving from one little knot to another, with a kind word for all.

Every heart was filled with delight, and a few ventured to give expression to their feelings. It had been so beautiful, the decorations, the statues, the banners, the procession. They had never heard such singing; it might have been the angels that came down to carry Our Lady up to heaven, singing in triumph.

Many of those present had a considerable distance to go, and this was why Father Donnatti had had Benediction after Mass. He knew that there were many there who could not return in the evening, so he meant that all should fully participate in the blessings of the day.

Kate and Denise were talking kindly to some of the women and children, while Eva condescendingly bestowed smiles and a handful of small coins on the latter, who regarded her with open-mouthed admiration.

Eva was not too prodigal with the goods that God had sent her, but it was so nice to act the Lady Bountiful in a small way; besides, those ignorant little creatures evidently admired while they stood in awe of her grace and beauty, and Eva liked to be admired and appreciated; but she could not bear to pat the little boys on their shoulders, or to smooth the heads of the little girls with a gentle, caressing touch, as Aunt Kate and Denise were doing; doing so might soil her gloves, and she just *hated* to have her gloves made dirty by contact with such rough-looking little things.

Many were the admiring glances and murmured blessings that followed the D'Arcy party to their boat, the priest walking with them to the water's edge, while in a few gentle words he thanked them for the happiness which they had that day bestowed upon his poor people.

"For myself," he added, "it has been one of the happiest days of my life, in very truth a *red-letter day*."

"Then I think I may venture to say we have all shared your feelings, Father," Kate responded, with her bright, winsome smile, her handsome eyes glancing rapidly round the little circle; and every voice answered that glance, "An exceedingly happy day;" but even as Denise's tongue formed the words, her heart cried out sadly, "Oh, why did mamma not live to share in this day's happiness?"

Ah, why indeed? Who could tell?

"Your life must be very lonely and barren here!" Frank Brand remarked, making an effort to say something, "isolated as you are from all congenial society."

"I have not much time to feel lonely; my people are pretty widely scattered over this district, Mr. Brand, and I like to visit them all frequently. It is true that they are for the most part rude and illiterate; but the duties of a priest are always congenial. *Society* and I have been so long apart that we have mutually agreed to forget each other."

"When a refined and intellectual man can conform his mind to such duties, it is perhaps the safest plan he *can* pursue," Frank answered, with a laugh, "but it takes some drilling, I have no doubt."

The spark of antagonism which had so long lain hidden away in the young man's breast had ignited and was burning fiercely long before they had quitted the chapel, and he had come forth a very different Frank Brand to the Frank Brand who had entered that building a few short hours before.

He had entered it, pleased to be in the near vicinity of the woman he loved; he quitted it, feeling enraged with himself and every one else, but too thoroughly a gentleman to make a display of his feelings, yet resolved to leave

Beechville and its neighborhood in a day or two, go to Long Branch, Newport, or the Catskill Mountains. It did not matter much where he went for a few weeks, if only he could overcome this foolish infatuation; if not—well, if she loved him and became his wife, she *must* conform to his religious views.

He did not pause to ask himself what peculiar shape *his* religious views took. It was just possible that even to himself he could not have given that question a satisfactory answer; he might decline to answer such a very impertinent question, satisfying himself with the assurance that, like every other Christian gentleman, he had religious views; but as he was the keeper of his own conscience, it did not matter to any one what those views were. He believed in the sacredness of the married state, and in the perfect union of mind and soul as being to married life what perfume is to the flower—the essence necessary to perfection.

"It is a wife's duty," he argued mentally, "to be guided in all things by her husband. '*Omnia vincit amor*,' 'Love conquers all things,' and love shall conquer her religious scruples," and with these consoling thoughts he subdued his irritation and shared in the general talk.

"Ave! Ave! Mother bright,
Guard us through the coming night."

Denise looked up with wide-open, startled eyes, then shrank back pale and trembling, and leaning over the side of the boat, gazed down into the sunlit waters.

"O Mr. Clifford!" Eva cried, bending eagerly forward, "do you know that? We used to sing it—that was long ago when dear mamma was alive, you know; she liked to hear us sing it, it sounded so beautiful when Lottchen sang with us. It is so long since we have sung it now, though."

Mr. D'Arcy touched the rippling masses of his daughter's shining hair with a caressing hand.

"Some day you must all sing it for me," he said gently.

"It is Lottchen's song, papa," Eva answered. "How did you know it, Mr. Clifford?"

Kate D'Arcy fanned herself slowly, but somehow her hand would tremble and her color would keep coming and going in time to the beating of her heart as she listened for the answer to unconscious Eva's question.

"My dear Miss Eva, I must plead ignorance," Clifford answered. "The one occasion upon which I heard that sung was last February on the streets of London. It was sung by a young girl; she had the most splendid voice which up to that hour I had ever heard. You remember it, Brand?"

"Yes," Brand answered. "Her voice was something magnificent, I tell you; it took the breath from us fellows."

"A rather remarkable song, I should imagine, for a London street singer," Mr. D'Arcy observed.

"I should scarcely class this girl with street singers; although a girl possessed of such a voice who could deliberately run such a risk must have been endowed with a large amount of courage, and what Englishmen call pluck."

"In other words, Mr. Clifford, you think it required some audacity on the part of a young girl to sing on the streets of London?" Kate asked, a crimson spot on either cheek and her blue eyes flashing as she sat erect.

"I think, Miss D'Arcy, that the streets of a large city are scarcely the place for any girl of delicacy or natural refinement to select for the exhibition of her talents. I look upon such an act as dangerous alike to mind and morals," he responded severely.

"If that is really your view of the case, Mr. Clifford, I

consider it a very unjust, one-sided view. In all large cities there are many very strange cases which you who have been born and reared in the lap of luxury cannot understand. How can you, how can we judge the motives which impelled that young girl to, as you say, 'exhibit her talents on the streets of London'? Perhaps driven by hunger, what was still more likely, in a moment of despair, she had remembered only that God had bestowed that gift upon her, and that through it she might save the life of some one very dear to her, a—a parent—a brother—a sister who at that very hour was perhaps slowly dying of hunger and cold, in some miserable place which they called by the sweet name of home. Do you not think that her heavenly Father, who understood the motive which prompted the act, would protect her? Ah, there are so many uncrowned saints in this world that only the judgment day will reveal to us. But I am afraid, Mr. Clifford, we all of us require to be purified by suffering and poverty, before we can understand the true meaning of charity to our neighbors."

A faint glow overspread Mr. Clifford's haughty face as he listened.

"I stand corrected, Miss D'Arcy," he answered, with a courteous bow. "You are right—I am afraid charity is not my peculiar virtue—it was a case on which I had no right to sit in judgment. The girl's voice was so—so utterly above that kind of thing, even at the time it struck me that she was running a great risk in exposing it and herself in such a place."

"I think," Frank remarked, a little eagerly, "that the poor girl must have been driven to it, for she was awfully shy. You remember, Clifford, that after you joined us, when you sent your man requesting her to sing again, she disappeared, and never returned all the time we remained at the Albany. She had certainly a magnificent voice."

"Yes," Clifford slowly answered as the boat neared the bank.

"Poor girl!" Kate said, with a laugh, "she doubtless never dreamed of the honor in store for her, when she should form a subject of conversation for us, at this distance of time and place."

Only Kate could understand the agony, the shame, the humiliation which Denise endured as she listened, with heart and brain throbbing, to every word that fell from Marmaduke Clifford's lips, to his voice so full of scorn, so pitiless, so utterly cruel, and she longed to take the poor girl in her arms and comfort her.

Mr. Clifford extended his hand to assist Denise from the boat; a faint color flashed into her white face and a proud light into her eyes, and with a coldly uttered "Thanks!" she declined the proffered help and shrank to her father's side. Mistaking the action for girlish shyness, he turned to Eva, who was laughing and chatting with childish *abandon.*

Chapter XIV.

"Oh, how full of briers is this working-day world."
—*As You Like It.*

"Now is now and then is then;
Seek now all the world throughout,
Thou kenst not clowns from gentlemen."

"OSCAR, Oscar, good fellow, bring me my basket."
A panting, rushing sound, and a huge dog bounded to the side of a young girl who was stooped in the act of fastening up the tendrils of a vine which the wind and rain of the previous night had beaten down.

"My basket, Oscar, bring it. There is no use, I am not going out for a walk until I have first fastened up those vines; just see how badly they have been hurt, and we could not leave them like that, you know."

Oscar drooped his feathery tail, disappointment and disapprobation strongly expressed in his handsome canine face; but in an instant, with newly awakened intelligence, he bounded through an open window into the house, and was soon back, carrying a small basket, which he deposited beside his young mistress with a satisfied wag of his tail, fully conscious of having done his duty.

"Good dog—splendid fellow! You shall not be deprived of your scamper; when I have tied these up we shall go."

Oscar wagged his tail with redoubled energy and patted his young mistress' arm with one great paw as she took from the basket a pair of scissors and carefully snipped the broken tendrils.

"Oh, yes, I know you are very pleased, but you will soil my gown, old fellow. Now that's accomplished, and we shall be off."

She rose and turned to pat her four-footed favorite, but he had again disappeared through the open window, and she smiled, knowing that he had gone to fetch her hat.

It was fourteen months since Lotta von Rosenberg had come to preside over her uncle's household, and during these months her life had been a very active one, her time fully employed. On her first arrival she was met by Mrs. Morgan, a stout, elderly woman who for six years had had undisputed management of all household matters. In consequence of which lengthened reign, the woman had come to regard herself as sole mistress of the farm, and resented Lotta's coming to rule over her, almost insolently refusing to wait upon her. But her rage knew no bounds when Lotta distinctly intimated that her uncle should no longer sit at the table with the "helps," and insisted upon having his and her meals served in a room which, under her directions, Dan soon converted into a very cozy dining-room.

It was in vain that Mrs. Morgan did everything in her power to thwart her young mistress, who calmly issued her orders, never once condescending to notice the woman's bitterness and ill-temper.

For the first three months Mrs. Morgan fought a hard battle for supremacy, but only to submit in the end. She could not endure to meet the full glance of the beautiful hazel eyes, always so serene and smiling. She hated Lotta with an intense hatred; she hated her for coming to interfere with her authority, she hated her high-bred voice, her lovely face, her graceful figure, her dainty, refined ways; she sneered at the small white hands, at the creamy pallor of the perfect complexion, and called it sickly; but above all, she hated Lotta for the calm dignity of tone and manner under which she writhed, but which she felt herself powerless to resist.

Mr. von Rosenberg told Lotta to make whatever changes she thought necessary in the house; as all he had was hers, she might as well have the house and gardens fixed up to please her own taste. He knew the house would want a good deal of setting up to make it fit for her, but there was plenty of money, and she must have whatever she wanted. If Mrs. Morgan gave her any trouble he would send her away and get some one else in her place; but helps were very hard to get. Americans would not become servants, and any emigrants who came out West were for the most part unfit for domestic work.

Lotta went on a tour of investigation through the house. The rooms, though clean, had a dreary, cheerless appearance, and to one who had always been accustomed to comfort and a certain amount of luxury the prospect was certainly discouraging; but she made no complaint against Mrs. Morgan, and at once decided to retain her if she could succeed in moulding her to her wishes. She knew that the woman's services were indispensable.

After considerable trouble and scouring over the country, Mr. von Rosenberg succeeded in finding a girl who, on receiving the promise of a very liberal remuneration, consented to "come for a spell," as she expressed it, "and help Miss von Rosenberg. She objected some to going out, but when a neighbor was in a fix she didn't mind helping them through."

So Malinda Greely had taken up her abode at "Fall Farm" for a month or two, and had long since ceased to talk about going away.

After a time Mrs. Morgan became outwardly submissive, with a mingling of would-be defiance and sullen respect; but for Lotta the battle was not won.

The interior of the house soon took on a new aspect; every apartment gave token of a refining hand, and Mr. von Rosenberg expressed his pleasure and satisfaction, and placed Dan at Lotta's disposal to assist her in the management of the garden, shrubbery, orchard, and poultry-yard.

Dan was delighted with this arrangement, and when his young mistress, who dearly loved a gallop, rode out, he constituted himself groom, although his apparel was by no means consistent with his pretensions.

At Father Burke's request Lotta visited the poor of the district, and soon realized that there was quite a number of idle, lazy, improvident families in the vicinity, although there was every facility for improving their condition. She did her best among them, and readily responded to the good priest's desire for Sunday classes and weekly meetings.

After a time she had the pleasure of knowing that her efforts had not been in vain, and that knowledge repaid her.

Mr. von Rosenberg was a devout lover of music, and when the weather was propitious his every leisure hour was spent upon the piazza, while through the open windows floated sweet strains from Mendelssohn, Beethoven, or Mozart, and he smoked and dreamed dreams of the long ago, when he was a youth in the fatherland, a gay *Bursche*, as merry and wild as any in the university. Sometimes during the long winter evenings they talked of her father. It gratified Lotta to see the deep interest with which her uncle listened to the story of his brother's life; again and again he would recur to it, making her repeat all she knew.

He gave her a *résumé* of his own life since coming to America, and in their mutual confidences uncle and niece became more closely united.

As Lotta now stood on the broad piazza half shaded from the brilliant sunshine by the clustering Madeira vines, there came to her, borne on the balmy air, rich aromatic odors from pine and evergreen and the musical murmur of a distant waterfall.

She did not notice that Oscar had returned, carrying her hat and gloves, and was standing by her side, his great eyes fixed upon her face, mutely waiting until she would notice him.

To a lover of nature no fairer scene could be presented than that upon which Lotta was gazing, but a shade of mingled displeasure and annoyance suddenly crossed her face as her eyes were attracted to two men who were coming toward the house.

She stooped and patted the dog's head gently.

"Ah, Oscar, good dog, there is an end to our scamper for just now; delays are dangerous. Had we not waited to fasten up the vines, we might have escaped this visitor whom your master is bringing to us."

"A letter for you, Lottchen, *mein Kind*," Mr. von Rosenberg called up to her, "and Mr. Haviland brings for you a message from the good mother."

Lotta, leaning over the balustrade, saw the letter in her uncle's hand. She knew it came from Denise or Kate D'Arcy, and forgetting her momentary annoyance, she gathered up her trailing skirts, ran swiftly down the steps, and stood pleased and excited at her uncle's side.

"A letter for me, uncle? Oh, thanks."

"Mr. Haviland brings a message for you, Lottchen."

"Ah, yes, I beg pardon. Good-morning, Mr. Haviland."

She looked so eager, so happy, with such a glad light in

her beautiful eyes as she received the letter, that a bitter jealous pang pierced the young man's heart and darkened the smile on his face as he took her extended hand.

"Good-morning, Miss von Rosenberg; my mother commissioned me to deliver a note to you. I am going to Pine Gully about the purchase of some cattle, and she knew I should be passing this way."

He partly drew forth a note, hesitating and glancing at the house.

"Will you not come in? It is cooler inside than here. My niece has some splendid peaches and iced cream; after your ride they will refresh you; besides, it is a good six-miles' ride to Pine Gully," Mr. von Rosenberg said hospitably.

With a regretful little sigh Lotta dropped her precious letter into her pocket for future perusal and led the way into the house.

"You are so happy and comfortable here, Mr. von Rosenberg, I envy you!" young Haviland remarked as they sat discussing Lotta's peaches, iced cream, and biscuits.

"*Ach, ja*, I am happy with much comfort since Heaven sent me my little Lottchen."

"And I should be the happiest man on earth if Heaven would bestow just such a gift upon me as your niece, Mr. von Rosenberg."

"*Ach! gut*, my young friend, you would not match my Lottchen in the States; but there are plenty nice girls about here who would make you a good wife. Choose one of them and settle down."

"None of the girls to whom you allude would suit me, Mr. von Rosenberg; there is but one in all the world, and if she will not accept me I shall never call another woman wife."

"*Ach, ja*, that is good, my young friend. Adam had just one Eve; there is just one Eve for each one of us, and yours will be coming some day soon. Lottchen, *mein Kind*, will you please me with some music? I have a little time on my hands."

Lotta gladly quitted her seat, thankful to escape, and felt like laughing aloud as she saw how dexterously her uncle intercepted Herbert Haviland as he prepared to follow her to the piano, engaging him in a conversation on cattle, crops, and seasons, past, present, and to come. But notwithstanding the young man's desire to propitiate Mr. von Rosenberg, he was inattentive and *distrait;* he could hear only the delicious strains evoked by Lotta's white fingers from the superb piano which her uncle had purchased for her in New York.

Mr. von Rosenberg, as he talked with animation on the advisability of a new water-course which was to be of infinite benefit to the neighborhood, watched his visitor's face with inward amusement. He liked every one to admire and appreciate his beautiful niece, but no one should take her from her old uncle; on that point he was determined; besides, there was no young man whom he had yet seen who was worthy of her.

From where he was seated Mr. von Rosenberg had a good view of the white road that wound past the farm, and along this road a man was advancing with quick, swinging strides.

"Here is young Pivot coming to bring me the good uncle's answer," Mr. von Rosenberg remarked presently, an amused twinkle coming into his blue eyes. "We would have to cut past their place, and he has a right to share the cost, as he would the profit and convenience."

"Yes, most decidedly!" Bertie answered, with a start and a flush. "I think I will take myself off to Pine Gully, and as I have not yet given my mother's note to Miss von Rosenberg, with your permission I will do so now."

He rose as a young man entered.

The new-comer was not by any means bad-looking; most people would call him handsome. There was a reckless daring in the bold eyes, in the pose of the head and massive throat, which was innocent of necktie, in the arrangement of the ruddy-brown hair, which was swept back from the broad brow, the lowness of which, with heavy eyebrows meeting across the nose, gave a sinister expression to the face.

There was a certain rude grace about the man, although he lacked the polish of young Haviland, whom he affected to despise.

Ever since the coming of Lotta to the farm there had sprung up a silent and bitter rivalry between the two young men.

As Luke Pivot entered the room, Herbert Haviland approached Lotta.

"I have not yet given you my mother's note, Miss von Rosenberg; but first let me thank you for the pleasure I have had in listening to you. I have never heard any one play as you do. But I have not yet had the pleasure of hearing you sing. May I hope that some day soon that happiness will be mine?"

"I have not once sung since my dear father's death," she answered, letting her hands drop into her lap.

A sad, wistful look crept into her clear eyes as her mind flew back to that last evening when she had sung to her dying parent Father Faber's beautiful hymn—

"Hark! hark! my soul."

Herbert Haviland, watching her face, read something of her silent sufferings.

"Pardon me if I have inadvertently recalled painful memories," he said regretfully; "you know—O Lottchen, do not be angry with me—you know I would give my life to make you happy."

She raised her eyes, a swift, angry light flashing into them, her eyebrows arching in haughty surprise; but as she read the misery and entreaty in the young man's face, she said gently, but with icy coldness:

"You are very kind, Mr. Haviland, but my dear uncle leaves me nothing to desire in the way of happiness. I have no wish left ungratified."

"I know that your uncle understands the value of his treasure, Miss von Rosenberg, but can you blame me if I also, knowing its value, should long to appropriate it?"

"It is a vain desire, Mr. Haviland. I have already told you it can never be realized. Why will you——" She stopped short as Luke Pivot crossed the room to them.

"My aunt's having a quilting-bee at our place on Thursday next for old Nance Dewar; I've been asking your uncle, Miss von Rosenberg, to let you come over. I guess there'll be a dance and a supper in the evening. I reckon it'll not be quite so smart an affair as you're used to, but you won't turn your back upon what's done for charity, even if you don't care a red cent for the fun. Say yes, and I'll bring my new buggy over for you after breakfast."

Young Haviland waited with suspended breath for the answer, while Luke Pivot stood eager, flushed, and just a little abashed before the girl, to win whose love he was determined to overcome every obstacle.

She looked so dainty, so refined, so much the superior of any girl he had ever seen, that a hazy notion of the presumption of his request dawned upon him.

"If your aunt expects me, Mr. Pivot, I shall be sorry to disappoint her, but Thursday is my class evening, and

Father Burke and the children could not get on without me; the loss of one evening might entail the loss of several. The little ones would be glad of an excuse to absent themselves."

"Father Burke be——" Luke Pivot burst out, with a heavy frown, but instantly seeing Lotta's eyes flash open with a look of haughty displeasure, he amended, apologetically:

"I reckon Father Burke could do without you for once in a while. Don't disappoint your friends, Miss von Rosenberg, for a lot of ignorant little shavers. We'll all feel honored by your presence."

"It is because they are ignorant that I could not think to disappoint the children, Mr. Pivot. Please to convey my regrets to your aunt that I am obliged to decline."

The young man stood, with flushed face and ominous frown, twisting his hat between his strong, sunburnt hands.

He saw the triumph in his rival's face and felt like strangling him where he stood smiling before him; but he made an effort to hide his disappointment and rage.

"Then it's to be 'no'?" he said, with an affectation of indifference. "I guess my aunt and the others will be cut up a bit, but I shan't feel it, for I'm going with the old man to Webster's farm on that day, and won't be back till all the fun's over."

"Then what is the use of worrying over other people's troubles when you won't be there to share them?" Haviland remarked, with an irritating laugh.

Pivot's bold eyes go to the speaker's face with a menacing glance.

"Possibly I mightn't either, if I hadn't a kind of regard for my aunt, and I reckon I don't care to see the old lady put out. But there, I've got my answer."

"Best make up your mind to take your answer when you get it, Pivot; it is the most sensible thing you can do."

"I guess I've not asked your advice yet, Mr. Haviland. When I do it'll be time enough to give it."

"Perhaps you would not get it then."

"I'll get it when I want it, you bet."

Lotta rose hastily from the piano as her uncle joined them, and laying his hand on Luke Pivot's arm he remarked pleasantly:

"You will say to the good uncle that I should like him to look over to-morrow and see the plan I told you of, will you not?"

"Yes, we'll come over to-morrow, I take it," Luke answered, the scowl disappearing.

"You must taste our peaches before you go," Mr. von Rosenberg added. He read the feelings of the two young men and dreaded seeing them quit the house together.

"Thanks, I'll not refuse. I hear you grow the finest peaches out here," Luke responded eagerly.

Herbert Haviland, recklessly bent on irritating his rival, followed Lotta.

"Before I go let me give you this, in the hope that you will not refuse the request which it contains," he said, in an audible whisper, as he slipped his mother's note into her hand.

"I hope your mother has not also a bee on hand, Mr. Haviland?" Lotta answered, in her clear, refined tones, turning the note in her hand, "as I am going to be very busy for the next fortnight."

Bertie laughed to hide his confusion.

"I will venture to assure you it is not a bee, Miss von Rosenberg," he responded lightly. "My mother would not put your feelings to such a test."

After that little thrust at his rival, Bertie said good-by and was gone.

Poor Bertie!

An hour later, when Luke Pivot rode away from Fall Farm, he clinched his fist and muttered with a savage oath:

"You'd better take care, Bertie Haviland; for if you come sparking around with your fine airs, thinking to win that girl from me, I'll have your heart's blood."

Chapter IV.

"Our morals are corrupted and vitiated by our admiration of wealth."—CICERO.

"How convenient it proves to be a rational animal who knows how to find or invent a plausible pretext for whatever it has an inclination to do."—FRANKLIN.

"QUITE a success!"

"Yes, decidedly the ball of the season! But the D'Arcys always do give the smartest 'society' entertainments. I tell you, they're having a gay and giddy time."

"What superb emeralds and diamonds Miss D'Arcy wears to-night! Did you ever see anything to equal her *parure?* By Jove! those gems are worth a fortune."

"Rather! Did you hear that she has refused Clement Russel?"

"No, really?"

"A fact! Clement's awfully cut up about it, too. How hot it is! There's no end of pretty girls on hand. Everybody's here to-night—all the upper crust of New York."

"Yes, by Jove! It was difficult to get an invite. They're kind of sassy, these D'Arcys, on the strength of having good blood and that kind of thing."

"Yes, and they've got the suet as well as the blood. D'Arcy's been fortunate, I tell you. I hear he has bought out old Van Hoeton's shares."

"That affair's settled, then?"

"Yes, and they're sure to pay him. Everything turns to gold in Gerald D'Arcy's hands."

"He had a hard fight for it, though. But that young fellow, his son, has splendid brains—just the sort of fellow to make a pile; no chance of shipwreck when he's at the helm."

"That's so—splendid young fellow! Did you see the Southern heiress, Miss Vanstone? I heard she was coming to-night."

"Lord, yes! D'Arcy opened the ball with her."

"The dickens! you don't say so! Gerald D'Arcy of all men dancing! But perhaps it was young Connor?"

"Not a bit of it. It was the elder D'Arcy who opened the ball with Miss Garnet Vanstone, and quite young and handsome he looked. Oh, he's having a dizzy old time of it, I tell you."

The speaker's companion gave utterance to a prolonged whistle. Then both laughed.

"By Jove! look there!"

They were seated in a convenient corner, filled with flowering shrubs, from whence a good view of the dancers could be obtained. It was a brilliant scene—brilliant with the wealth and *élite* of New York society. Fragrant odors filled the atmosphere, mingling with the crash of music, the flash of jewels, the sheen of costly silks and satins, and the harmonious measure of the dancers' flying feet.

But the above ejaculation was called forth by the sight of Gerald D'Arcy, with a young lady on his arm, passing out of the ball-room.

People called Garnet Vanstone beautiful, and if a complexion of dazzling fairness, golden hair with ruddy tints, large amber eyes, *nez retroussé*, a round, dimpled chin, and full, handsome figure which moved with a slow, indolent grace, would constitute beauty, then she was, indeed, beautiful. She was dressed in white silk and cloudy gauze; white lilies and green grasses nestled in its shining folds; diamonds flashed on her round, white throat and arms and in her shapely ears.

"The atmosphere of these rooms is oppressive," Mr. D'Arcy said solicitously. "If you do not fear the cold, I could find you a sheltered seat upon the piazza which commands a fine view of the river. The moon has risen and the effect is simply magical."

"Thanks. I should enjoy it very much," Miss Vanstone returned in clear, languid tones, and having led her to a seat, Gerald D'Arcy hurried away to procure a wrap.

Presently he returned, carrying a warm, wadded *sortie de bal* in which he carefully wrapped her; then he drew her hand through his arm and led her out upon the piazza, whose floor was covered with rich Turkey rugs, and costly blooms added their fragrance to the witchery of the moon-lit night. Leading his fair partner to a wicker chair piled with Oriental cushions, Gerald D'Arcy placed one beneath her satin-shod feet, and, standing by her side, looked out across the river with its twinkling lights to the snow-capped heights beyond.

The clear stars flashed brightly down on the woman's face, looking out, so dangerously fair, from beneath the fur-lined hood, on the tall man by her side, on the brilliantly lighted mansion, on snow-clad roofs and spires, and on the mammoth city, with its pulsing human life, its joys and suffering, its pleasures and pains, its wealth and poverty, its virtue and crime, flashing down from their purple background as calmly bright, as serenely cold, as if sin or sorrow were unknown, as if earthly joys were everlasting and human hearts never break; while from the ball-room out upon the frosty air came a crash of music and a breath of rich odors.

And little more than three short years before Honoria D'Arcy lay dying in a London attic-room, dying of want, of privation, but most surely of all dying of a broken heart.

Of what was Gerald D'Arcy thinking as he stood there under the moonlit heavens with that look of unrest on his usually *débonnaire* face and in his blue eyes so persistently turned from the face of his beautiful companion, who was gazing thoughtfully out upon the river?

Was he thinking of sweet, gentle Honoria O'Connor, whom he had wooed and won on the banks of the Shannon, now sleeping the last long sleep so far away, or of the handsome sons and fair daughters she had bequeathed to him, a sacred trust, a living memory of her—of haughty, reserved Connor who had served him so faithfully for the past three years; of quiet, studious Teddy in far-away Europe, in the quaint old Spanish city, perfecting his education; of bright, generous Denise; of beautiful Eveline, with her clever, quaint sayings and odd mingling of childishness and worldliness—or was he weighing the step he was about to take and all the consequences likely to result therefrom?

Would he draw back before it was too late?

Did he hesitate, dreading the answer which the beautiful Southern heiress might return to the words he had brought her there to hear?

Whatever his thoughts, they were presently put to flight by the languid voice of his companion. The sound of those sweet tones dispelled his waking dreams and banished all indecision; the moment that was his to draw back, if he contemplated so doing, had passed away forever.

. . . .

"Oh, Mr. Brand, is it really you?" cried a ringing voice in an ecstasy of delight, and from the midst of a wilderness of tall palm ferns and costly exotics rose a slender, girlish form in a white, cloudy dress, with a face fair as the fairest of the flowers by which she was surrounded.

"What! not really my little friend Miss Eva, quite a grown-up young lady?"

"Yes, I am just myself, Mr. Brand. I do not think that any one would be so benighted as to desire an exchange of personalities. But where have you been all these ages and ages? It is over two years since you last called," Eva responded, with the childish freedom of those by-gone days when Frank Brand was her special friend and favorite and when he was an almost daily visitor at this house, from which he had so long absented himself, to Eva's intense astonishment.

He advanced now with extended hands and genuine admiration in his honest eyes.

"Are you pleased to see me?" he inquired eagerly. "I fear you are nearly right about the time, but I must disagree with you upon that other point; for I am convinced there are many young ladies who would gladly exchange personalities with you, if such an exchange could be effected." He was anxious to avoid further questioning, but he should have remembered that Eva would not be turned aside.

"We will not discuss that point, if you please, Mr. Brand," she said, frigidly drawing up her slender figure and looking away from the outstretched hand.

"I want to know why you have stayed away so long. Papa could not tell, Connor could not tell, and no one seemed to know."

It was impossible to evade Eva's straightforward pertinacity.

A question so directly put must be answered in some way; and poor Frank, unused to subterfuge, flushed and stammered like a school-boy.

How could he confess the truth?

How tell her that he had dreamed his dream and been rudely awakened—awakened to the humiliating knowledge that for him, at least, "love had not conquered all"? That he had laid his hand and heart at the feet of Kate D'Arcy, only to be rejected, not because she did not love him, but because she loved still better the Faith of Christ?

"I respect and esteem you, Mr. Brand," she had said, "perhaps I do even more. But a barrier stronger than death separates us: that barrier is Faith! A union blessed by God must be a union in which husband and wife have but one Faith, one soul. Remove this barrier by becoming a Catholic; then ask me that question and I will answer you."

He had left her resolved to conquer his love and, if possible, never to look on her face again.

He was thinking of that last interview as he stood there with Eva's large, clear eyes seeming to look him through, and vainly striving to appear composed.

"Don't lay all the blame at my door, Miss Eva," he pleaded very humbly. "I called frequently, but unfortunately could never find any one at home. You have been having such gay times, I began to fear you had quite forgotten old friends. But I must remind you that you have not yet said you are pleased to see me."

"I think in order to punish you I should not say I am pleased to see you; but I am: still, it was not treating us like friends to stay away so long. You might have found us at home some time, you know," she responded quaintly.

Frank colored ever so slightly as he gallantly raised to his lips the little gloved hand so grudgingly laid in his.

"If you only knew how awfully busy I have been," he protested mendaciously, "you would not be so severe, unless you desire to score me out of your friendship."

"Oh, not I. But it is odd that you have never been to any of Aunt Kate's parties until to-night. Now, I should not treat you so if I had been your friend."

He flushed guiltily at that allusion to Kate.

"Then you are not my friend?" he asked, to cover his confusion. "Your words make me feel very miserable and lonely."

"Yes, I am your friend, Mr. Brand, but I am not a gentleman, you know; and therein lies the difference."

Frank laughed his old pleasant laugh.

"You certainly do not look like one; but if we are still friends I am well content. I suppose every one has been telling you how beautiful you are?"

Had the last remark been uttered by any other than Frank Brand, Eva would have resented it as an impertinence, but from the first she had looked upon him in the light of an elder brother and treated him much as she treated Connor; so instead of resenting his words she laughed a sweet, mocking laugh that almost took away his breath.

It was so unlike Eva.

"Oh, yes," she answered naïvely, "people are always giving me to understand that I am beautiful; but if papa were not so rich they would not see that I am even pretty."

"At least their flatteries have not spoiled you?"

"Why should they? Beauty, like riches, might take unto itself wings and fly away; now, if my beauty should take a notion to fly away there would be nothing left. You see, I am not like Denise: she is both good and pretty, while I am mean and selfish and would not be poor again for all the world; and if I were poor, apart from those who have always loved me I would not have one true friend on earth, and all those who now bow down before me would forget my very existence. Another and brighter star would rise in the fashionable firmament. It is like playing at 'up cardinal, down king,' you know."

To say that Frank Brand was surprised by her words would be to but faintly describe his feelings. He was shocked and inexpressibly pained by this startling cynicism in one so young and fair. It was usual for her to say the most unheard-of things in that pretty, quaint way of hers, but surely this was a new development.

"I hope you do not include me in the category of your summer friends?" he asked reproachfully.

"I do not know. I used to think different, but of this I am convinced: the friends who bask in the sunshine of our prosperity are too often found wanting when weighed in the balance of our adversity. People are better to be poor, after all."

"My dear child, why do you talk in this strain? Heaven forbid that you should ever have occasion to put me to the test, but if you should, I promise you shall find me the same true friend in adversity as in prosperity, in gloom as in sunshine."

He held out his hand to her, his blue eyes eloquent of sympathy. She looked so fair, so lovely, standing there against a background of ferns and flowers, surrounded by all the accessories of wealth, costly mirrors giving back the graceful white-robed figure, the perfect face, the slender, locked hands, the glittering hair looking in the softly subdued light like threads of palest gold.

Of all the fair women who crowded that stately mansion, this daughter of Gerald D'Arcy was by far the fairest.

Frank noted with a feeling of apprehension that her clear eyes looked strangely dark and brilliant and her delicately tinted cheeks glowed like the heart of a crimson rose.

"What can have caused this change?" he asked himself.

"This is such an unusual state of mind for Eva." Then as she gave him her hand he asked abruptly:

"How is it I find you here alone? I expected to see you among the dancers."

"Oh, I was tired of dancing," she answered, with a little feverish laugh. "I wanted to get away from the crush and the glare, and we came here to rest. I sent my partner, Mr. Falconer, for an ice; he has been gone quite half an hour. I know it is very hard to get through the crush, but isn't it an awfully long time to stay?"

"Let me get you an ice; I shall not be long."

"Thanks, no; I don't care for it now. Have you seen Denise and Aunt Kate? Isn't she just lovely?"

Frank was very busy with the buttons of his gloves.

"Do you mean your sister or Miss D'Arcy?" he inquired, with a constrained little laugh. "On which am I expected to pass judgment? I think they're both 'just lovely'!"

Before Eva could reply a gentleman entered the conservatory, followed by a servant carrying refreshments.

"I fear you will never forgive me, I have kept you waiting so long. But I assure you it was not my fault. I had three different ices knocked out of my hands; then I went in search of some of the waiters and found Adam, who has been more fortunate than I," Mr. Falconer said.

She deigned no answer, and the man having placed the heavy silver salver on a small table disappeared.

"Surely you are not vexed with me for being away so long, Miss Eveline," the young man entreated earnestly.

"Vexed!" with a haughty lifting of the perfect eyebrows. "Oh, of course not, Mr. Falconer, but one might be excused for imagining you had gone in search of the proto-Adam. I do not care for the ices now. This gentleman is an old friend—let me introduce you."

"Mr. Falconer and I are acquainted, Miss Eva," Frank Brand said pleasantly; at the same time extending his hand to the young man, in whose evident distress he felt a generous sympathy.

"Will you take me to Miss D'Arcy, Mr. Brand?" Eva said, laying her gloved hand on Frank's arm.

"But our dance, you know?" expostulated Mr. Falconer.

"I shall sit out this dance with Mr. Brand. I have not seen him for a very long time, and I want to tell him about Father Donnatti," she responded coolly.

"May I have the next?" he implored.

She glanced indifferently at her *carte de danse*.

"Mr. Felix Rooney's initials are down for the next," was the serenely indifferent answer as she moved away on Frank's arm, leaving Paul Falconer standing there, pained and disappointed.

If he could but have known it, his tardiness had had nothing whatever to do with Eva's singular mood. She had sent him for the ices in order to be rid of him. She wanted to be alone, to think over the whispered comments which had reached her during the evening—comments which had set her pulses throbbing and her heart aflame with a very storm of indignation. And in that half-hour of self-communing all that was mercenary, all that was selfish and worldly in Eva's nature, the fruit of the seed sown by former poverty, burst forth strong and vigorous, to remain branded on her soul forever.

Chapter XVI.

"Yet she was pale, and sooth a tear
 Was trembling in her lucent eye,
As though some thought to memory dear
 Was rising with a sigh."

"A faithful friend is the elixir of life, and his counsels as gold to the indigent."—MRS. W. M. BERTHOLDS.

MISS D'ARCY was surrounded by some of the most distinguished men of New York. She appeared to be deeply interested in the conversation of a white-haired senator who was relating an episode of the War of American Independence, but there was a look of haunting dread and anxiety in the handsome eyes that so frequently glanced down the crowded ball-room.

Who in that brilliant assembly would imagine that once upon a time—a time not so far distant—this richly attired woman, clad in a rusty shawl and faded gown, used to steal away to Father Brady's poor chapel for an hour's quiet prayer? Although no poverty of apparel could rob Kate D'Arcy of the "Hall mark" of gentlewomen, yet, romance-writers notwithstanding, beauty adorned is *beauty perfected*. If a change had come to her in the last three years, to all appearance that change was for the better. Gerald D'Arcy had not forgotten her loving devotion to his wife and children during the years of his separation from them, and despite her remonstrance he had settled a handsome annuity upon her. The magnificent diamonds and emeralds she was wearing were his gift, as was the jewelled fan which she raised to her swiftly paling face as her brother and Garnet Vanstone re-entered the ball-room.

Her hands were cold and trembling, the senator's voice sounded far away, the music strangely harsh, her brain reeled, and for one brief instant there was darkness, a sense of coming oblivion; then a sweet voice near her said:

"See, auntie, I have brought this truant to you, but please don't be awfully severe upon him."

Eva's voice and words instantly dispelled the faintness to which Kate had so nearly succumbed.

She looked up with a wan smile and slightly dazed expression, but at sight of Frank Brand a warm blush chased the pallor from her face.

"I should punish you, Mr. Brand, but for Eva's advocacy," she said, giving him her hand.

And Eva wondered what there was in her aunt's words to make Frank Brand look so happy.

The senator's story ended at last, as all things will, and a crowd of young men gathered round Eva. Frank Brand had come to the ball at Gerald D'Arcy's pressing invitation. He was angry at himself for yielding, and made up his mind to leave at the earliest opportunity; but as he stood behind Kate's chair he forgot to carry out his resolve, forgot the determination he had formed at their last parting, and he still lingered.

Suddenly he saw Connor, who had just entered the ball-room, and his heart glowed with a feeling of fraternal pride in his friend.

"He is the handsomest man here to-night," he thought proudly. "He looks like a young prince. What can his father have been thinking of?"

Kate's heart seemed to stand still, then began to throb wildly, when she saw Connor approaching, and as he paused before her her eager eyes searched his face almost fearfully.

But it was evident that Connor had not seen his father and was still blissfully ignorant of that which was an open secret to almost every man and woman present—that which was to alter the whole course of his life.

"I have been looking for you all evening, Connor," Kate said, tapping his arm with her fan. "How are you so late?"

"I had some business to attend to; duty before pleasure, you know, dear," was the smiling reply.

A look of keen pain came into Kate's eyes, but Connor was already talking to Frank Brand and failed to notice her agitation.

To Frank Eva was an enigma. He watched her with ever-increasing wonder.

How dazzlingly fair she was!

The feverish unrest of look and tone which had so startled him while talking to her in the conservatory had vanished; her lips and eyes were smiling, her brow serene and unclouded.

"She is so naïve, so impulsive, so unsophisticated, a creature of variable moods," he thought.

A crowd of eager admirers surrounded her; Mr. Felix Rooney, to whom she was engaged for the next dance, hovering near, the most devoted of slaves. She permitted him to hold her bouquet while she talked, sometimes smiling behind her fan at his fatuous endeavors to appear witty, her unconscious victim often joining in the laugh against himself when she condescended to hold him up to the ridicule of those around him in that clever, charmingly fresh, and thoroughly childlike way of hers which most people found so irresistible.

She had forgotten to tell Frank Brand about Father

Donnatti's late severe illness, and that the good Father was going to Europe in the spring to recruit his health, and would visit Salamanca and see Teddy in the old Spanish university.

"Oh, I shall tell him to-morrow," she thought as she floated away in the arms of Mr. Felix Rooney to the exquisite strains of *Soldaten Lieder*.

"That dance is about to begin, Connor," Kate said quickly, "and you have not sought out a partner. Shall I find you one?"

Connor laughed and shrugged his shoulders.

"Oh, don't trouble about me, dear," he returned carelessly. "For the present I shall content myself with looking on. Have you any engagements, Brand?"

"None. Unless Miss D'Arcy takes pity on me I shall not dance to-night."

Kate blushed vividly in spite of herself.

"Since you put it in that way, Mr. Brand, I shall be obliged to keep you a dance," she said graciously, and held out her programme to him.

Brand took the dainty satin-fringed card and glanced over it. Hastily scribbling his initials against two dances, he returned it with a bow.

"It was good of you to oblige me!" he said as Kate's partner came up to claim her for the dance that was just forming.

She smiled, took her partner's arm at once, and they swept away, leaving the two young men standing there, with more than one pair of bright eyes turned expectantly upon them.

"Come!" Connor said hastily. "Let us get away from the crush and the glare of these crowded rooms. I must speak with you where we won't be interrupted."

Brand nodded, and without another word they left the

ball-room and passed through an anteroom into the lofty hall. Half way down Connor paused, and sweeping aside the rich *portières* draping a velvet-hung arch, led the way into a small but elegantly furnished apartment where a number of wax-candles cast a mellow light on surrounding objects and a large fire burned in a low open grate.

"Have you spoken to Denise to-night, Brand?" Connor inquired as he wheeled forward a luxurious easy-chair for his friend and leaned his elbow on the over-mantel. He had not overcome his dislike of the splendor by which he was surrounded; it irritated and galled him; the memory of his mother's patient sufferings and death was never more vividly present with him than when, as now, he stood in his father's palatial home.

"Yes," Frank responded, flinging himself into the chair and stretching his long limbs with an air of lazy enjoyment. "I spoke to her for a few minutes between the dances. How pretty she is! But, I say, old man, is anything wrong?"

"I fear there is. I have had a letter from Teddy; the poor boy is not well—been overworking himself, no doubt. You know Teddy would not complain so long as he could hold out."

Frank nodded assent, an uneasy look coming into his eyes. He was wondering how Connor and Teddy would receive the announcement of their father's engagement to Garnet Vanstone.

"He certainly would not," he rejoined gravely. "Somehow I have always fancied that Teddy is the kind of material out of which the early martyrs were made. But was it wise to send him so far away?"

"It was his wish and we did not like to oppose him. I shall speak to my father to-morrow, and he or I shall take the first steamer to Europe and bring Teddy home."

To-morrow! Even the wisest mortals are incapable of foretelling what to-morrow may bring forth.

"That will be your best plan," Frank said cheerfully. "Teddy will be better beside you."

"That is just my opinion, and I will know no peace of mind until he is here. But as nothing can be done in the mean time, I have decided to refrain from mentioning the matter to any of the others until to-morrow. Now, I have brought you here, Brand, to have a long talk and to ask your advice."

"If I can help or advise you in any way, old man, you have but to command me," Frank said warmly. They talked long and earnestly, and when Brand returned to the ball-room and sought Kate's side, he was barely in time to claim his dance.

When the guests had all taken their departure and the last carriage had rolled away, Mr. D'Arcy approached his sister.

"I must congratulate you, Kate, on the success of your ball," he said, with his gayest smile, but there was a touch of uneasiness in his manner not usual to him. "You quite surpassed yourself. It was a most brilliant affair, I assure you; and I must say, my dear, I never saw you look one-half so handsome," he added gallantly.

"I am glad you are pleased, Gerald," was all the answer Kate returned.

"Pleased! I am delighted! Everything went off splendidly; there was not a single hitch from first to last," he rejoined enthusiastically. "I hope your duties as hostess have not too utterly exhausted you, for I am going to ask you to give me a few minutes before retiring. I have a communication to make."

It was coming, then, that which she most dreaded! She was about to hear of his engagement to the Southern heiress, Garnet Vanstone. She shivered as if an icy blast had suddenly swept over her.

"Is this communication of such vital importance that you cannot wait a few hours?" she inquired wearily. She was very pale, but he did not see it.

"To *me*, yes!" he returned coldly.

She inclined her head proudly. "I am ready," she said, and followed him to his study, declining his proffered arm.

He rolled forward a chair, placed a hassock under her feet, then he stretched himself comfortably in a low chair facing her and at once plunged into the subject uppermost in both minds. He was master in his own home—master of his own actions, she knew, and had a perfect right to please himself; but had he not also a yet stronger right to consider his children? He paused at length and awaited her reply.

"You do not congratulate me, Kate," he said sharply, irritated by her silence.

"Congratulate! Ah, Gerald! have you then so soon forgotten poor Honoria, your faithful wife, the mother of your children, who loved you even in death and whose last words were a blessing and a prayer for you?" No pen could do justice to the reproach and pathos of tone and gesture which accompanied Kate D'Arcy's words, but her brother felt all that words, tone, gesture conveyed. Hastily quitting his seat, he began to pace the richly carpeted floor, which gave back no sound to his quick, uneven steps.

For several seconds the deep silence was broken only by the silvery chimes of the bronze clock on the writing-table announcing the fact that it was half-past four o'clock, after which silence once more reigned.

Kate's thoughts were with the past—that bitter past.

"What will Connor say? How will it all end?" she asked herself. "Will it be war à outrance between father and son?"

A faint moan escaped her, and Mr. D'Arcy, turning abruptly, came to her side.

"Why will you torture yourself and me, my dear girl, over what is beyond recall?" he cried passionately. "You know that I loved my poor Honoria with all my heart, that I still love her memory, and shall never cease to reproach myself for having caused her a moment's suffering. Look up, Kate, and listen to me. I have asked Garnet Vanstone to be my wife; I have told her how I loved Honoria and she has accepted me. I know that men younger, richer, handsomer than I have wooed her in vain, and I feel sure that Honoria will not sleep less peacefully in her grave that there is still left a ray of happiness in this life for me."

She raised her eyes and looked at him steadily.

"Suppose the case had been reversed, Gerald," she said: "how would you contemplate the possibility of Honoria placing another father over your children?"

He looked at her in speechless indignation for a moment, then gave utterance to a short, impatient laugh, his face paling perceptibly.

"Such a question, and from you of all others!" he cried. "*You* who knew Honoria so well know there could be no such possibility. Such an act would be utterly incompatible with her true and loyal nature. But why waste time on useless discussion? It is not like you, Kate. Can you not see that my honor is involved in this affair? Besides, it is time you had some rest: you are utterly exhausted and there is something else I wish to say. Are you listening?"

She inclined her head coldly and he continued:

"I am happy to say that even before I expressed a wish

to that effect, Garnet spoke of her desire to embrace our holy Faith. As she has not been influenced in her decision by any words of mine, I have all confidence in her becoming a good Catholic, and——"

He was silenced by an imperious gesture of Kate's white hand. She had risen hastily as the full meaning of his words became clear to her startled senses, and was standing before him proudly erect, the flash of her blue eyes outrivalling her costly jewels, which blazed and scintillated in dazzling splendor, her face flushed, her lips wreathed in a smile of ineffable scorn.

"Am I, then, in my senses? Can it be Gerald D'Arcy, the son of *my* father, to whom I have been listening while he proudly tells me that he has asked a woman—an alien to our holy Faith—to become his wife, to fill the place of Honoria D'Arcy and be a second mother to her children, not knowing, probably not caring, whether or not this woman would willingly be other than alien to the end, because, forsooth, she is beautiful? I will not insult my father's son by even a thought so degrading as that her wealth could influence him. Can adversity have so changed the brother of whom I was so proud that the Faith once so dear to him has become but a secondary consideration when it is likely to clash with the gratification of his wishes?"

Chapter XVII.

> "So dark a mind within me dwells,
>   And I make myself such evil cheer,
> That if I be dear to some one else,
>   Then some one else may have much to fear,
> But if I be dear to some one else,
>   Then I should be to myself more dear."
> —Tennyson's "*Maud.*"

FOR an instant Gerald D'Arcy shrank before his sister's flashing eyes and scorn-lit face; it was so unexpected that he stood stunned, bewildered, self-convicted.

The prize for which others contested—the prize most difficult to win had always appeared the most valuable in his estimation. It had pleased and flattered him to be first in the race for Garnet Vanstone's favor. His was a kindly, if selfish, nature with warm and generous impulses.

He had been disappointed in his children; not but what each and every one of them yielded him the most unquestioning obedience and deference, but their affection for him lacked the warmth and spontaneity which his heart demanded. He never blamed himself, never imagined that his neglect and indifference were at the root of the evil of which he mentally complained.

Garnet Vanstone's beauty had enthralled, fascinated him; her conquest was a pleasurable excitement; but it would be difficult to say if his heart was really touched. Certain it is, the question of Faith had had no place in his rosy dreams of the future.

Kate's words had hurt him cruelly, not the less so that he felt they were merited. But not even to her could he acknowledge his error.

"On my honor, you wrong me, Kate," he cried impulsively, anxious before all things to stand well in the eyes of this his only sister, whose respect was very precious to him.

"I should not have made her my wife until she had, of her own free will, been received into the Church. Do not doubt me, I beg! But for Heaven's sake, Kate, never again mention Honoria's name to me if you wish to see me happy."

The pain and self-accusation in tone and look as he uttered that last sentence went straight to his sister's impulsive heart, and all anger, all scorn died out of her face and voice.

"Heaven knows I do wish to see you happy," she said gently. "But oh, Gerald, my dear, could you not have found happiness in the midst of your children? What will they—what will Connor say?"

Her words were as a sword-thrust to her listener—they were the words which he most dreaded to hear.

"What will Connor say?" Yet he resented them almost fiercely.

"I have hitherto regarded myself as the master of my own actions, responsible to God alone, and possessed of the rights to exact obedience and respect from my family. Now"—with a short, sarcastic laugh—"it appears that the order of things is reversed. I no longer govern, I am governed by my children. I must yield obedience to their wishes, must consult them on that which concerns *my* happiness alone——"

"Ah, Gerald, how unjust you are!"

But he went on heedless of her interruption:

"I have yet to learn by what authority a child is permitted to question the divine right of parents, or since when it has become the duty of a father to render an account of his actions to his children. The past is unalterable; I shall abide by that which I would not change if I could. Have no fear that my children will again suffer from neglect of mine or from the step which I am about to take. I have provided for each so that no change of fortune can touch them. How long do you imagine I could count upon having my children around me? You know how many good offers of marriage I have already had for the girls, and last night young Falconer begged me to use my influence with Eva in his behalf. He is not very rich, but I think he would make her a good husband; he is a fine young fellow and I like him better than any of her other suitors. Then there is Connor: with that face and figure of his, how long do you think he will remain unmarried? I confess he puzzles me, he appears so indifferent to female attractions and prefers hard work to pleasure.

"But some day he will meet his fate; with so many fair women around him he cannot fail to do so. Teddy I hope to have with me for some years; but in any case my marriage will not make any change in the harmony of our relations; everything can go on as heretofore. This is Garnet's wish as well as mine. I know you regard my *fiancée* with prejudiced eyes, but I feel confident that she will love my children if they will let her and be a true sister to you for your own sake; and if you ever loved me, Kate, let this be the last you will say on this subject."

Deeply wounded, but too proud to resent his words, she bowed coldly.

"I should like to be the first to tell Connor," she said.

Her brother winced, although this was exactly what he

most desired; yet making Connor's feelings and opinion of such paramount importance irritated him.

"Certainly, if you so wish," he returned graciously, controlling his rising anger.

"I want you to call on Garnet to-day, Kate, and I should like Denise to accompany you."

"Do you think I would torture the child even to please you, Gerald?" she asked indignantly. "Denise is truth itself and could not act a lie to save her life. Will it be nothing to her, think you, to learn that a strange woman is about to take the place of the mother she loves in your heart and your home? Let her have time to recover from the first effects of what will be to her a terrible shock before you ask her to congratulate her mother's rival."

Mr. D'Arcy bit his lip and flushed angrily.

This was going to be harder than he had anticipated.

"I hope you don't contemplate inciting Denise to rebellion?" he interrogated coldly.

"As if Denise would rebel!" she retorted scornfully. "Ah! Gerald, my brother! you neither understand nor appreciate the blessed gifts that God has bestowed upon you in your children!"

He was silent, but the cloud on his brow deepened.

"We are straying from the point," he observed presently. "I have asked you to call upon Garnet for her soul's sake, if not in compliance with the rules of good breeding. I know you will not grudge the time spent in winning a soul to God, and you can initiate her in the doctrines of our holy Faith, if you will, after which you can make her acquainted with Father Rylands. I feel sure she would have been charmed with Father Donnatti, he is so gentle, so forbearing, and Garnet has been a favorite of fortune from her birth, unaccustomed to contradiction or——"

"If in taking this step Miss Vanstone is actuated by the love of God alone, she will listen with submission to the words of His priest," Kate interrupted.

"You are severe. Remember, to those without the Church the entrance is not rose-strewn; there are prejudices to overcome and humiliations to be borne in the conquest of self, and unquestioning obedience to spiritual guidance. You who have been born in the Faith cannot understand what such an ordeal will be to a girl like Garnet. I wish her to be thoroughly instructed before being received into the Church. I ask you, Kate, will you do this, not for my sake, but for the love of an immortal soul?"

"If any effort of mine will benefit a soul I shall not shrink from the task, however difficult," Kate answered calmly, and with her brother's thanks sounding in her ears she quitted the room.

It was Connor's custom to breakfast early and start for the city before the family breakfast-hour; but on this particular morning he was both surprised and disappointed on entering the breakfast-room to be informed by a servant that Mr. D'Arcy had already breakfasted and gone out.

Connor had hoped to see his father alone, that he might tell him about Teddy without alarming his aunt or sisters.

He ate his breakfast hastily and struggled into his furred great-coat, but even in his hurry he did not forget to utter a pleasant "Thanks!" to the footman who handed him his hat and gloves and held back the door for him to pass out.

"By the way, Casey," he observed, pausing in the vestibule, "will you say to Miss D'Arcy that I shall be detained in the city till a late hour?"

"Yes, Mr. Connor," the man answered, with a profound bow, and nodding a hasty good-morning, Connor dashed down the wide steps, out into the keen, crisp air of the early morning. No matter how great the storm, Connor always walked to the office; when his father had expostulated with him, he had smilingly declared that the exercise braced his nerves for his day's work.

This morning as he hurried along his mind was occupied with thoughts of Teddy, ill and alone in a strange land, far from those who loved him; and he wondered uneasily if his father would call at the office, as he sometimes did in the course of the forenoon. But he was doomed to disappointment; the forenoon and afternoon passed without bringing Mr. D'Arcy to the office.

Immediately after breakfast, to Eva's intense delight, Mr. Brand had come in his elegantly appointed sleigh to take them out for a ride; but Kate's heart was crushed and sore since that interview with her brother, so pleading an engagement as an excuse for remaining at home, she committed her nieces to Frank's care with many injunctions for their safety.

The look of keen pain which darkened Frank's clear, honest eyes when she declined to accompany them somehow soothed her vexed spirit.

He had been so eager and smiling, declaring with almost boyish delight that the weather was delightful, the snow in beautiful condition, the horses quite safe and gentle, and for once Kate felt gratified when she saw the smile vanish and the light fade from his face at her refusal.

From one of the windows of the morning-room she watched the trio while Frank carefully arranged the costly fur draperies around his two fair companions, and waved them a smiling adieu as the elegant equipage with its handsome horses glided swiftly from view, its silver bells making sweet music on the clear air; but although she had denied herself the pleasure of accompanying them, she retired to her room strangely comforted.

She had promised to call on Garnet Vanstone, and that promise must now be fulfilled; afterward she could tell Denise and Eva of their father's engagement to the heiress.

Ordering the carriage, she made the necessary changes in her dress and was soon being driven to Madison Avenue.

An hour later, when the sleighing-party returned, their faces glowing with excitement and delight, they found Kate awaiting them in the drawing-room.

"Oh, auntie, it was just heavenly!" Eva cried rapturously. But her ecstasies were short-lived.

At that instant a message from Mr. D'Arcy requesting her presence in the study came upon Eva with the effects of a cold *douche*.

She flushed, then paled, her eyes dilating with a sudden terror, and for a brief space seemed to falter. It was her last moment of indecision. A cold gleam shot into her eyes; a clear, metallic laugh that startled her hearers rippled over her lips as she started from her seat.

Blowing a kiss from her finger-tips to the three who were regarding her with looks of pain and wonder, she swept to the door; but as she reached it she paused and glanced back over her shoulder.

"*Au revoir*," she cried, with a reckless laugh. "When you see me again I shall have crossed the Rubicon and burned my boats behind me!"

Then she was gone.

Chapter XVIII.

"True nobleness doth those alone engage,
Who doth add virtue to their heritage."

"Each former feeling's old control is from the spirit gone,
And all the idols of the soul are gathered into one."

EVA and her father were alone in the study. There was a silence between them which had lasted several minutes, during which time Eva had sat with her hands idly, gracefully folded, her glance bent on the rich carpet, and, strange to say, her thoughts travelling back to the past, that bitter, cheerless past which had filled her young heart with a shrinking horror of poverty.

She had tasted the sweets of wealth, she had enjoyed the adulation, the luxury, the homage with which it had surrounded her; and as she now thought of that past a hard look—a look not good to see—stole into the beautiful, childlike face.

Mr. D'Arcy sat opposite his fair daughter, his elbows resting on the writing-table, his face hidden in his hands.

Suddenly he raised his head and regarded her searchingly, a mixture of pain and disappointment in his glance.

"Eva, my dear child," he began. With a start she looked up and met his eyes. "I find it exceedingly difficult to believe that a daughter of mine could voluntarily make such a choice as that which you have just announced to me. I cannot realize that *you*, my Eva, have accepted Felix Rooney from among your many suitors. I had hoped you would have preferred young Falconer, who is decidedly handsome and a gentleman. You are still very young, Eva—only nineteen; pause, my dear, and consider the matter well before you take such an irretrievable step. Marriage should not be lightly entered upon; remember it is for time and eternity; its responsibilities cannot be evaded or cast aside as you would cast aside a dress or a jewel of which you had grown weary. Consult your own heart and try to realize all that it would mean to a girl of your birth and refinement to yield a life-long wifely obedience to the son of such a man as old Barney Rooney, who began life as a collector of soap-fat and accumulated his vast wealth Heaven alone knows how!"

It was as if he had suddenly dealt her a blow when that allusion to the source of Barney Rooney's wealth passed his lips.

She shrank back, lifting both hands with a swift movement to her face, over which the warm blood rushed in a crimson flood to the roots of her golden hair; seeing which Gerald D'Arcy, who hated giving pain and loved to "sun him in the light of *happy faces*," paused and waited for her to speak.

Presently the white hands fell away from her face, and Eva looked up, a smile dawning in her eyes.

"Mr. Rooney is the richest man in New York, papa," she said sweetly. "He owns millions and millions of dollars, and if I marry Felix, who will get it all, he has promised to settle twelve thousand a year pin-money on me. I am to have the finest horses and jewels in the city, and he will build the handsomest residence in the States for us.

"Felix recognizes the fact that he is wofully deficient in good-breeding, and you know, papa," with a little mocking laugh, "a *man* who is willing to confess himself *outré* and *exceedingly* bad form is already more than half-way on the road to perfection. It is true that Nature has denied Mr. Felix Rooney the attributes of a Bayard, but when we have travelled a year in Europe the results will astonish you. Oh, you may depend he will emulate Chesterfield, and return to the States a—gentleman!"

"Good heavens, Eva, a gentleman! Felix Rooney transformed into a gentleman! No power of the alchemist could effect such a transmutation as that of changing such base metal into gold! But if your happiness is at stake, Eva, I shall say no more; I desire, above all things, to see my children happy. If you really love this man well enough to become his wife, to endure all things cheerfully for his sake, as is the duty of a wife, and if he should meet with reverses to willingly share poverty and hardships with him; to——"

She sprang to her feet, flinging out her white hands with a gesture of horror and repulsion, her voice ringing out clear and sharp.

"No, no, no!" she cried, "I would *not* be poor again, for the love of the fairest Absalom on whom the sun of heaven ever shone! I should hate the man who brought me to that! I should die if I had to return again to the cold and hunger, the struggling for even a morsel of bread while others went without. I could not deny myself food that others might eat, as Denise and Aunt Kate have done times without number. I have endured hunger until my brain reeled and my senses seemed deserting me, yet I had more to eat than they."

Mr. D'Arcy listened like one suddenly smitten with dumbness—listened, drinking in every word.

"I have been thankful, oh, so thankful! when Lottchen von Rosenberg has asked me to her rooms to sit with her, because of the warmth and comfort which I knew awaited me there, and because Lottchen would insist upon me dining or taking tea with her, as the hour might suit; but Denise would not join us, although there were times when she had tasted nothing, or next to nothing, all day.

"How I hated myself for the meanness which urged me to accept what I had not sufficient self-respect to refuse; but Lottchen did everything so sweetly, so graciously, appearing to be the recipient of favors when in reality she was conferring them; and the delicacies which she never failed to bring mamma could not have been refused by the proudest lady in the land. But I believe at this moment I should in any case have accepted her favors just the same.

"Do you think that after such an experience I would return to such a life for the love of any man? No, a thousand times! I feel that what I am saying will make me appear contemptible in your eyes, but remember, please, that I am not a saint, as dear, beautiful mamma was. I could not, knowing myself dying of a twofold starvation, bear the knowledge with smiling resignation and die blessing the cause of it. Neither am I of the material from which heroines are made, as is Denise, for though I should see all around me dying, I could not sing on the streets to procure them food and fuel, as she did for mamma and Teddy."

"Oh, my God!" burst from Gerald D'Arcy's white lips. They were the first words he had uttered—words wrung from his tortured heart.

But blind to his agony, she went on passionately, recklessly, and told him all the miserable story.

"Denise never dreams that I know why she was so long absent that day," she added. "It was not until Bella Norris came to pay Miss Carlyon's bill that Denise told Aunt Kate what she had done. How auntie wept over her! They did not know that I heard every word, and never shall, for I could not endure to humiliate Denise by so much as a word.

"Ah, papa, you are astonished that I, *your* daughter, should of my own free and unbiased will accept Felix Rooney; but while those trials have only served to develop all that was good and perfect in Aunt Kate and Denise, they have brought to the surface all that is mean and despicable in my nature.

"Though I may despise myself, I can no more change my nature than the leopard his spots. I know myself to be ease-loving and utterly selfish—not a very exalted character, you will admit; my only *real estate* my beauty, but the man whom I have chosen does not look beyond that. I could endure *anything* but a return to poverty and privation; even the offensive ignorance of Mr. Felix Rooney or the sordid coarseness of his father.

"I shall not marry any man who is not willing to settle upon me a sum sufficient to secure me against all future contingencies. Felix is willing to do this, therefore I have consented, with your approval, to become his wife. He will be possessed of more wealth than any other man in New York. I have beauty, birth, and grace—I think you will admit that the advantages are about equal. He cannot despise me for the lack of virtues to which he is himself a stranger; and I shall be happy."

She stood before her father a picture of rare girlish beauty, so fair, so ethereal as to seem scarcely a creature of earth; her blue eyes black and glowing with intense self-scorn, yet never for an instant wavering in her resolution.

There was an unyielding will beneath that fair exterior—how unyielding Gerald D'Arcy never dreamed, or that the rumor of his engagement to Garnet Vanstone had precipitated her acceptance of Felix Rooney.

"No strange woman shall reign over *me* in my father's house," she had thought, while jealously watching her father's very marked devotion to the heiress; and that thought had decided her.

Love was an unknown quantity in Eva's calculations; she *would* marry the *richest* man in New York, and such Felix Rooney would one day be.

After that one exclamation wrung from the depths of his agonized soul, Mr. D'Arcy uttered no word, but sat there white and still, his haggard eyes fixed on Eva's face. But when her voice no longer sounded in his ears, the fixed look left his eyes and he flung out his arms with a gesture of despair.

"Ah! merciful Heaven!" he cried passionately. "What a heartless wretch I must have appeared to my beloved ones, leaving them to suffer like that! No wonder, though, my children should hate me!"

"Oh, papa, dear, you wrong us, indeed, indeed you do, by such a suspicion. We are all convinced that you were blameless. Mamma and Aunt Kate said so all the time. How could you know that auntie had lost her money? I should not have told you about these things, which are all past and beyond recall, but, oh, papa, you cannot conceive what a miserable coward I become when I look back upon that past. Say you forgive me, papa, darling, for having pained you so cruelly in my selfishness."

Frightened at sight of her father's strong emotion, Eva had flung herself at his feet, clasping his knees in an agony of remorse, her beautiful eyes softened and brimful of tears.

Gerald D'Arcy looked down on the lovely upturned face, so childlike, so full of pleading, and the despair in his own gave place to regretful tenderness.

He raised her gently and placed her in a chair.

"Forgive you, child?" he said sadly. "What have I to

forgive? Am I to forgive you for telling me the simple though most bitter truth, all of which I should have been told when first we met? It was a mistaken kindness to spare me. I am no tyrant, child. I know now that in my short-sightedness I have been all to blame.

"You have made many things clear to me. I can now understand the cause of Connor's coldness—I had almost said dislike of me. Had I been told all this at first, how different our future might have been! But regrets are worse than useless now."

Rising hastily, Eva crossed over to her father, and kneeling by his chair, rested her clasped hands upon his knees.

"I have been very wicked, papa," she said simply, "and I want to kneel here, that I may feel sure you have forgiven me. Do not send me away, please. Now, papa, I cannot let you misapprehend Connor; he is all that is good and noble and generous, and I want you to believe that we all love you very, very dearly, indeed."

"And yet, my poor little Eva," he rejoined, tenderly smoothing her shining hair with his shapely hand, "you have no faith in my affection for you."

"Oh, papa!"

"Hush, my dear! In the past I unfortunately gave my children cause to doubt me; but, thank Heaven, I was not wholly to blame, nor have I neglected their future. Trust me, Eva; your dowry will be worthy the daughter of an English peer; do not, then, I beg of you, wreck all your future by making a mercenary marriage, from which all your finer instincts must recoil. I would rather see you the wife of a poor man of good family and respectable antecedents, though I had to give him a helping hand to fortune, than give you to this man if he could place you on a throne."

Eva bent her golden head and kissed the hand that rested on her own.

"I know you are the dearest and best of papas, and that in all you have said you have been actuated by a desire for my happiness alone; but indeed, papa, darling, I should be much happier with Felix than with—with any one else, and I have promised him, you know. Say 'Yes,' papa."

It was hard to resist those pleading eyes, but heart and soul recoiled from calling Felix Rooney son; and Gerald D'Arcy wondered, almost savagely, from whom his beautiful, graceful daughter could have inherited such a perverted taste.

How was he to inflict such a brother on his other children? and stately Garnet Vanstone, how would she regard the prospect of such a son-in-law?

Eva silently watched her father's face and read there the struggle waging in his breast.

"If you are *convinced* that this marriage alone will give you happiness," he said at length, "I love you too well to make you miserable. Let it be 'Yes,' then, Eveline, but I must express my regret that your choice should have fallen on one whose only claim to consideration—nay, even to toleration—is his wealth. You are so utterly unlike the man that I cannot believe my senses, but you have my consent and blessing, Eveline. God grant you may never repent of your singular choice."

"I have promised him my answer to-morrow at twelve o'clock."

Eva rose quietly and kissed her father's cheek.

"Thank you, papa, you have made me very happy," she said, in strangely subdued tones.

"I want you to promise me something, please. It is that you will *never* repeat to any one what I have told you about—about, you know, dear, about Denise singing——"

He interrupted her with a gesture of infinite pain.

"Ah, no," he cried bitterly, "do not fear; my poor, brave Denise has been sufficiently humbled!"

She caught both his hands in hers and kissed them passionately.

"You are too good to me, papa," she said, her voice choked with emotion. "Heaven knows I am not worthy to be *her* sister or your daughter!"

Then she turned and passed from the room.

She had crossed the Rubicon and burned her boats behind her.

When the closed door shut her form from his sight, Gerald D'Arcy dropped his face upon his folded arms and wept bitter tears—such tears as only a strong man weeps in his agony of grief and repentance.

Eva had indeed made many things clear to him.

He knew now why Connor had so firmly refused to accept more than the salary of a manager, and yet no manager ever before worked for an employer as Connor worked for his father, who had with a feeling of resentful pride accepted his son's decision—Connor could not forget his mother's sufferings; and somehow the knowledge made Mr. D'Arcy's heart glow with an added pride in his first-born and a yearning desire to win his affection.

The memory of all that had been said that afternoon while crossing the river at Beechville came back to him now. He recalled Clifford's strictures on the girl he had heard sing in front of the Albany, and Kate's loyal defence; and for the first time he understood why Denise had rejected Marmaduke Clifford, the man whom above all others he would have been proud to call son.

Kate found it the most difficult and bitter task she had ever undertaken to acquaint Connor with his father's engagement to Miss Vanstone.

In what words she told him, she could never afterward remember. But so long as life should last she would never forget Connor's blank, incredulous horror, or the storm of wrathful indignation that swept over his face, until she literally cowered away before his blazing eyes.

And oh, the scathing scorn in the few words he uttered —few, but they held in them the very bitterness of death. In vain she wept, in vain she implored. He stood before her cold, stern, immovable, the handsome mouth curved in haughty disdain, the handsome eyes looking like flames in the pallid face.

When he left her, Kate fell upon her knees and wept out her anguish in a very abandonment of despair. She was still kneeling there when a low tap sounded on the door, and Denise asked softly:

"Please, auntie, may I come in?"

The door was softly opened, the silken *portière* swept aside, and Denise with pale, troubled face entered.

"Is Connor very angry, auntie?" she faltered.

"Ah, hush, my dear, hush! he is going away. The steamer sails to-day, and he is going to—to Teddy," Kate responded, striving to speak calmly but breaking down utterly. Denise waited to hear no more. One wild look she cast on the weeping woman, then dashed from her presence out along the corridor, pausing only when she reached Connor's door, upon which she knocked for admittance.

But when she looked upon his pale, set face and flashing eyes she realized with a sinking heart that she was powerless to dissuade him from his purpose.

"I will ask papa to let me go with you to Teddy, Connor, dear," she urged passionately when all her pleading had failed, but the tone in which he answered, "No, you shall not!" silenced her entreaties.

In his stern face she read only too clearly his fixed purpose. He was about to bid an eternal farewell to that house and to the father whose last act of folly had cost him his son's respect.

It was later than usual when Mr. D'Arcy awoke next morning. He had attended a meeting on the previous evening, at which he had been detained till a late hour, and had had no opportunity of seeing any member of the family when he returned home. He was resolved to seek an interview with Connor, and if possible break down the barriers of coldness and formality which had grown up between them.

He was not a man to borrow trouble or to sup on dire forebodings; but, despite his naturally easy-going disposition, a thought would occasionally obtrude itself, like a spectre at a feast—a thought what Connor would feel and say when he should hear that *he* was about to contract a second marriage; and at such times his heart would contract with a feeling of positive dread.

He awoke languid and out of sorts, and glanced around the room. On a table near the bed was a silver salver, on which lay a letter and small parcel neatly sealed at both ends.

He reached out his hand toward the letter, then drew it back with a strange sense of fear upon him and rang a hasty summons.

"What is this, Adam?" he asked as his man entered the room. "Did you give my message to Mr. Connor?"

"Mr. Connor sailed for Europe yesterday, sir; but he left that letter and packet for you."

Before the man had finished speaking Mr. D'Arcy had sprung out of bed and seized his dressing-gown. Something had gone wrong, he knew; but what that something was he did not at first comprehend. He turned to Adam with a gesture of dismissal.

"That will do. You can go and get my bath ready. I shall ring when I want you."

As soon as the man disappeared Mr. D'Arcy seized the letter, his hand trembling, a terrible misgiving filling his heart as he tore it open, scarcely noticing an inclosure which fell to the floor.

There were only a few sentences written on the thick, creamy paper, and these were faultlessly, coldly respectful.

Connor had resigned his post of manager, and hoped that his vacant place would soon be filled by a competent person. He had left everything in good working order; all papers, bills, receipts, and contracts for the working of silver and other mines, together with a considerable sum of money, just received, were locked away in the large iron safe in the inner office; the key of the safe would accompany this letter.

He was going to Teddy, whose last letter to himself he begged leave to inclose.

Not a hint that he had heard of his father's approaching marriage, but what need was there for words? It was not in Connor's nature to descend to reproaches. But the coldly ceremonious tone of that brief epistle told all too plainly that the iron had entered into the writer's soul, as Mr. D'Arcy fully realized with a yearning tenderness for his first-born and a keen sense of irreparable loss. Pale to the lips, he picked up Teddy's letter and read it slowly—a long letter this, full of brotherly love, mingled with a tender reverence for his elder brother and a touching dependence on his counsel and advice.

With a profound sigh, Gerald D'Arcy returned both letters to the envelope, which he locked away in his desk.

"I must not lose the trust and love of my children," he

cried passionately, "and, Connor, my boy, if I cannot have your affection, neither can I afford to forfeit your respect. You have left me meaning never to return; but first you have gone to Teddy, and I shall follow in the next steamer.

"I can trust Brand to look after my affairs while I am absent; he would do more than that for Kate's brother.

"I will have time to settle everything and see Garnet before the next steamer sails."

Chapter XIX.

"Could ye come back to me, Douglas, Douglas,
  In the old likeness that I knew,
I'd be so gentle and loving, Douglas,
  Douglas, Douglas, tender and true."

"I THINK the translation runs, 'The Cross is a shield in all danger, a consolation in all sorrow, and the brilliant lighthouse which in the night guides us toward the eternal splendor.'

"To me you have been the lighthouse which pointed out the way to eternal happiness. Why will you not let us tread the path of life together? You have ignited the sacred spark of Faith in my darkened soul; do not deny a little ray of hope to my hungering heart."

On a path at the base of a hill two persons were standing—one a girl, slender, graceful, high-bred in tone and gesture; a girl whom one would not expect to meet in this western wild, and meeting would pause to wonder what chance had brought one so fair so far from the boundary line of "good society."

That she was not American one could see at a glance; that she was English one might also guess, but English with that indefinable grace and tone which only foreign travel and mixing in foreign society could impart.

The other was a young man, decidedly good-looking, tall, with good breadth of shoulder and depth of chest; his supple, shapely limbs showed to advantage in his tight-fitting riding-suit; in his left hand he held a soft felt, broad-brimmed hat, his right hand was extended toward the girl in humble entreaty.

At a little distance a splendid chestnut cropped serenely the rank herbage skirting the road on one side, feeding while he waited for his master to remount him.

On the ground at the young man's feet lay a silver-mounted riding-whip.

They were surrounded by the glowing glories of October, whose soft light fell around them, whose health-giving breath wafted sweet odors to where they stood.

The sides of the rocks were hidden from view by long drooping branches of hemlock, woven into fantastic garlands by Nature's cunning hands; far up to the summit of the hill the stately pines rose in solemn grandeur, while here and there luxuriant evergreens peeped forth.

They made a striking picture standing there, the bright sunlight falling upon them: the tall, stalwart young man, eager, ardent, imploring; the girl in a gown of pale blue cashmere and satin of the same hue, a soft, white, fleecy scarf fastened with careless grace round the slender neck and secured on the left shoulder by a large gold cross of Celtic design; a wide-brimmed hat covered the graceful head and shaded the ivory-white face; the clear eyes, filled with pain, were gazing away beyond her companion as she swung a basket which she carried a little impatiently to and fro. Above the clear blue sky, behind the tall pine-topped hill with its glowing drapery of rich vegetation forming a fitting background.

At his last words she turned her eyes upon him.

"You pain me exceedingly by speaking in this way, Mr. Haviland," she said, a faint *soupçon* of anger in the clear, refined tones. "I think it is very unkind of you to persecute me and torture yourself needlessly. You promised me never to allude to this subject again. As a friend I like you very much indeed, but I can never like you in the way you want me to."

"Then you *have* a lover more fortunate than I?" he asked, in a tone of hopeless despair.

"A lover! I have never had a lover in my life," she answered, looking clearly and frankly into his troubled face.

He raised his head proudly and threw back his shoulders as if freeing himself from a heavy burden.

"Then, Heaven helping me, I shall not despair. I know that I need not fear Luke Pivot, for with all his love for you he cannot win you. There, do not fear that I shall persecute you, as you call it; but with an open field I shall win you yet. I will strive to deserve you, and wait so patiently, thankful for the precious gift of your love, however long I may be in winning it, and you know, '*Qui patitur vincit.*'"

"I regret to hear you speak like this, Mr. Haviland. I should like to spare you all unnecessary pain. Try to believe me when I assure you that though you may be willing to endure, yet you cannot conquer in this particular instance; for when, after an acquaintance of three years, I can regard you only as a friend, my feelings for you will never grow warmer. Then do not further torture yourself by following an *ignis fatuus* that can lead to nothing but disappointment. I suppose you know the saying of the ancients, '*Ex nihilo nihil fit.*'"

He threw out his strong, shapely hands with an imploring gesture.

"One moment! Do not leave me like this. See! I shall not stop you against your will; but only grant me another instant."

Moved by his tone and gesture, she paused in the act of leaving him.

"I think it is unkind of you, Mr. Haviland," she said, a little less scornfully, "to desire to prolong this interview. Apart from this subject, I will have much pleasure in listening to anything you may have to say, but——"

"I do not dispute the wisdom of the ancients," he interrupted with passionate vehemence. "Nor do I expect that out of *nothing* I could possibly extract *something*, but *you* are not that invisible *nothing*—you are all the world to me, you are the sun that lights my days, your displeasure the cloud that darkens them; you have a heart and I mean to win it—stay! you *are* going to listen, and I *shall* speak only this once; try to be patient, and I swear that I will never speak to you again like this. I loved you the first moment I met you in New York. When you came to your uncle's home I tried to win a return of my love from you, but I saw you were indifferent. I endeavored to discover some means of pleasing you, for *your* sake—not for my soul's, Heaven help me! I began to study the Faith you love; I thought that by embracing it I should be a step nearer to you— I see you are displeased, but, before Heaven! this is how I first came to take an interest in it, for your sake alone! Thinking to please you, to win a place in your heart, I began thus; now I have finished by believing in it, loving it with all my soul—loving it for its truth and beauty. In a few days Father Burke will receive me into the Church, and I owe it all to you; it was my love for you which turned my soul to God! You were my beacon-light, your hand pointed the way, although unconsciously. Do not cast me into despair: give me some hope that one day I may win you. I would lay down my life for you, Lottchen—don't be angry with me for calling you by that name; only this once let me call you Lottchen, and I will never presume to do so again until you give me the right— no, do not say you will never do that. I call Heaven to witness that if the laying down of my life would save you from harm I should yield it up gladly."

She would have been less than woman had she remained unmoved by the force of his great love for her; but deep down in her heart Lotta felt that she did not and never would reciprocate his love. Very gently but very firmly she told him this, leaving him no room to hope that she would change. Then she spoke to him of that other greater and more perfect love.

"Let me tell you how delighted I am to know that you are about to enter the Church," she said, giving him her hand, a radiant smile lighting up her beautiful face. "God grant that the thorny path which you have chosen may blossom into the flowers of eternal life for you."

"Thanks; you *are* pleased, then?" he asked, holding her hand and looking down into her smiling face, a great joy lighting up his own.

"From my soul," she answered, withdrawing her hand from his clasp, "and the angels in heaven are pleased also."

"Ah, yes, I know," he responded, a shade of sadness chasing away the smile.

"But," Lotta asked, suddenly remembering, "what do your parents say about your change of Faith?"

He laughed a short mocking laugh.

"Change of Faith? I never knew the meaning of the word faith before; true, I had unbounded faith in myself, but I did not trouble about religion in the past. As to my parents, the old man thought I was mad and told me so, called me a fool, and a few very polite epithets; my mother and the girls were horribly shocked, but they knew that there was no use talking to me."

"Do not lay aside your crown because the thorns may pierce your flesh; only by sufferings patiently borne can we hope to gain the eternal splendor," she said encouragingly.

"I must go now. I have been gone so much longer than usual, and uncle will be uneasy. I think my trusty squire Dan has forgotten me."

"Let me see you home," he said eagerly.

"Thanks, Mr. Haviland, but I will take the wood road; it is the shortest way home. Good-by—a pleasant ride home."

"If I could hear you call me Bertie just once?" he said imploringly, as for one moment he held her hand in a firm clasp.

She looked at him with a flash of indignant surprise.

"It is useless to hope for that," she said coldly.

He released her hand in silence, and she turned from him with hasty steps into a rough, narrow wood road. As she entered beneath the shade of the trees, she turned and glanced to where she had left him; she could not understand what had impelled her to do so.

He was standing gazing after her, his right hand thrust into his breast; his left hand, still holding his hat, drooped listlessly by his side, the sun glinting down upon his uncovered head.

She saw him standing there in the pride of his strong young manhood, saw him as she would see him till the last hour of her life, and as she would never see Bertie Haviland again in this world.

With a feeling of pity for the man she had just left, mingling with a strange foreboding of coming evil, she pursued her way, picking her steps carefully over the uneven road.

"I wish he would try to be content with my friendship," she thought, with an impatient sigh. "He has always been so kind and attentive that I have come to like him almost as well as I should have liked a brother. I am so sorry that I dared not speak more kindly to him just now; he is the only friend I have had since coming here, and now I must see him as seldom as possible. What is the meaning of this strange foreboding? Possibly the effect of coming from the sunlight into this gloom. I wish I had taken the open road; I shall never come this way again."

As she advanced the gloom became deeper, and she wished that she had not left Oscar at home.

Suddenly she paused with a startled look in the wide-open eyes and listened attentively; then she laughed at her own fears and continued on her way.

"What a coward I am to-day!" she thought, trying to reassure herself; "it is some of the men from the village shooting down a wild turkey."

But notwithstanding this assurance, she hesitated more than once before she reached a clearing, where, gleaming whitely in the sunshine, she could see the road which skirted the wood, and the sight brought a feeling of relief to her. She would soon be home now. But here she again came to an abrupt pause, fully convinced that what she had been striving to persuade herself was but the result of her foolish terror was really some one rushing after her along the road she had just come, calling upon her to stop.

She could not recognize the voice of her pursuer, but she stood like one spellbound, unable to move.

She knew that it was a man who was dashing along at that headlong pace, but all power of motion seemed gone from her limbs, until she recognized Dan's figure and knew that it was Dan's voice, hoarse with terror and shouting, which cried out as he came full into view:

"Stop, Miss von Rosenberg, darling, for the love of the Holy Mother. Come back—you're wanted."

"What is the matter, Dan?" she asked in a tone of cold

displeasure, regarding him with indignant surprise. "Why do you come crashing and shouting after me in this way when you did not come to me in proper time?"

From her first coming to reside on the farm, Dan had never failed in obedience and respect to his young mistress. He was her veritable slave; she was to him a beautiful young princess whom it was his pride to obey; he followed her about like a great Newfoundland dog, made happy by a word of commendation and miserable by a word of reproof.

But on this occasion, to Lotta's surprise, he returned no answer to her indignant inquiry. Without a word of apology he stretched out his hand to take her basket.

"Ah, now, ma'am, for the love of Heaven don't wait here a minute longer," he said in a tone of humble but earnest expostulation, "but come back. Shure, young Mr. Haviland is lying shot dead through the heart where ye left him."

"Merciful Heaven!" burst from Lotta's white lips, and flinging her basket from her she dashed past Dan, who followed quickly in her steps, and rushed on unheeding the roughness of the way, thinking only—

"Dead! dead! and I have spoken such hard, cruel words to him. Ah, Blessed Mother, pray for him! Pray that I may be yet in time."

She stopped short, almost dashing Dan to the earth as they came in sudden collision.

"Have you been to the village, Dan?" she asked.

"I have indeed, ma'am; I went be the road and missed ye."

"Was Father Burke still there when you came away?"

"He was, ma'am, but he was jist comin' away to see ould Pat Murphy."

"Go at once and bring him to me! Tell him what has

happened, and as you hope for mercy in your last hour do not delay a moment."

Dan thrust his hat on his head, his big eyes opening wide in surprise.

"Niver fear, ma'am, I'll run every fut of the way," he answered readily, and had darted off before he had finished speaking.

She followed, never pausing for breath.

On, on until she was out from the gloom of the wood, out into the sunshine, out on to the white road, her eyes strained toward the spot where she had last seen Bertie standing gazing after her. He was no longer there, but close to a group of men stood his horse, drooping and dejected.

Everything was blurred and indistinct—she could only see the still figure over which they so anxiously bent.

As she sank on the ground beside them she grasped the arm of one of the men and tried to speak. He read the unspoken question in the imploring eyes.

"No, thank Heaven! he is not dead, my dear child!" he answered gently; "there is still life. I have sent for Dr. Edwards, but I fear he is away at Pine Gully; I met him going there this morning."

She did not know that the low-spoken words were uttered by Father Burke, or that it was his face into which she had just looked. She only knew that Bertie Haviland was not dead, and she bent her face in her hands and murmured a heartfelt thanksgiving and a prayer that he might be spared.

Some one touched her on the arm, and looking up she met Father Burke's glance of pitiful sympathy, and for the first time became aware of his presence.

"His eyes are open now. Will you see if he recognizes you?" he said.

She nodded silently, and bending over the prostrate form looked into the dull eyes, watching with suspended breath for some sign of recognition, but in vain!

"Bertie, don't you know me? It is I—Lotta."

She spoke the words softly, but they sounded clear and distinct on the still air.

An instant of breathless waiting followed.

Gradually consciousness dawned in the dull eyes, slowly they turned toward her, a faint smile creeping into them and around the white lips, which moved without making any sound.

"Oh, if we had some wine, some brandy—anything—anything to revive him," she said desperately.

"Here is some water, ma'am," Dan said, coming to her side a little shyly, carrying his hat, filled with clear water, between his hands.

It was no time to be fastidious.

She dipped her handkerchief into it and touched Bertie's lips and forehead with the cool water. He looked at her gratefully, and seeing that he wished to speak, she bent her ear to his lips.

"It has come sooner than I thought, Lottchen," he gasped painfully.

His words pierced her heart cruelly.

"You must not talk," she said, gently smoothing the damp hair from his forehead. "Father Burke has sent for Dr. Edwards."

He turned his eyes from her face, a quick light flashing into them.

"Would you like to see Father Burke? Shall I bring him to you?" she asked eagerly.

She read assent in his eyes, and motioned Father Burke to approach.

Bertie's lips moved again; she bent her head to listen.

"Don't—go—far—away—Lottchen."

"No," she answered softly.

She did not care what he called her now. If only he would recover and forgive her late scorn, he might call her Lottchen for the rest of his life. She felt that if he died she would have been the cause of his death; she knew without being told whose rifle had laid him there.

He smiled faintly up into her troubled face, his eyes following her lingeringly as she moved away, giving place to Father Burke.

Dan stood at a little distance awaiting orders, a look of genuine sympathy on his honest, homely face; the other three men had gone to the wood to cut down branches to form a litter.

"To whom does the nearest house belong, Dan?" Lotta asked anxiously.

"Siah Butterby's on the farm, ma'am, ye know; but shure it's only a shanty, and there's not a spot fit to lay a dying dog on in it, if ye had any falin' fer him."

"But Mr. Haviland will not die now, Dan, and he must not be taken there. Would it hurt him very much to have him taken to the farm?"

"Well, indeed, ma'am, His Reverence is afraid to move him at all, at all, till the docther comes, though ye know, ma'am, he's a bit of a docther himself. I think His Reverence wants me."

Chapter XX.

"White as a white sail on a dusky sea,
When half th' horizon's clouded and half free,
Fluttering between the dim wave and the sky,
Is hope's last gleam in man's extremity."

"No future hour can rend my heart like this save that which breaks it."

ON that sad and memorable October afternoon the tall pines on the hill-top looked down on a strange, weird sight. Four rude-looking men with uncovered heads surrounding a wounded man, supported in the strong arms of a stout, motherly-looking woman, down whose homely face great tears were unrestrainedly falling.

By her side, his right hand resting lightly on the shoulder of the prostrate man, knelt Mr. von Rosenberg, his head uncovered, his usually ruddy face pale, his clear blue eyes troubled and anxious.

On one side knelt Dan, a look of reverent awe on his weather-tanned face, his hat, filled with water, held between his strong brown hands; while at a little distance Lotta knelt and prayed—prayed with all her soul that Bertie Haviland might live.

Last, though not least, of this striking central group stood the "stoled priest," in the act of administering the Sacrament of Baptism to the wounded man—at his earnest request—to whom Mr. von Rosenberg and Mrs. Morgan were sponsors, and for whom they spoke the words which his fast-failing strength would not permit him to utter;

while, far away, a fugitive was flying from justice, and a haggard-faced man, upon whom a lightning flash seemed suddenly to have fallen, withering and blighting him in its descent, rode wildly in the direction of the silent group.

"Thank God!"

The words, so full of gratitude, fell from Bertie Haviland's pale lips, startling every one.

"He *will* live, Father?" Lotta whispered joyfully to the priest, who was carefully folding up his stole.

"Yes, my child, he will *live in Heaven*, but Time does not hold many more hours in his sand-glass for my poor young friend. Try to take comfort from the knowledge that through the Sacrament of Baptism, which our Heavenly Father has mercifully seen fit to bestow upon him, his soul is now clothed in a garment white as an angel's before the Eternal Throne. This most miserable event has only hastened the consummation of that for which he has been some time preparing, and let the knowledge that he has been *fully* prepared give you fortitude to bear this trial which has come into your young life."

"If he dies, Father, I shall feel that I have been the cause of his death," she said.

"My dear child, you must not indulge in such thoughts; you are entirely blameless. The ways of Heaven are inscrutable; what seems to our weak human judgment a calamity is often a mercy in disguise. Remember God does all things well."

She knew he was right; but she turned away sad at heart, and approaching the injured man seated herself on the ground by his side and gently supported his head, while Mrs. Morgan moved to a little distance where she could cry quietly.

There was a slight flush on Bertie's pallid face and a

new light in his eyes. Lotta looked at him with sudden hope. "You are better?" she questioned eagerly.

"Better! Ah, yes, the sick made whole, Lottchen!"

"I spoke to you cruelly a short time since; say you forgive me, Bertie, and if Heaven spares your life I will give you the right to call me Lottchen while we two live," she said earnestly.

Poor Bertie! How could he understand the refined and highly sensitive nature of this girl, who, through a mistaken sense of responsibility, had resolved to immolate herself and atone to him through all her future life? He looked up at her, a great joy shining in his eyes.

"My darling! I have nothing to forgive. I know that in your priceless innocence you are as far removed above me as the stars of heaven are—above—the——"

She saw with terror that he had spoken too much, that her words had excited where she had hoped they would soothe; and she gently interrupted his faltering speech.

"I forbid you to speak another word just now. See, here are the men coming to take you away."

Four men approached, and four pairs of strong arms raised him gently from the ground and placed him with almost womanly tenderness on the litter. She saw with a shrinking heart the deathly pallor return to his face and the spasm of pain that distorted it, but she did not know that as the procession moved away he became unconscious.

She hurried on before to prepare a room, Dan coming behind holding the bridle of Bertie's horse, which followed slowly after.

When the wild rider reached the deserted spot, there was only a pool of blood to tell where his son had lain.

A number of men and women from the village were excitedly hurrying toward Fall Farm; but unheeding the murmur of sympathy which greeted his appearance, Squire

Haviland drove his spurs fiercely into his horse's sides and pursued his way, coming up to the procession as it halted in front of Mr. von Rosenberg's door.

He dismounted quietly now, while the men lowered the litter and entered the house through the wide passage into a room where Lotta and Mrs. Morgan awaited their coming.

As the squire reached the door of the room into which his son had been carried, Father Burke and Mr. von Rosenberg came to his side.

"My dear sir, I need not tell you that your son is in a most dangerous state," the former gentleman said, in tones of deepest sympathy; "the least excitement may prove instantly fatal. The ball cannot be extracted until Dr. Edwards arrives. We dread——"

"Let me go to him!" the squire burst out hoarsely, passionately; "he is my only son, dear to my soul as was Absalom to his father David. Do not keep me from him lest I curse you!"

At that moment the men, having tenderly deposited their insensible burden on the bed, passed silently from the room, and Father Burke detained one of them to question him.

"Your son is insensible, squire, and will probably remain so for some time," he said gently, turning to the stricken parent. "I think you may safely see him, but I need not warn you to control your feelings when he returns to consciousness."

He opened the door softly, and the squire, silent, subdued, utterly broken down, entered the room.

He saw nothing but a white bed, on which lay his only son, and struggled hard to repress all outward expression of the passionate anguish which was rending his soul as he gazed on the still form, stricken down in all the glory and pride of his early manhood by the hand of an assassin.

Father Burke and Mr. von Rosenberg were walking impatiently to and fro under the piazza, casting anxious looks toward the road, when they were rewarded by seeing Dr. Edwards, his horse covered with foam and dust, riding furiously into sight.

They went to meet him, thankful for his coming, and while he wiped the perspiration from his heated face, they told him in a few words what had happened, and resigning his steaming horse to the care of Dan, he followed the two gentlemen into the house.

But medical aid availed nothing to Bertie Haviland, whose hours on earth were numbered.

The following evening, supported in Lotta's arms and surrounded by parents and sisters whose silent anguish was pitiful to behold, he took his last look of earth and sky. All the pain and suffering of the last twenty-four hours were gone, and peace had taken their place.

The mother, who loved this her only son with all of a mother's undying love, knelt by his bed, clasping his cold hand in both her own; the rugged countenance of the squire worked convulsively as he watched the face of his dying Absalom.

After he had received the Viaticum from the hands of the priest he had rallied a little, seeing which a vain hope had sprung up in the breasts of those around him; but the dying man knew better, and told them so, with a smile not of earth's on his face.

"Father, mother, do not deceive yourselves with a false hope; I shall not live. It was hard at first, but, thank God, I am now ready to die. There is something I want you all to promise me. I know you will not refuse my last wishes."

He listened with a faint smile to the low murmur of assent.

"I want you to promise me that you will leave the man

who shot me down to the justice of God—you must not speak, father; if he comes in your way, promise me that you will not deliver him up to justice and that you will let him go uninjured. Remember, 'Vengeance is mine, saith the Lord.'"

Squire Haviland struggled hard to subdue his wrath before answering this appeal; he had sworn to have the life of his son's murderer, and how was he to break this oath?

"It is a hard promise to make, harder still to break the oath which I have taken; but you shall not die, Bertie, my son, feeling that your father had refused your last wish."

"Thanks, father! God will not hold it against you, seeing that you will be more justified in the breach than in the observance of that oath. There is something else. I want you all to love Lottchen, and when a better man wins her for his wife let him be as a son to you; love him for my sake."

Mrs. Haviland sobbed audibly, and only her fear of agitating him kept her silent.

"*You are my only son*," the squire responded, with a sudden burst of emotion that would not be subdued, "but if the young lady will let me, I will love her for your sake."

Lotta looked at the speaker through a mist of tears, and silently laid her white hand in the squire's large palm. The action was more eloquent than words, and so the compact was sealed.

Bertie Haviland was laid to rest in his quiet grave, at the head of which a white stone cross stood, with the name and age of the dead man and the legend "*Requiescat in pace*" engraven on it.

No other grave was tended like this one, and here Lotta never failed to come and offer up a prayer for the soul of the man whose life had been the price of his love for her.

Squire Haviland returned to his home with his sorrowing wife and family, crushed and broken-hearted, with all pleasure in life's joys gone forever.

It was soon well known throughout the county that Luke Pivot had committed the cruel deed. Many were the vows of vengeance that were breathed against him, and had he been discovered there is no doubt he would have been made to pay the penalty of his crime without the aid of judge or jury, after the fashion of Western law.

His aunt dying shortly after Luke's disappearance, his uncle put up the farm and stock for sale and went to reside with a sister in York County.

That golden October had rolled away into the past; winter had come and gone; the early spring with its capricious winds and clouds, its mocking sunshine and bitter driving rains, had once more come to revisit the earth.

After the long repose of winter, Mr. von Rosenberg waited somewhat impatiently on the slowly advancing spring. He longed for the commencement of out-door work, and went about the farm out of temper with the weather and the compulsory delay; he liked his hands to be early at work, and had a certain pride in always having the finest crops in the county.

Within the farm-house was warmth, comfort, and neatness, so different in every detail to its appearance on the first day of Lotta's arrival—even to sullen Mrs. Morgan, whom Lotta had succeeded in subjugating by having nursed her through a fever in the fall of the previous year with a tenderness which had changed the woman's feelings from intense hatred to the most devoted affection.

Lotta was standing at one of the windows of the quaint, wide dining-room, looking out sadly on the bleak, dreary prospect beyond, the lowering clouds, the drifting rain, the leafless trees on which the brown buds were not yet unfolding their tender shoots to the biting winds.

In the distance she could see the waterfall foaming and dashing over its rocky impediments, casting out a fine, misty spray before it descended to its basin, from whence the waters flowed in a wide, troubled stream to the river. She could see the pines on the distant hills nod and sway in the blast, and she shivered as if the cold wind from without had pierced her.

She was not the Lotta of a few months ago; her form was more slender, her face had lost its softly rounded outline, and there were dark circles under her beautiful, sad eyes.

The memory of that October day was ever present with her; she blamed herself continually with having been the innocent, though actual cause of Bertie Haviland's death.

What was once a source of pleasure and excitement had ceased to interest her. She attended to her household duties as usual, but only through a sense of duty to the uncle who had given her the affection of a father and the shelter of his roof, supplying all her wants with a lavish hand. Mr. von Rosenberg saw with pain and dismay the change that had come over his niece, and was resolved as soon as the weather would permit he would take her away somewhere.

Notwithstanding this, Lotta never looked more lovely than on this bleak day in early spring, in a gown of cardinal-colored cashmere and velvet, with soft ruffles of creamy lace at wrists and throat, dead-gold earrings and necklet, and her little feet incased in dainty French shoes.

With a sigh she turned away from the sight of the nodding pines, and her glance fell on the tall figure of her uncle coming through the driving rain to the house, a large woollen muffler hiding the lower part of his face, his hat crushed down to meet it, and his trousers thrust into the tops of his boots.

He entered the house after carefully cleaning the mud from his boots and unwinding the muffler from around his neck, and Lotta hurried into the hall to meet him.

"Oh, uncle, how could you stay out in that dreadful rain? Come in beside the fire at once; and, Mrs. Morgan, please come and take my uncle's overcoat to the kitchen fire."

Mrs. Morgan hastened to obey, and Mr. von Rosenberg regarded his niece with a look of comic dismay.

"*Ach! mein bestes Lottchen*, don't come near to me and get your pretty hands wet—*Ach!* that is so good!" He shook himself free of his wet coverings, which he handed to Mrs. Morgan, and followed Lotta into the cheerful warmth of the dining-room.

"Why did you stay so long, uncle?" she asked, drawing him over to the chair she had placed for him. "There, sit down beside that warm fire, and Mrs. Morgan will bring in the tea."

He dropped into the cozy arm-chair with a sigh of intense enjoyment.

"*Ach! ja, Lottchen, mein Kind*, this is good!" he said smilingly. "I have news: *mein* Lottchen will not be so lonely soon—Butternut Farm is sold; I was talking to the lawyer from the city. It seems to me it might be your good friends who have bought it; the lawyer said the gentleman was named D'Arcy."

"Oh, uncle! not Butternut Farm!" Lotta cried in startled tones; but at that instant Mrs. Morgan entered with the tea-tray.

Chapter XXI.

"Gloom is upon thy lonely hearth,
  O silent house once filled with mirth,
  Sorrow is in the breezy sound
  Of thy tall poplars whispering round.

"The shadow of departed hours
  Hangs dim upon thine early flowers;
  Even in thy sunshine seems to brood
  Something more deep than solitude."
                      —*The Deserted House.*

BUTTERNUT FARM, lately the property of Seth Pivot, was of large extent. The house was situated in a beautiful little valley, three miles distant from Lotta's home, and although the owners of Butternut Farm had been her nearest visiting neighbors previous to the terrible tragedy of Bertie Haviland's murder, she had never since then even approached the valley.

  Mr. Pivot had been proud of his farm, of his wide, well-cleared land laid out in broad, neatly fenced fields of waving grain, of his reaping-machines, his threshing-machines—Mr. Pivot patronized every new machine capable of accelerating labor—of his cattle and horses; he was proud also of his house, which stood in the loveliest and most sheltered part of the valley; it was a long, low building, with a wide piazza in front, covered with Virginia creepers and odorous Madeira vines.

  At the back of the house rose a hill covered down to its base with a scrub of dwarf butternut-trees. In front of the house was a smooth, well-kept lawn, and at one side a grove of elms of youthful growth, reaching down to the border of a fair lake, cool, clear, fathomless, reflecting in its dimpled surface their graceful, curving branches and slender, drooping twigs. On the other side of the house was a large old-fashioned garden and orchard, the former intersected by long alleys formed by pretty rows of maple trees; at the foot of the garden a magnificent cedar tree, with great outspreading branches reaching nearly to the ground, formed a beautiful arbor furnished with rustic seats and an equally rustic table.

But now the house with its pretty lawn, its shrubberies, orchard, and garden looked neglected and forsaken. The honeysuckle, broken, storm-tossed, trailed unheeded on the ground; the lilac and snowball bushes, just putting forth fresh green leaves, shared in the general look of neglect; the alleys and lawns were strewn with dead, bleached leaves and here and there a few broken twigs and branches.

The man in charge of the farm lived a short way up the valley, close to the entrance of which, on a rising ground, near to a clump of cottonwood trees, were clustered several rude shanties formerly occupied by the farm helps, but now standing deserted and forlorn.

One bright, sunny day a change came to the lonely dwelling in the valley.

The windows were unshuttered and open, admitting into the long-disused rooms the delicious breath of May, fragrant with the fresh green odors of reawakened nature; the doors were laid back invitingly, and there floated out on the sweet air the sound of voices masculine and feminine, mingling with laughter fresh and musical and pleasant little shrieks of dismay.

In the shrubbery and garden over a dozen of men were

working with a will, planting, setting, pruning trees, fastening up broken vines and carrying away the litter. The lawn in front of the house was strewn with a quantity of rich, old-fashioned furniture upon which two pairs of brawny feminine arms were trying their powers of persuasion with the most satisfactory results.

In one of the apartments, from which the furniture had all been removed, Denise D'Arcy and Lotta von Rosenberg were standing, leaning on long-handled dusters, which together with their short-skirted gowns, wide aprons, and sleeves rolled up to their shoulders was strongly suggestive of work; in front of them stood Connor, wearing a linen duster, his shapely white hands soiled and otherwise betraying evidence of hard usage.

With his body half-way through the open window, Frank Brand, looking none the better for his contact with dust and cobwebs, was amusing himself humming a tune and watching the performance of the two women on the lawn, with an occasional word to those within the room.

"Well," Denise said, complacently looking around her, "I think, Connor, you must allow that Lotta and I have done a very commendable morning's work, and that the walls of this and the adjoining rooms look very pretty. You may laugh at our head-gear if the sight affords you amusement, but I assure you, sir, we present a very respectable, workman-like appearance."

"Why not say workwoman-like?" Connor asked teasingly.

"For the reason that I do not think the word sufficiently expressive; but I have called a rest and we are going to strike for dinner. I wish, Mr. Brand, that you would ask one of those women on the lawn to inquire if Miss D'Arcy will give us any dinner to-day, or if we are to be starved out."

Frank Brand, who had become what Eva had once laughingly named him, "*l'ami de la maison*," drew in his head and shoulders with alacrity.

"My dear child!" he answered gayly, "it would be such a pity, you know, to send either of the good women away from a recreation which they appear to enjoy so heartily; therefore with your permission I shall myself seek the culinary regions and prefer your very reasonable and seasonable request."

Frank's speech was greeted with a burst of laughter, and as he disappeared Connor called after him:

"Please remember our wants, and don't remain in the 'culinary regions' till supper-time."

A moment later Mrs. Morgan's stout figure appeared in the doorway.

"I guess, ladies and Mr. Connor, if you wants dinner you'll have to take it in the kitchen. I reckon you've had a purty long spell working and wouldn't be the worse for something to eat."

"Thanks, Mrs. Morgan," Connor answered politely; and Mrs. Morgan, who was already charmed by Connor's manner, vanished with a satisfied smile.

"Allow me the pleasure, ladies?" Connor said, with mock ceremony, bowing profoundly as he offered an arm to each of the two girls.

"Thanks," Lotta responded, a little maliciously, "we must decline to accept such attentions from a gentleman in *dinner dress;* we are only helps, you know, going to the kitchen for our dinner."

The kitchen had been partially set in order, and presented a more habitable appearance than any other part of the house, and a happy party were soon gathered round the dinner-table.

"I think you have been very fortunate in securing this

place, Connor," Mr. Brand remarked, in the midst of a very animated flow of small-talk. "A few years of good management and it will be quite a handsome estate, something to be proud of, old man."

Connor smiled.

"I shall certainly do my utmost to improve it. I question if in all the States I could have found a spot more exactly to my mind."

"It is lovely! lovely!" Denise cried enthusiastically. "I cannot imagine how the owners of such a place have been induced to part with it."

The smile faded from Lotta's face, the color from her lips; she bent hastily over her plate, and Frank answered gayly:

"My dear child, have you yet to learn that there are causes for every effect in this world if we could but discover them? But I think in this case the cause is very apparent: the poor old man was lonely after the death of his wife."

"Thanks, Mr. Brand, for your very lucid explanation; and please excuse my density, which yet I need scarcely regret, since it has served to afford you an opportunity of displaying to your admiring listeners your great powers of observation," Denise retorted mischievously.

Lotta's agitation had passed unnoticed by all save Connor and Frank.

Denise and Lotta were alone together under the great cedar tree in the garden. The former was saying:

"I could never tell in words all that I suffered after Connor went away; although he said he was going to Teddy, I felt sure he would never return to us. I do not think my fears were in the least lessened when papa told Aunt Kate that he had arranged everything and was going in the next steamer to bring Teddy home. I dreaded with a great dread all that might ensue when papa and Connor should meet. I did not fear for Teddy, he is so gentle, you know, poor boy! I saw that auntie shared all my fears, but she was silent on the subject, so I refrained from speaking of my misery. Mr. Brand was so kind; he called to see us every day and looked after papa's affairs. Eva was so busy with tradespeople and milliners she did not seem to have a thought for anything but her *trousseau*. I don't know what we should have done, auntie and I, all through that time, if Mr. Brand had not been so attentive; he did everything he could to make the time pass pleasantly. But oh, Lotta! when they, papa and the boys, returned together, and I saw them drive up to the house, and papa alighting, looking so happy, and Connor helping Teddy out of the carriage, I laughed and cried for very joy. I don't know how it had been effected; but papa and Connor were quite reconciled. Connor went away somewhere a few days before the weddings came off—for Eva was married on the same day as papa, you know—and did not return until all was over and they had gone away. Papa and Mrs. D'Arcy were only a month absent on account of Teddy's health. Eva and Mr. Felix Rooney are going to travel over Europe before they return, and will be absent for twelve months. While papa and Mrs. D'Arcy were absent Connor managed everything as formerly; but it was understood that he would not remain in New York. He refused to use the money that papa had secured to him, but he consented to accept the loan of a certain sum, which, together with what he had saved from his salary, would be sufficient to complete the purchase-money of this place. Teddy remains with papa and Mrs. D'Arcy; she appears to like him very much. Auntie and I chose to come here and help Connor. We wanted to see you so much, dear; it was just like old times, coming to reside so near to you."

"You have not told me about Mrs. D'Arcy yet. Is she pretty, Denise?"

"She is more than pretty, she is beautiful, with a proud, lazy kind of beauty; not at all like dear mamma, but she can be very charming. I know I should have liked her very much if she had not taken mamma's place."

"Yes, I understand; and Eva, is she very happy? Tell me all about her husband."

"I would much rather not speak of him, Lotta; but since you have asked me I will tell you. Eva's marriage has been a great disappointment to papa and the rest of us; Connor could not be even civil to him. Mr. Felix Rooney's possessions can be enumerated thus: great wealth, unbounded self-esteem, and a ridiculous affectation of elegant gentility. He is short and slender, and though not coarse-looking, nature has marked him with the sign-manual of his birthright, for in every feature she has traced with indelible obstinacy *parvenu*, and, Lotta dear, if you could but see his father! *Canaille* is written in capital letters all over his person, from the crown of his horrid-looking head down to his great, broad, misshapen feet! I could never understand what could have influenced Eva in making such a choice; you remember how beautiful she was, despite her poor dress, when we lived in Charlotte Street; but the Eva of those days would give you but a very faint, very imperfect notion of the Eva of to-day. She is like some rare exotic in beauty and delicacy of coloring."

The season was a busy one, full of activity and life. The hands on Fall Farm had scarcely breathing-time, but Mr. von Rosenberg had insisted upon the D'Arcys and their guest, Mr. Brand, staying at his house until their own was set in order, so they drove to the valley every morning, returning in the evening to Fall Farm.

These were happy days for every one. Lotta was beginning to look more like her former self, although she avoided visiting Butternut Farm whenever she could find an excuse for so doing.

But a day came when everything was declared to be satisfactorily completed, and Frank Brand could no longer delay his return to the city and business; then life fell back into its usual routine for Lotta, except that Kate and Denise were her frequent visitors, but during the busy weeks that followed her meetings with Connor were not so frequent.

Chapter XXII.

"When I stood beneath the fresh green tree,
   And saw around me the wide fields revive
With fruits and fertile promise; and the spring
   Come forth, her work of gladness to contrive,
With all her reckless birds upon the wing,
I turned from all she brought, to all she could not bring."
                        —CHILDE HAROLD.

"Despair is never quite despair;
   Nor life nor death the future closes;
And round the shadowy brow of care
   Wild hope and fancy twine their roses."
                        —MRS. HEMANS.

FATHER BURKE'S chapel was a rudely constructed edifice, situated outside of the village boundaries, on a rising ground, and was shaded in front by two magnificent elm trees, beyond which a tolerably large space of ground was cleared and neatly fenced in; it was the prettiest and best-cared-for spot in the vicinity.

Here, after Holy Mass on Sundays, the little congregation gathered in clusters to discuss the events of the past week or news from home.

It was Sunday morning. The sky was cloudless and blue as a sapphire; the sun was pouring down his rays on the parched earth with pitiless splendor; the leaves upon the trees hung limp and drooping; the grass looked dry and shrivelled; the birds sat listless and silent on the trees.

Within the little chapel the heat was overpowering, and

at the conclusion of Mass there was a simultaneous rush made for the cool shade of the great elms without. Rough men regarded Connor with admiring envy, he looked so cool and elegant in his white summer suit, and Mr. von Rosenberg told him so as he greeted him cordially.

"Did you drive over? Lottchen talks of walking home, but it is a long walk by the road under this sun. My Lottchen has never gone by the wood-road since poor Bertie Haviland was murdered just below the hill yonder. *Ach!* it was sad—it went near to killing my Lottchen."

This was the first that Connor had heard of the tragedy which was known far and wide throughout the country. "This, then, was the meaning of the change in her," he thought, a sharp pang piercing his heart.

The smile faded from his face, a gray pallor replacing it, and Mr. von Rosenberg wondered at the sudden change.

He looked like one who had received a terrible shock.

"I did not know there had been a murder," Connor said, in a strangely altered voice.

Mr. von Rosenberg's reply was cut short by the approach of Father Burke, who greeted them heartily notwithstanding the heat.

Kate and Denise had seized upon Lotta and were urging her to accompany them back to Butternut Farm and to coax her uncle to join them.

"I have a fancy for being at home to-day," Lotta said, shrinking as usual from going to the valley, "so come with me to-day and we will go with you next time."

"It is too hot for further argument, so we will let Connor decide," Kate answered.

"I have such good news, Lotta, you really don't deserve that I should tell you, since you prefer turning your back upon paradise, *i.e.*, Butternut Farm," Denise said, her eyes sparkling with delight, "but I will be more merciful than you deserve. Connor has had a letter from papa. He thinks that Teddy, who is anxious to see us all, would be better at the farm during the heated season, and as Mrs. D'Arcy objects to Teddy travelling alone until he is stronger, they are all coming; so you will soon see your old admirer, Teddy, and Mrs. D'Arcy."

"Dear Teddy!" Lotta exclaimed, a glow of pleasure lighting up her beautiful face, "it will be such happiness to see him again."

"Teddy is a lucky boy! for once I envy him," interjected Connor.

Lotta turned with a start and a vivid blush and smilingly extended her hand.

"Good-morning! Don't indulge in envy and all uncharitableness. Do you find the heat very intolerable? I dread leaving the shade of these drooping branches and committing myself to the mercy of that piercing sun. Are you not well?"

He forced a laugh.

"I am very well, thanks. Father Burke has just been asking me the same question. I suppose I must be of the salamander species, since I do not find the heat affect me very unpleasantly."

"Still, I should not advise you to trust too much to such a questionable supposition, Mr. D'Arcy. It is a rather dangerous experiment to stand so long with your head uncovered, even though you are partly in the shade; a sunstroke is not a very pleasant thing to endure, and your salamandrine proclivities may not preserve you against one," Father Burke remarked amusedly, as he came slowly up to them by the side of Mr. von Rosenberg.

"Do put on your hat, Connor, dear!" Kate and Denise cried eagerly, but Connor only smiled indifferently, stepped out of the sunshine under the shade of the elm tree, and stood beside them.

"Lotta wants us to go home with her, Connor; I said that you should decide."

"Then I decidedly favor Miss von Rosenberg's wishes, whatever they may be," Connor answered at once.

"Thanks. Shall we walk to the end of the village, or would you prefer driving all the way?" Lotta asked brightly.

"I shall be guided by your decision; I have no choice in the matter."

"Let us walk a little way," Denise said eagerly, and so it was decided.

Lotta was hurt and puzzled by the constraint in Connor's tone, and seeing with surprise that he persistently avoided looking at her, she went hastily to where her uncle stood.

"We are all going home now, uncle," she said. "Are you ready?"

"*Ach! ja, mein Herz*, I am ready," he answered, gently patting the hand she had laid on his arm.

Then he told Dan to drive to the outskirts of the village and await their coming.

A general hand-shaking followed, a confused interchange of ideas on the heat, parting adieux with Father Burke, and they were off.

They passed through the village, where a number of brown-faced, rough-looking men were scattered about on the burnt-up semblance of grass that grew, or rather wilted, under the scorching sun.

Little children were playing on the dusty road in front of some houses, for the most part ragged, dirty, unkempt; but there were sturdy little fellows and pretty, healthy-looking little baby-girls among them.

As they passed along the village street they were followed by glances of admiration from the men—the women and children rushing to their doors to get a better view of the ladies and "that han'some young gent from Butternut Farm."

Yet "that han'some young gent" did not look strikingly happy as he walked between Lotta and Denise, whose appearance created feelings of admiration and envy in more than one girlish breast as they looked with jealous eyes after the graceful figures, losing sight of the simplicity of the apparel in the elegance of the wearers.

"Jem-mi-mo! thar's style for you; mebbe some o' you gals could try it on. I'll bet you five dollars agin' Mellisa's new breastpin that all you wimming would give yer ears to make sich a figur' as any o' them three gals. Whew! wouldn't ye, though; but that would be agin' natur'," cried one of the loungers on the grass to the occupants of the doorways as the observed of all eyes passed out of sight.

"You shut up, Zeke Carter! ye're jist as mad as a hornet that yer can't spank out as that han'some young feller down in Butternut Farm can. Sakes alive! if you was jist as rich and han'some, 'stead of bein' as poor as Job's turkey, you'd be lookin' for the President's darter. But you jist let my Mellisa alone; I guess you'd a sight better. She wouldn't throw away her chances on the likes of you, you bet."

"Wa-al, Mrs. Purson, you is sharp, to be sure! you *raly* hit it right smart that time. I reckon if I war sich a swell as that thar young Butternut feller, I'd no more look at your Mellisa nor he do. I'd jist be tryin' his game, which be makin' love to that purty gal of old von Rosenberg's. Thar ain't her equal in the States, no matter how you fix it. Them Butternut gals are purty, you bet;

but they wouldn't be no more'n the light of a dozen tallow dips to a New York 'lumination to her. I'd have that gal afore all the gals in the States."

"And git yerself shot as young Squire Haviland done, and sarve you right for bein' sich a consarn'd fool!" And with this parting shot Mrs. Purson retreated into her house, banging her door violently behind her.

"I say, Mrs. Purson, you'll want the hinges o' yer tongue 'iled after that," her tormentor called loudly after her amid a chorus of laughter and uproarious applause.

All unconscious of the wordy warfare which their appearance had evoked in the village, Lotta and her friends went serenely on their way.

At the outskirts of the village were two roads; the broader, leading out to well-cultivated land, lay before them under the blazing sun, straight, white, for the most part unsheltered, rich sections of grain parched and drooping on either side. The other was a well-beaten track, bordered by a low scrub of box-elder and sugar-maple, which gradually increased in size and terminated in a large wood, behind which rose high hills crowned with pines. Here they found Dan waiting their coming, with the wagonette and the horses drawn into the shelter of the sugar-maples.

Mr. von Rosenberg was enjoying his after-dinner *siesta* —he had had a musical treat—had listened entranced while Connor and Lotta sang the duet, "O lovely Peace," from Handel's "Judas Maccabæus," and tears stood in his eyes as he listened to Gounod's "Ave Maria."

Then Denise played the solo from Rossini's "Stabat Mater," with a soft, exquisite touch, until his eyelids drooped, then closed over his heavy eyes, and his head came in contact with the back of his chair—seeing which Lotta lightly dropped her cobweb handkerchief over his face, lest the flies that would float dreamily in through the open doors and windows might disturb his repose.

Connor strolled out to the shrubbery to think over the bitterness that had found its way into his heart, and Kate, taking Lotta's arm, drew her out upon the piazza, leaving Denise to the undisturbed enjoyment of her music.

She sang softly and played dreamy accompaniments in a minor key, although Lotta had assured her that the music of an orchestra would fail to disturb her uncle's slumbers.

So Denise played on, until all the brightness faded from her face and her eyes were filled to overflowing with tears, and the pair upon the piazza talked in low, subdued tones, and Connor flung away the end of his second cigar and continued to pace the shrubbery, brooding deeply.

"It is more pleasant now. I think it will be refreshingly cool for our return home!"

Kate and Lotta looked up, startled. Connor was standing tall and stately before them.

"Really, Connor, you here! I thought you were smoking in the shrubbery," Kate remarked, with a smile.

"I have been in the shrubbery just fifty-seven minutes, my watch says; but if you desire to banish me for a longer period of time, I shall——"

"Fifty-seven minutes! You astonish me, Connor! I did not think you had been gone fifteen minutes," Kate said quickly, seeing a look of pain in her nephew's eyes. "You can have my seat, Connor, while I go and look if Denise has followed Mr. von Rosenberg's example and fallen asleep under the combined influence of heat and music."

But Connor did not avail himself of the invitation, but leaned on the back of the chair which his aunt had just vacated.

"I hope you enjoyed your fifty-seven minutes in the shrubbery, Mr. D'Arcy?" Lotta asked, with a smile.

"I do not think that misery is at any time enjoyable, Miss von Rosenberg, even in a shrubbery with the sun laughing down upon one through the green leaves."

"Misery?" in a tone of incredulous surprise, the beautiful eyes opening wide as she looked at him.

He nodded slowly, gazing sadly down into her upturned face.

"Yes, fifty-seven minutes of bitter misery, trying to reconcile myself to the inevitable, trying to look my shattered hopes of happiness bravely in the face, trying to gather up my broken idols and bury them out of sight. It is not a very easy achievement, Miss von Rosenberg, when a man has cherished these hopes for years, made them the motive power of all his actions, to rise unhurt and serene out of their ruins."

"I—I do not understand, Mr. D'Arcy. I am truly grieved, believe me, if you have met with any disappointment, if anything has occurred to make you miserable," she said, with earnest sympathy.

"It used to be Connor in the old days, Lotta," he said reproachfully. "Do you know what it was to me then to hear my name from your lips? It was life, hope, strength. When I saw you no more, all hope, all brightness vanished from my life. I resolved to see you again no matter what obstacles I should have to overcome. The hope of seeing you made me relinquish every other hope. The sight of your face reconciled me to a mode of life utterly uncongenial to me. I went heart and soul into the work before me; only this morning I looked with pleasure on the house which I had made my home, on its fair surroundings, on my fast-ripening grain, on my fields of rich pasture land and handsome cattle, because I had hoped that one day you might care enough for me to come and share them with me. Now I know that hope was as delusive as a mirage of the desert. A few short hours ago my heart was filled with pleasant anticipations of all the future might hold for me; now it holds only the ashes of hope, for I know that you have never loved me."

She rose to her feet, the color fluctuating painfully on her cream-white face.

"How do you know, Connor, that I have never cared for you? I did care for you; I do care for you now more than I have ever cared for any created being; but, oh, Connor! I can never share your home, for the grave of Bertie Haviland lies between us!"

Chapter XXIII.

"Love is no wandering vapor,
  That lures astray with treacherous spark;
Love is no transient taper
  That lives an hour and leaves us dark."
                      —PRINGLE.

"A certain miracle of symmetry,
  A miniature of loveliness, all grace,
  Summed up and closed in little!"
                      —TENNYSON.

"ME-ES DENISE, Me-e-es De-ni-ise!"

"What is the matter, Sara?" a sweet voice cried in answer, and a large sun-hat protruded from among the leafy branches of a great peach-tree.

"Dey's all here, Mees Denise, please, Mistah D'Arcy, an' de madam, an' Mistah Teddy, an'——"

A scream of delight came from the tree, a rustling of branches, a shower of leaves and rich, luscious peaches fell to the ground; and a white figure sprang out and down into the arms of a gentleman.

"O Teddy darling! darling Teddy!"

The sky was blue, a deep sapphire blue, with never a cloud to soften or subdue its intensity. The sun was sinking below the horizon like a huge ball of fire; the locust piped shrilly, knowing with insect instinct that there was likely to be a continuation of dry weather. In the rich pasture land, which, being situated near the bend of a small river, was well irrigated, the cattle lay panting and exhausted under the trees, whose thick, wide-spreading branches afforded a grateful shade for the tired animals.

Not a breath of air stirred the drooping leaves on the trees, but it was pleasant in the orchard at Butternut Farm, where Sara stood, eyes and teeth shining with delight, as she saw her young mistress throw her arms around the neck of the gentleman who had caught her just in time to save her from a severe fall.

"De lor', how she will take on!" Sara ejaculated, thrusting her apron into her mouth to stifle an explosive burst of laughter as she ran out of the orchard.

But Denise saw her mistake the instant she raised her eyes to the face bending over her.

"Mr. Clifford!" she gasped, shrinking away, her sweet face crimson with pain and confusion as he placed her safely on *terra firma* and released her; then raising his hat he stood with uncovered head bowing before her.

She did not raise her eyes and kept her blushing face averted.

"You are not hurt, I hope?" he asked anxiously.

She tried to look at him—tried to laugh at her mistake, but in the effort burst into tears.

"Denise! Good heavens, child! if I had thought my presence would have distressed you like this I should have remained away forever. I have followed you here, *carissima*, in the hope that you may have reconsidered your answer to me, for I love you so utterly that I can find no happiness apart from you, and I refuse to accept your answer as final."

He had taken her hand in his while speaking, but she snatched it hastily away.

"You are cruel!" she cried out passionately, "to follow me like this, and I shall *not* listen to you."

She darted past him out of the orchard through a little gate into the garden, along a shady alley leading to the house, never once pausing for breath until, in turning a corner, she blindly dashed up against some one coming from the house—a man, she knew, for his arms closed round her hastily. She struggled violently to free herself.

"Oh, don't!" she cried shrilly. "How dare you?"

"Why, Denise, what is wrong, dear?"

She uttered a little hysterical scream, and in a paroxysm of tears and laughter her head sank on Teddy's shoulder.

Teddy's restoration to health had not been so rapid as his favorable surroundings might have warranted; the want and privation which he had endured had told severely on a constitution naturally delicate; but notwithstanding the fatigues of his recent journey he was all excitement to see Lotta, and at an early hour the following morning, accompanied by Denise, he rode over to Fall Farm.

The following days were spent by the new arrivals in going over the farm suggesting improvements, examining every spot of interest in the neighborhood, scrambling up the hills, rambling through the woods, rowing on the river, and in the cool of the evening lounging on the broad, vine-wreathed piazza.

Mr. Clifford had avoided Denise ever since that little scene in the orchard, in his cold, proud fashion emulating her evident desire to shun him; and when Mrs. D'Arcy proposed a pic-nic and expressed a wish that Miss von Rosenberg should make one of the party, Denise gladly accompanied Teddy to Fall Farm.

"Oh, Teddy, see, there is Lotta!" Denise cried, suddenly reining in her horse.

Teddy looked excitedly in the direction pointed out.

It was Lotta sure enough, Lotta on horseback riding away from them in an opposite direction, closely followed by Dan; they were keeping in the shade of the trees growing close to the river's bank.

Teddy shouted shrilly, using his hand for a speaking-trumpet, and waving his straw hat, but in vain; there was only a flash of color as she came for an instant into the sunlight before she disappeared from sight.

"What shall we do now?" Teddy asked with marked disappointment and regret. "Shall we try to overtake them?"

"It would be no use, dear, she was at too great a distance when I first noticed her. I wonder where she can be going that she rides so swiftly?"

"Then, since we cannot overtake her, shall we return?"

"No, we will go on to the farm and leave Mrs. D'Arcy's note with Mrs. Morgan for Lotta."

They found Mrs. Morgan busy as usual, but she welcomed them with evident pleasure, fussing about and begging of them to partake of some refreshments after their long ride; to which Teddy, always thoughtful for the feelings of others, consented, and they sat down in the cool, shady room, with the fragrant breath of the vines coming in through the open window, to partake of Mrs. Morgan's home-made wine, rich milk, delicious peaches, honey, maple molasses, and biscuits.

She told them that Squire Haviland had had a fit, and owing to the excessive heat his wife feared he would not recover, and she had sent for Miss von Rosenberg.

She told them a great deal more also, and when her visitors rose to depart they knew quite as much as Mrs. Morgan did of the death of Bertie Haviland and its cause.

The brother and sister rode silently along for some time.

"Denise," Teddy said suddenly, "do you imagine that

that is the reason why Lotta comes so seldom to the valley? You know you told me she has not been four times to see you."

"I am afraid it is, Teddy, and—and that she has refused Connor; he has never been the same since we spent the Sunday with Lotta three weeks ago."

Nothing more was said by either until they neared home, when they caught sight of an approaching wagon.

"Oh, there's Connor going to the depot," Teddy cried. "If father will let me I'll go with him."

But after a glance at Teddy's flushed face, Mr. D'Arcy decided that he had already ridden far enough.

"You will be better in the house, Teddy," he said; "the sun is too strong for you." And with a kind word to Denise they drove away.

The wagon turned down the hillside to the highway at its foot, where, about a hundred yards away, a double-track railway crossed the road. In the distance they heard the shrill scream of a locomotive.

"That will be the train from Philadelphia now, father," Connor remarked.

"I think not," Mr. D'Arcy responded. "I fancy it is the train for, not from, Philadelphia."

They turned a curve in the wagon-road as he spoke, and were startled to perceive a man rushing madly forward toward the railway crossing.

"What is the matter? Has there been an accident?" Connor asked.

"The cars have run off the track, the locomotive is smashed, and I guess some of the passengers are scalded to death," he answered breathlessly.

"Where did it happen?"

"Down the line a bit, I reckon, mister," the man called back as he ran on.

"Had we not better tell Amos to take the wagon down the line, father?"

"I think so, Connor; it is lucky you have the wagon here," Mr. D'Arcy answered.

About half a mile down the line they came upon the scene of the catastrophe.

The man had not exaggerated.

The engine and several of the carriages were wrecked, and some of the passengers badly scalded.

The utmost confusion and disorder reigned on every side—children crying, women screaming, men rushing hither and thither shouting and swearing, while others were trying to rescue the injured from the débris, and in a ditch three men and a woman lay dead or insensible, surrounded by some of the contents of the wrecked baggage-car.

A woman on her knees was sobbing over a baby-boy of some two years. The little face looked so still, so waxen; the soft baby hair clung damp and disordered to the white brow; his garments, which were of the richest material, were covered with dust and drenched with water.

"I hope your baby is not dead, madam. Let me take him from you while I assist you to rise," Connor said very gently.

The woman raised her tear-stained face, struck by the rich, musical voice and tone of genuine sympathy.

"Oh, sir, he is dead!" she cried piteously, "my beautiful darling! But I am only his nurse, sir. I was walking about with him when it happened, and he was laughing and talking so prettily, and now—now he is dead! What will the earl—what will the countess say? And Sir Arthur —it will break Sir Arthur's heart!"

"Where are your master and mistress?" Connor asked

as he assisted the woman to rise and looked down into the sweet baby face, touching the little hands tenderly, seeking for some sign of life.

"They were in the train. Oh, what shall I do?" with a sudden burst of newly awakened terror; "perhaps they are dead also!"

Connor looked around him anxiously.

"Can you sit on this tree-trunk while I go in search of them? Let me help you. You are not fit to stand."

She thanked him gratefully.

"Now," he said cheerfully, when he had assisted her to a seat on the stump of the tree, "I will find out what has become of your master and mistress. Take courage—the child may be only stunned after all!"

A few yards down the track two men were bending over a woman's motionless form, and Connor paused beside them.

"Is she dead?" he inquired.

"Wall, I guess, mister, she looks more dead'n alive; don't you think so?"

Connor did think so; and he bent and gently wiped the dust from the white face.

A low ejaculation of intense surprise escaped him.

"What is it, mister? Is the lady a friend of yours?" one of the men asked, a little curiously.

"The lady is a stranger to me, my man; but see, she is reviving."

A pair of dark eyes opened wide and a faint sigh escaped the parted lips, to which the color was slowly returning, and a clear, high-bred voice asked sharply:

"What is it? Where am I? What has happened?"

"There has been an accident, madam, but you are quite safe," Connor answered reassuringly.

The white lids closed over the dark eyes.

"Jest you swaller a leetle sup o' this water, marm," one of the men said with rude kindness, holding a gourd-shell filled with deliciously cold spring-water to her lips; "it'll bring you about right smart."

With a sudden energy she thrust the gourd away, flashing upon the man a glance of cold surprise and great displeasure.

"Where is my woman? Where is Lord Riversmede?" she inquired haughtily.

"You forget, madam, that we are all strangers to you and cannot possibly answer your questions, and that those good men were simply performing an act of humanity in striving to restore you to consciousness," Connor said, indignant at her rejection of the man's well-meant attentions.

"As you've gotten over that faintin'-spell, marm," one of the men said, "we'll jest leave you to this gentleman and give help whar it's more needed."

The lady looked at Connor a little less haughtily, but with evident surprise.

"I remember all now," she said. "Will you assist me to rise? Thanks! Lend me your arm, please."

She was trembling violently, and Connor raised the gourd of water from the ground and held it toward her.

"You will find this water very refreshing," he said; "let me beg you will taste it."

She assented with a languid inclination of the head, and he held it to her lips while she swallowed a little of the water, which appeared to revive her.

"There is my husband, Lord Riversmede," she said hastily. "Will you tell him to come to me, please?"

He left her resting on a pile of luggage which had been collected from amid the general ruin, and presently returned with a rather handsome, rather *blasé*-looking man of fashion, an unmistakable English aristocrat. He had evidently been hurt, for he walked with a slight limp and held on by Connor's arm, and altogether looked very much the worse for his enforced visit to the ditch.

"Well, Edith, my dear, all right, eh? Rather seedy-looking, though; a little smashed up myself, don't you know. But I say, Sir Arthur's badly hurt—got a leg broken or something of that sort; deuced pity—can't get a conveyance of any kind to have him taken to the village. Shocking affair, isn't it?"

"But, Percy, who is taking care of grandpapa?"

"I really don't know; you sent for me, you know, my dear. Ah, by Jove! where is the boy and his nurse?"

"Have you not seen Wilson all this time, my lord? For Heaven's sake, go and look for my child!"

"The child is with his nurse farther up the line," Connor interposed. "I will take you to them, my lord."

"Thanks; you are very good," he responded.

Then turning to his wife:

"You'll be quite safe here, Edith, my dear, till I come back. Drew is looking after the traps. It'll be all right, you know."

"Yes," she assented indifferently.

"My wagon is here, my lord," Connor said as they moved away, "and if your friend has received any injuries I shall have much pleasure in placing it at your service. The village is two miles distant; my farm is just half a mile from the depot; it would be the shortest distance to have your friend conveyed, and Dr. Edwards can attend him there."

"Ah, thanks; you are really very good, Mr.—a—a——"

"Connor D'Arcy."

"Then, Mr. Connor D'Arcy, I accept your kind offer for Sir Arthur; but what is Lady Riversmede to do, my good sir? She could not walk two miles."

"If she can sit in the wagon beside Sir Arthur, I have no doubt we can find a room for her ladyship at Butternut Farm."

His lordship made a grimace of comic horror.

"The Countess of Riversmede go in a wagon to a Western farmhouse—Jove!" he thought.

But he answered good-naturedly: "Thanks; you're awfully kind, but don't you think it will be a great bother for you?"

"Not at all. I see my father down there. I have no doubt he will ride at once to the farm and tell the ladies that we are going to bring home company."

"Awfully good of you—we must try to manage it some way. In a fix like this her ladyship must not be too fastidious."

Connor bowed and turned his head aside to hide a smile as he wondered what her *fastidious* ladyship would think of the house in the valley and its inmates. Certainly her mode of conveyance—a heavy country wagon—would not be very suitable for a lady.

"Oh, my lord, the little Lord Arthur isn't dead!" the nurse cried hysterically as they approached her. "He opened his dear little eyes and smiled up at me, my lord, but he looks dazed like."

His lordship looked down into the face of his son and heir a little uneasily.

"He looks very pale, doesn't he, Wilson?" he asked apprehensively. "But I suppose it's all right—don't understand much about children, you see. This—this gentleman," with a swift glance over Connor's person, "has kindly offered his conveyance to take us all to his house. You had better take the boy to the countess—she's most awfully uneasy about him; and look here, Wilson, tell her ladyship we are going to see about Sir Arthur, and—and I'll be with her directly."

Fortunately Sir Arthur had not broken his leg, but his knee was severely injured and he had received a few bruises.

To her husband's intense annoyance, Lady Riversmede insisted on keeping her room until Sir Arthur should be sufficiently recovered to permit them continuing their interrupted railway journey to Philadelphia.

Her ladyship's nervous system had received a shock, but otherwise she was uninjured.

"My dear Edith," her husband expostulated one morning, "wouldn't it look better if you didn't keep your room quite so much? You have been here a week and you are better now, you know, and the doctor says the little fellow's getting quite strong and Sir Arthur is getting on splendid. They—they have all been—er—er—very kind, you know. It looks so—so—er—overpowering, always keeping your room like this; it's deuced ugly, you see, receiving favors and—er—er—snubbing your entertainers; 'pon my soul I hate to see you do it, Edith."

Her ladyship arched her delicate eyebrows in cold surprise. "Really, Lord Riversmede, I am at a loss to understand what you expect me to do. I shall certainly remunerate these people for all the trouble they will be put to through me. I am quite sure that grandpapa will not leave without paying them handsomely. What more can they require from us? *You* nor *they* cannot possibly expect that *I* will mingle in their amusements or eat at their table."

"Now, Edith, don't be absurd! I assure you they are not the sort of people you seem to imagine. I will certainly be surprised if they accept any remuneration from the Countess of Riversmede or Sir Arthur Cardlyon. They are not farmers. Mr. D'Arcy and his wife are here on a visit to his son, who owns this place—that splendid young fellow who brought us here, you know, and—and have you seen the ladies yet, Edith?"

"Ladies? No, decidedly!" a cold smile curving her lips; "nor do I imagine that a Western farm, however good the soil, could produce such a *rara avis*. I certainly saw a young woman on my first arrival, in a white alpaca gown with black lace and blue velvet trimmings, who asked me if I should like some refreshments brought to me here, or if I should prefer joining the family when I had taken a bath. I remember thinking that her dress looked neat and cool, but I did not particularly notice the wearer."

"Ah, that is Miss D'Arcy, my lady, a pretty, graceful gentlewoman."

"Don't 'my lady' me, for Heaven's sake, my lord! You remind me of Wilson or some of the menials at home."

"I beg your pardon, Edith, but I am convinced that if you had taken a proper look at Miss D'Arcy you would have seen at once that she is all I say; and, by George! there are three of the prettiest women in this house that I have seen since coming to the States, and positively quite as well bred as—as—er—as yourself, Edith, my dear."

She regarded him with haughty surprise and scorn.

"I bow to your verdict, my lord," she retorted with fine irony. "I believe it is generally conceded that Lord Riversmede is an indubitable authority in such matters."

Yet, notwithstanding her scorn, Lady Riversmede was piqued into seeing and judging for herself, and she sent a gracefully worded message to Miss D'Arcy to the effect that as Lady Riversmede felt quite recovered she would be very happy to join the family at dinner, and hoped her presence would be no inconvenience.

In a few minutes Wilson returned with the answer:

"Miss D'Arcy would be very happy. Lady Riversmede's presence could only be a pleasure."

Chapter XXIV.

> "To have met the joys of thy speaking face,
> To have felt the spell of thy breezy grace,
> To have lingered before thee, and turned, and borne
> One vision away of the cloudless morn."
> —MRS. HEMANS.

> "Knowledge comes, but wisdom lingers, and he bears a laden breast,
> Full of sad experience moving toward the stillness of his rest."

LORD RIVERSMEDE, Mr. D'Arcy, and Connor were enjoying a lounge and a chat on the piazza, while up from the maple alley came the whiff of a genuine Havana, telling that Marmaduke Clifford was having a smoke *à la solitaire*.

A soft breeze was stirring the vines and wafting rich odors past the three loungers, in through the open windows to the room beyond, where three ladies and a noble, patrician-looking old gentleman were seated.

Sir Arthur Cardlyon was still a strikingly handsome man, very suave, very courteous, very haughty; at present he was pale and languid, from recent pain and confinement. He reclined in a low cane chair, a soft cushion supporting his head; his injured limb, carefully swathed, rested on a pile of cushions.

At a little distance sat the countess in a soft greenish-blue gown that fitted to a fault; rich old lace at her throat and wrists, yellow gleams from her broad gold bracelets, and the flash of a solitaire diamond on one long, slender white hand, in which she held a fan of peacock feathers. Near one of the open windows Mrs. D'Arcy, in a creamy-white gown, gold bangles on her round white wrists, deep purple flowers, heavy with a subtle perfume, fastened in the lace at her throat, and a book lying open on her lap, was idly fanning herself as she talked in her soft, languid Southern tones to Sir Arthur.

The third lady was Kate D'Arcy, also in white, a soft satin-like India muslin, her white fingers moving swiftly on a piece of exquisite lace-work.

They made a pretty picture, the grand old man with his silvery hair and fine, high-bred face, and those three fair women with the sun falling in a long bar of gold on the polished floor, and the faintly stirring vines without casting pretty, quaint shadows on its polished surface, shadows that

"Come tremulous with emerald-tinted gleams."

In another fortnight at farthest the harvest would be ready for the whirring, clattering reaping-machines, and there would scarcely be breathing-time for any of the workers and helps on the farm.

But Connor had lost all pleasure in the wide-spreading fields of grain and rich pasture-land.

What were crops and pastures to him as he gazed with gloomy eyes out over the valley?

He had gradually withdrawn, leaving his father and Lord Riversmede to continue their conversation alone, and was leaning over the balustrade with a sad, far-away look in his gray eyes, into which a new light suddenly flashed, a dusky flush overspreading his face.

Three horses and three riders were sweeping down the valley at a rapid rate.

No need to tell him the names of those riders. Denise

and Teddy had been spending the last week with Lotta, and all three were now riding toward the house.

He waved his straw hat to them, and with that happy light in his eyes and a faint flush lingering on his face went to meet them.

"This is indeed a pleasure," he said as he assisted the girls to alight and bestowed a fervent hand-shake on Teddy, who declared he had been having a splendid time, a statement which his improved looks fully indorsed.

Both girls were heated with their rapid ride, and pulled off their hats to fan themselves with as they ran past Connor into the house, and he, in the joy of seeing Lotta there, forgot to tell them that Sir Arthur Cardlyon and Lady Riversmede were in the drawing-room.

Denise hurried Lotta along the wide, airy passage, threw open a door, and before they became aware of the presence of strangers, both girls were standing in the midst of the occupants of the quaint, wide, low-ceiled drawing-room.

"We have come for just one hour, Aunt Kate," Denise cried gayly.

"Great heavens!"

As that exclamation escaped the baronet's white lips he suddenly sprang erect, his slender white hands grasping the arms of his chair, his dark eyes, startled, intent, fixed on Lotta.

Taken utterly by surprise, the two girls paused for an instant arm in arm, the sun glancing lovingly around them, their trailing skirts gathered up and held with negligent grace, their hats swinging carelessly by their sides, their shining hair tossed and tumbled, clinging in pretty, tangled masses to their white foreheads, a breezy negligence at once fresh and charming pervading their whole appearance.

The silence scarcely lasted an instant; but in that one instant the baronet had recovered his graceful self-possession, and sinking back in his chair with a deprecatory smile said languidly:

"I trust, ladies, that I have not startled you, or rather let me apologize for the suddenness of the exclamation wrung from me by pain. I did not imagine"—very sadly —"that physical pain had so weakened me."

"It is I, sir," Lotta answered, in her sweet, clear tones, "who should apologize for so unceremoniously entering the presence of an invalid; but my excuse, which I hope you will kindly accept, is that neither this young lady nor myself were aware that Mr. Connor D'Arcy's guests were sufficiently recovered to leave their rooms."

The baronet's eyes glowed, his clear-cut lips twitched slightly as he listened. There was a tone, an echo of the past, in that sweet voice which took him back to the years that were gone, when a lovely girl with the face and form of this girl standing before him would come and lay her soft cheek against his, clasp her slender hands around his arm, and with pretty, childish audacity beg for some trifling, girlish favor.

That girl had been his fairest, best-beloved daughter, on whose beauty he had built such brilliant hopes, and whom he had cast out from his heart and home forever when she by her one act of disobedience had doomed those hopes to disappointment.

The momentary yearning, the momentary pain, called into life by that glimpse of the past died out as Lotta ceased speaking.

"Do not apologize, my dear young lady," he said with gentle suavity, waving his white hand deprecatingly. "You see, my little accident has made me weak and nerveless; but I would not have foregone this pleasure, this charming little surprise, even at the price of a much greater pain. May I ask the favor of an introduction to your two lovely young friends, Miss D'Arcy?" with an irresistible smile to Kate, who instantly complied.

"My niece, Denise D'Arcy, Sir Arthur Cardlyon."

That name fell on the ears of the two girls with singular distinctness; to Lotta it sounded as if a thousand elves took it up and mockingly repeated:

"Sir Arthur Cardlyon!"

She wondered at her power of self-repression as she realized that for the first time she was face to face with the man whom she knew to be her grandfather, and felt that the recognition was mutual.

She stood calmly, quietly dignified, watching his suave smile, listening to his gracefully worded apology for retaining his seat; his clear, evenly pitched tones, his prettily uttered compliment.

"Denise D'Arcy—a name just suited to one so bright and piquant as yourself, my dear young lady! Now, I beg you will not take offence at an old man for speaking his mind, for, you see, this," touching his white hair with his white fingers, "is my letter patent; and let me venture to add, the sight of your fair young face has given me much pleasure."

Denise bowed gracefully and uttered a few words expressive of her pleasure at seeing the baronet well enough to quit his room.

Then he raised his eyes to the calm, proud face of Lotta, raised them with a cold, glittering, society smile, which hid his keen, anxious scrutiny. He had no fear of this girl claiming kinship with him, even should she know herself possessed of the right to do so.

"Miss von Rosenberg, Sir Arthur Cardlyon; and let

me add, Sir Arthur, a very dear and valued friend of 'auld lang syne.'"

"Miss von—a—a——"

"Miss von Rosenberg, Sir Arthur!" Kate repeated, this time so distinctly that he could not again feign ignorance of the name.

"Thanks. Miss von Rosenberg, I am very happy to have met you."

She bowed deeply, profoundly, and turned away to be introduced to the countess, and he sank languidly back with a faint sigh of utter exhaustion.

The countess, who for an instant had been startled out of her frigid serenity, smiled graciously, slightly inclining her head in acknowledgment of the introductions. As Denise for the first time met the unsmiling eyes, looked upon the coldly statuesque face, there came back to her with overpowering distinctness the scene in the Mayfair drawing-room so long ago.

She sees the rich velvet pile of the white carpet faintly flecked with gold, and delicate border of deep purple pansies, the great mirrors in which her shabbily dressed person was reproduced with such startling frequency, the costly furniture and hangings, the gleaming statues; nothing is forgotten, even to the ruddy glow of the bright fire and the beautiful bride-elect whom she now recognized in the Countess of Riversmede.

The cold, the hunger of the dear ones at home, her own anguish and despair were all vividly before her in that swift, lightning-like flash of memory.

There was no recognition in her ladyship's glance.

Denise D'Arcy, the pretty, refined-looking seamstress, was forgotten before she had well passed from the presence of Edith Cardlyon.

But that sudden flash of memory, that picture from the

never-to-be-forgotten past, sent the eloquent blood for an instant from Denise's bright face, and brought the flash of a tear into her clear gray eyes.

"'Faultily faultless, icily regular, splendidly null,'" she murmured softly as she turned from her ladyship.

Chapter XXV.

"Thus said the Duke—thus did the Duke infer."
—*Richard III.*

"I was one
Who loved the greenwood bank and lowing herd,
The russet prize, the lowly peasants' life,
Season'd with sweet content, more than the halls
Where revellers feast to fever height. Believe me,
There ne'er was poison mixed in maple bowl."

"MAY I ask the favor of your company, Miss von Rosenberg, while I rest in this cozy nook?"

"Certainly, Sir Arthur. I shall have much pleasure."

The still clear eyes of the baronet were turned with a swift, penetrating glance on the sweet young face of the girl beside him.

"Thanks; you are very good. Few young ladies care to be troubled with the society of the old; you appear to be one of the few."

"I do not know, Sir Arthur. I have really had no experience, but I think it might prove a very pleasant trouble."

"A *very* surprising sentiment, truly, from the lips of a young lady in this progressive nineteenth century."

"I should not wish to believe so, Sir Arthur."

He smiled blandly, deprecatingly.

"Will you lend me your arm? Thanks. You see my knee is still a little uncertain. Pardon me, I would suggest that you place yourself on this side; you will not then be exposed to the vertical rays of the sun. Now I think we can rest here quite comfortably."

A week had passed since the day on which Lotta had first seen her grandfather. The D'Arcys and their guests were having a picnic, and Sir Arthur, who was able to walk with the aid of his gold-headed cane, had graciously consented to make one of the party.

They had chosen a spot of rare beauty near to a lovely lake, surrounded by great trees and fairy glades opening out from the dim woods beyond.

When they had alighted from the wagonettes, Sir Arthur seized upon Lotta in his suave, courteous way, declaring he would like a rest, and with slow deliberateness selected a pretty nook formed by the stumps of some young trees which had been sawn off some distance from the ground, and were now covered with leaves and mosses, while above all a maple tree spread out its branches.

No one appeared to notice that those two had remained behind, and for a few minutes after the baronet's last words there was perfect silence between them, with only the distant echoes of their companions' voices and the soft rustle of the trees to disturb the solitude.

Sir Arthur attentively scanned Lotta's face, while she abstractedly watched the flickering shadows on the grass from sunlight and trees; but her eyes saw only that of which her mind took no heed.

Her heart was filled with contending emotions, a great tenderness for and a fierce indignation against the man seated by her side. She knew that he had recognized in her his dead daughter's daughter, and she was indignant that he should make no sign, ask no question, speak no word of tenderness to that daughter's orphan child. Her heart went out to this grand-looking old man, her dead mother's father, longing for one kind word, for one caressing touch of the thin, white hand, which she could have bent and reverently kissed when assisting him to his present seat; but she would speak no word if he did not, and they would part as they had met—strangers.

And while Lotta with swelling heart made that resolve, the baronet watched her with an approving glance, quite as much astonished as he was pleased by her exceeding grace and perfect repose of manner.

"Where has she acquired all this good breeding?" he asked himself. "She has greater perfection of beauty than the countess, whom she undeniably resembles—more life, more expression, more vitality. This girl lives, the countess merely exists!

"If she is, as I believe, my granddaughter, her beauty is hereditary; that and her grace come from the Cardlyons. But even natural grace must be perfected by cultivation in order to attain this degree of excellence, after the fashion of all rare plants. Weeds grow up rank and luxuriant without the aid of culture, but exotics—never. This must be the result of her mother's teaching." He was still in ignorance of his daughter's death, and a sudden irresistible desire came to him to learn something of his beautiful Verra.

But a new and startling fear arrested the words ere they could pass his lips. What if this girl should happen to have sisters less graceful than herself, or brothers, great, rough-looking fellows working on a farm?

That thought made him shiver with actual horror. Lotta looked up startled.

"I hope you have not taken a chill, Sir Arthur? It is not cold here," glancing at the sweet green grass and its sunlit shadows; "at least I—I beg your pardon, perhaps you are cold; I quite forgot that you had been ill," she said earnestly.

"No, my dear," he answered, with genuine kindness in tone and look, touched by her evident solicitude. "I have not taken a chill, and really do not feel like being an invalid any longer. I have left all that behind me."

"I am very pleased to hear you say so, Sir Arthur."

He looked at her with a glance of keen scrutiny.

"You are very kind, my dear young lady, to interest yourself in an old man. I know you could find more congenial society there," waving his white hand gracefully in the direction which the others had taken, the sun sending a blinding flash from his diamond ring; "but I am very grateful, believe me."

"I do not think you have anything to be grateful for, Sir Arthur. I like being here very much. I am so accustomed to look after my uncle's comforts that this seems only a part of my duty and is very pleasant."

"Your uncle's comforts! Part of your duty! I—I do not understand. Have I then been mistaken in thinking that your parents' home is here?"

"My parents' home, Sir Arthur, is, I humbly trust, in a happier land—a land where pride, ambition, and falsehood are unknown and where truth and fidelity receive their just reward."

He shrank away as if from a blow and put up one hand with a gesture of pain to his pallid lips.

The haughty old man was strangely moved.

Could the daughter he had loved and disowned, and who still seemed to live in this girl, be dead?

When he spoke again a faint thrill of pain still lingered in the high-bred tones.

"Pardon my thoughtless question, my dear," he said gently. "I am, as you know, quite ignorant of everything concerning your family. You and I, Miss von Rosenberg, seem to be quite old friends, and I am strangely interested in you. Will you excuse an old man's curiosity if he ventures to ask you a question? You will? Thanks. You have just given me to understand that you are an orphan. Are you, then, alone in this Western settlement? But perhaps you have some brothers—some sisters?" suggestively.

"I have no brothers, no sisters. I was left alone in the world, and Heaven knows," she cried with passionate intensity, "when I looked upon the dead face of my dear father, I would have thanked God with all my soul had he also taken me!"

Sir Arthur was both touched and startled by her vehemence. He had never heard so much *real* pathos and so much passion condensed in the utterance of a single sentence.

Edith, Lady Riversmede, was incapable of such depths of affection as this girl's tones evinced, and a strange desire that some one would mourn as deeply, as truly for him when he should be called away came to him.

"And your mother, did she die first?"

"My mother died when I was a very little girl; she followed her four little baby children, and papa and I were left alone. He never recovered the blow dealt him by her death, though he struggled to live and work for my sake; but if ever man lived on carrying with him a broken heart, that man was my dear father."

The leaves rustled faintly, the lake murmured softly, the sun danced merrily on its placid bosom, but a silence had fallen on those two which endured for several seconds.

"Had your mother no relatives who for her sake would have taken you to their home?" Sir Arthur inquired in strangely altered tones. "But I think you spoke of an uncle—your maternal uncle, perhaps?"

"No. My dear mother was disowned by her family because she preferred the love of a good and honorable man to empty splendor and the false glitter of fashionable life. The uncle with whom I reside is the only brother of my father. This kind uncle stretched out a hand of welcome across the broad Atlantic to his dead brother's child, the child whom he had never seen, took her to his heart and home, supplying all her wants with a lavish hand and giving her a father's love."

Sir Arthur was silent—it was not pleasant to hear this girl speak to him in this way; perhaps there was a little regret, a little self-reproach mingled with his indignation. He leaned back and just touched his lips with his filmy white handkerchief.

A pretty yellow oriole in a chestnut-tree near by poured forth its song; there was no sound of voices or footsteps to disturb its melody.

"Are you not a *little* unjust to your mother's family, Miss von Rosenberg?"

His tones were hard, cold, clear.

"I think not, Sir Arthur."

"You can scarcely understand the distinction of classes if you do not realize that they may have had a right to consider themselves disgraced by her folly."

Lotta half sprang from her seat, but sank back instantly, her eyes flashing, a swift rush of hot, indignant blood sweeping up over her face.

"Pardon me, Sir Arthur," she said proudly, "if I refuse to have my parents discussed, even by you; but this much I will say, my father was a gentleman by birth and education; his love could disgrace no woman. He was, in the words of Pope, 'An honest man, the noblest work of God.'"

A faint flush crept into the baronet's aristocratic face; somehow he could not quite persuade himself that he reached the poet's standard.

He was startled by Lotta's audacity. No one had ever dared to speak to him like this before; but though his pride was ruffled, he admired her none the less that she honored her dead parents, and he regarded her with smiling interest.

"Your mother's name was———"

"Verra Cardlyon!"

"And you know that I am your grandfather?"

"I knew you to be my grandfather when I first looked on your face, Sir Arthur. I have a likeness of you which belonged to my dear mother. You were much younger when it was taken, but the likeness is perfect. It was a birthday gift from you to my mother."

"Will you let me see that likeness? Am I asking too much?"

"Certainly not! Your wish can easily be gratified, since I always wear the locket which contains your portrait, because it also contains those of my parents."

She unfastened a locket from a fine gold necklet she was wearing and placed it in the baronet's extended hand.

"Perhaps you will also favor me by opening it?"

His face was very pale, and there was the faintest tremor in his well-modulated tones as he made that request. She took it from him without a word.

The locket was large and of the finest gold, not ornate, but simply exquisite; on one side was a cross, formed of a double row of small seed-pearls; on the reverse side the name, Verra, was engraved in old English letters. It opened with a double spring and had been made to hold four portraits. It contained but three—Sir Arthur Cardlyon's, the Herr von Rosenberg's, and his wife Verra's.

"This, you will see, is your portrait, Sir Arthur; these are the portraits of my parents."

He had regained his composure, and looked at all three with a serenely critical glance, then closing the locket, he returned it to her.

"Thanks! Yes, I am changed since that likeness was taken; my hair was not then white, but time changes all things, even a man's hair, my dear young— Ah, by the way, you really *are* my granddaughter! I never dreamed, when I conceived a most singular—I may say an irresistible—desire to visit the States, and the Earl and Countess of Riversmede kindly agreed to accompany me, whom I should meet there. But does it not seem strange that you have not told me your name?"

"Lotta, Sir Arthur; my dear parents called me Lottchen, as does my uncle."

The baronet frowned slightly and waved his white hand. "Kindly oblige me by not indulging in retrospection, my dear; it is not good form. I think, if I have your permission to express an opinion on your name— I have? thanks; then permit me to say that I consider the name of Lotta de-ci-ded-ly undignified. May I ask is there no other name, something more suitable for a young lady, by which your friends can address you?"

"My name is Carlotta, Sir Arthur."

"Carlotta! Ah, that is better. Now, I have a proposal to make to you, Carlotta. I am perfectly satisfied with the justice of your claims, and——"

"I make no claims, Sir Arthur; I desire to make none."

He waved his hand, much as one would wave off a troublesome fly, and the diamonds flashed in Lotta's eyes.

"One moment, if you please. I say that I am satisfied of the justice of your claims without demanding further proofs; you are my granddaughter.

"I may add, this is the first I have heard of your mother's death. I am willing to overlook her disobedience, to repair the past by taking you to the home which was once hers, and giving you all that she forfeited by her—er—er—folly.

"You are fitted to shine in society—it is your proper sphere. You will outrival the Countess of Riversmede; your beauty and grace will win for you, as my granddaughter, the best match in England.

"I have a grand old home to take you to. You shall have your mother's dowry, and more; all that I can will away from the others shall be yours. In return I ask only that you forget the past, that in future you hold no communication with the man whom you now call uncle or the people whom you now call your friends."

"And you are willing to do all this for me, Sir Arthur, and *trust me*, if I forsake my uncle and friends?"

She wondered at the calmness with which she asked the question, while her heart was swelling with indignation.

"Is not that word 'forsake' just a trifle too strong? You are going away with *me*, going to the home to which you belong. I should not ask you to leave without having first repaid them for all they have done for you—certainly not. We Cardlyons never forget to repay our indebtedness."

She lifted her eyes swiftly to his face, but he read something in their clear depths that did not please him, and he raised one white finger hastily.

"Do not answer me now," he said. "Take a little time to consider my proposal. Remember all that I have offered, all that I can bestow upon you; and realize, if you can, all that such a life would mean for you. Remember also, please, that I will *not* repeat this offer."

Chapter XXVI.

> "More beautiful she looked than flowers,
>   When newly wet with heaven's dew;
> Upon her face the sacred showers
>   Of truth had fallen anew."

ALL around was silence and repose; overhead a fleecy white cloud floated dreamily across the deeply azure sky. Bees hummed their drowsy chant as they floated past in their light irregular course, a squirrel sprang into sight and darted up a tree, a rabbit scuttled out of its hole and stopped to nibble at the rank herbage, eying the pair in the little hollow suspiciously. A soft, low sigh stole through the branches, but the oriole still sang his song in the chestnut-tree.

Lotta sat with folded hands and drooped eyelids. Her grandfather had requested her to take a little time to consider his proposal, but no amount of thought could change the nature of her reply, which would be the same years hence as now.

Faith, which was dearer to her than life; friendship, the love of her dear, kind uncle—these were the precious gifts she would be called upon to relinquish if she accepted his offer.

The price demanded was too heavy to pay.

She had but to utter one little sentence, and, as if by magic, the whole current of her life would be changed. But as she sat there she gave no thought to the brilliant destiny which awaited her acceptance.

She was praying Heaven with all her heart to direct her speech that the wording of her refusal should not anger this new-found relative, whose silvery hair appealed to her love and reverence—praying that no word of hers might thrust aside forever the olive branch of peace which he now held out to her.

In a few days he would pass out of her life; in all probability they would never cross each other's paths again; but he was her dear mother's father, and her heart craved a place in his affections.

All the anger and scorn with which she had listened to his suggestion of repaying with money the love and kindness which had been lavished upon her by uncle and friends had died out, and there was only a wistful sadness in her soul.

What could this haughty aristocrat understand of her uncle, with his large, warm heart and human sympathies, or of the D'Arcys?

The baronet was watching her from under his half-closed eyelids, but he was not quite prepared for her sudden upward glance. He saw she was about to speak, and buckled on his armor of well-bred indifference to meet her words.

"Do not think me ungrateful, Sir Arthur," she began, her sweet voice tremulous with emotion, "if I say that I cannot accept your offer. I appreciate your goodness and fully realize all that such a life would mean for me. But I was alone in the world when my uncle gave me that which money cannot repay—a home and a father's love. Like myself, he too was alone, having lost wife and children.

"I cannot repay his love and trust with ingratitude. I cannot forsake him for wealth or position. I have chosen my path, and, Heaven helping me, I shall follow it faithfully to the end. I thank you most sincerely, Sir Arthur. How grateful I am you will never know, although I cannot conscientiously accept your offer. And oh, sir, let me beg that you will try to think kindly of me in the time to come."

"This, then, is your decision?"

"My unalterable decision, Sir Arthur."

He was very pale, but he forced a smile to his lips.

"I may admire your fidelity," he said suavely, "although —pardon me—I cannot admire your taste. I hope you will never regret your decision. But if a time should come when you will no longer have a protector and I should be in existence, come to me."

Those words were not warmly or tenderly spoken, but they went straight to Lotta's heart.

Swiftly, impulsively, she stooped and pressed her lips gratefully to the baronet's hand.

"You are very kind to me, grandfather," she responded with emotion, "and I shall never forget what you have said."

She had called him "grandfather" for the first time, and touched, in spite of himself, by that and her graceful action, he turned hastily and looked away, just as Lord Riversmede and Mr. D'Arcy emerged from the wood and came toward them.

"Here you are at last!" the former cried good-naturedly. "Edith's been making no end of a bother over your mysterious disappearance, Sir Arthur; she thinks that Miss von Rosenberg and you have been carried off by some of the toll-taking gentry—'road-agents,' I fancy they call them 'out West'—so we concluded to 'scout around' in search of you. Been having a pleasant time, Sir Arthur? Awfully jolly place this for a rest, Miss von Rosenberg."

"It is lovely!" Lotta returned simply. "This spot will always be sacred in my eyes."

Sir Arthur looked at her with a gentle smile, and she knew that he at least understood her meaning.

From the first Lord Riversmede had been struck by Lotta's resemblance to his wife, and had taken quite an interest in her in his easy, pleasant way. But when Sir Arthur, with a graceful motion of his white hand toward Lotta, said in a matter-of-course tone: "I presume, Riversmede, you were not aware that this young lady, Miss von Rosenberg, is my granddaughter?" he looked at the speaker for an instant very much as if he thought that that gentleman had taken leave of his senses. True, the haughty old man was not given to jesting, and a glance at Lotta's face dispelled his lordship's momentary doubts of the baronet's sanity.

"By Jove, this *is* a surprise!" he exclaimed heartily, as he shook hands with Lotta. "Awfully glad, don't you know. Saw the likeness just at once. Give you my word, you're an out-and-out Cardlyon, Miss von Rosenberg."

"You have my warmest congratulations, Miss von Rosenberg," Gerald D'Arcy said, extending his hand, a glow of pleasure suffusing his face.

He knew how dear she was to Connor, and from the first had secretly cherished the hope of one day calling her daughter.

They were all seated on the emerald grass at the foot of a great oak, with the sunlight filtering down through the leafy branches, quivering over the uncovered heads of the gentlemen and weaving pretty, fantastic patterns on the gowns of the ladies. There were the flash of crystal and silver, the snowy sheen of damask; the odor of violets, the gleam of the sunlit lake, the music of birds in the air, the buzz and whiz and whirr of insect life from the great dim woods beyond.

Sara, in gay gown and scarlet ribbons, moved about like some bright tropical bird, her mahogany face all aglow with delight, a flashing, gleaming point of light wherever she appeared.

Lady Riversmede had laid aside much of her frigid *hauteur*, and was smiling and talking to Connor on one side and Marmaduke Clifford on the other. Under the shadow of her wide-brimmed hat and drooping feathers, her face looked more soft and gentle; and a cluster of great yellow violets among the lace at her throat showed with a pretty effect against her dead blue gown—*l'eau de nil*.

Mrs. D'Arcy, Lotta, and Denise wore purple violets, and red columbines glowed warmly against a background of feathery-looking ferns at Kate's white throat. The gentlemen also wore flowers, even to Sir Arthur, who had graciously permitted Lotta to fasten an exquisite combination of fern-like mosses and great purple violets in his buttonhole.

Listening to the even flow of his graceful conversation, looking at his handsome, animated countenance, no one would imagine that scarce one little hour before he had received one of the keenest disappointments of his life.

There was the shadow of a great pain in Lotta's eyes, which Connor was quick to perceive, and he knew that whatever had been said in the course of that half-hour's *tête-à-tête* with her grandfather had brought it there.

The D'Arcys one and all were charming entertainers, a fact which their guests appeared to recognize and appreciate. All coldness and constraint had vanished, and the pleasant hum of voices, with now and then a ripple of laughter, told that they were a very happy, very unconventional party.

Then Lady Riversmede expressed a wish to visit the lake, and they strolled down to the water's edge.

"Lotta, Lotta, come here quick!" Denise cried; "I have got such a pretty white rabbit in this hole." She was kneeling on the grass, peering into a hollow in a tree trunk, too intent upon catching her prize to notice that Lotta and Teddy were some distance away.

"Let me assist you to secure your prisoner." Denise turned quickly at the sound of that voice, sprang to her feet, and the white rabbit scampered off. Marmaduke Clifford was standing beside her, his hands filled with pond-lilies.

"Please don't trouble to follow him, Mr. Clifford," she said hastily, as he turned to pursue the runaway.

He looked regretfully at the flushed, annoyed face, which was instantly averted.

"I am exceedingly sorry," he said very humbly.

"Oh, it does not matter; no doubt, poor thing, it will be much happier in the enjoyment of its freedom."

"Possibly! It will be sufficiently stupid for that."

"Or sufficiently wise?"

He laughed pleasantly.

"I will not contest the point; you know it is scarcely in good taste to contradict a lady. I have brought you these pond-lilies from the lake; I thought you would like them."

"They are very beautiful," she said, blushing and hesitating, her gray eyes kindling with pleasure.

She took them with a shy "Thank you," and was moving away when he said:

"To-morrow I shall leave the valley and the friends I prize, and turn my face once more to the pine hills of Virginia; but the memory of this hour will be engraven on my heart. I will see you always as I see you now, with those lilies in your hands."

Her eyes were lifted with a swift, startled glance to his face, and averted hastily, but she was silent.

They were standing near the lake, the red sun flooding the distant hills with a golden glory and touching with a farewell kiss the limpid bosom of the lake, the trees on its bank casting long shadows athwart its placid surface, while a balmy breath, fragrant and odorous, stole from the woods to where they stood.

"Will you not wish me God-speed on my journey?" he asked, looking down on the averted face. "It is hard to leave the Happy Valley."

"I wish you had stayed away!" she cried passionately. "Why did you come here?"

"You know why I came; it was because I loved you. Now I am going away because I still love you."

"I told you long ago it was no use. Could you not have stayed away and spared me all this pain?" she said, a quiver in the sweet voice.

"If my going away gives you pain, Denise, why will you not give me the right to be always near you?" he pleaded.

"Because I could not live and endure your scorn, and because I know you would despise me," she said, snatching away the hand he had taken.

He looked in utter surprise at the fair face flushing and paling, the pretty lips tremulous with repressed tears; at a loss to understand her, but more firmly than ever resolved to win her.

"You speak so strangely, Denise," he said gently, "that I fail to understand you. But believe me, my darling, no man ever yet despised a girl for loving him, and your love would be the greatest earthly boon that Heaven could——"

She flashed round upon him with laughing defiance sparkling through tears in her beautiful eyes.

"I should certainly feel consoled by *that* assurance, but as I have never yet said that I have loved or do love, have cared or do care the *least* bit for you, Mr. Clifford, why you should assume that I do I cannot comprehend; but if I did care for you in that way, why should I refuse the honor you are so desirous of bestowing upon me?"

He flushed hotly at the tone and question, but he looked down steadily into the defiant face, as he stood towering above her in his superior height.

It was, perhaps, only natural that Marmaduke Clifford, rich, handsome, cultured, should be just a trifle spoiled by the adulation and—it must be admitted—admiration to which he was so long accustomed. When he first made the startling discovery of his love for Denise, he had imagined, in his lordly way, that she could not *possibly* decline the honor of becoming *his* wife; but she did decline, and very decidedly, too.

Three hours later he quitted New York, disappointed, angry, mortified, with an aching sense of loss and loneliness at his heart, but determined never to see Denise D'Arcy again until he could prove to her that her rejection of his suit had not cost him a single regret.

He saw women—as he had often done before—many degrees more beautiful, women who had always a smile for him, who would gladly have shared his name and wealth; but somehow Denise's truthful eyes with their ever-changing expression were always haunting him, her sweet voice ever sounding in his ears, and after two years' absence he was convinced that to him she was the one woman in the world worth winning.

He was not a man to yield tamely; opposition only served to arouse within him the determination to conquer.

"Suppose I leave that question unanswered," he said, a smile creeping round his lips and eyes; "or answer it with another—if you do not care for me just a *little*, Denise, why should my going away give you pain?"

She flashed a glance of indignant scorn at him, her face aflame.

"I did not think that you would be so mean and contemptible as to use my words as a means of humiliating me. I thought you were too honorable for that, but I find that your code of honor is not a very exalted one after all."

She turned and walked away, leaving him with flashing eyes and a dusky flush on his olive face.

Chapter XXVII.

> "Let no one ask me how it came to pass;
> It seems that I am happy; that to me
> A livelier emerald twinkles in the grass,
> A purer sapphire melts into the sea."
>
> —Tennyson's *"Maud."*

FOR an instant Clifford watched the graceful, girlish figure vanish fleetly through the trees; then he sprang after her and laid his hand upon her arm just as she was about to emerge into the pretty open glade where, under the shadow of the giant oak, they had all sat and dined.

He would not let her go away angry with him; he knew if he did that she would avoid him during the remainder of his stay.

"One moment, Denise!" he cried, "only one! I cannot let you go until you have pardoned me."

She turned swiftly.

"How dare you follow and detain me like this, Mr. Clifford?" she demanded haughtily. "I thought a gentleman could understand when his presence was no longer desired."

He did not release her arm, but stood looking down at the flushed, annoyed face.

"You are indignant, I confess not without reason; but do you not think that you have punished me sufficiently by showing me how contemptible I am? Only say that you forgive me, and I will not detain you longer. Do not let me go away feeling that I have offended beyond pardon."

He looked so humble and penitent that she regretted her scornful words, but her pride rebelled against forgiving him.

"I will forgive you the use you made of my words, Mr. Clifford," she said coldly, "if you will please to release my arm—you are hurting me!"

He complied instantly, bowing very low.

"Pardon me! and please accept my thanks for showing me what a savage I am."

She looked at him half amused, half indignant, then burst into a peal of laughter.

"Yes, you really *are* a savage! Now are you satisfied, Mr. Clifford?"

"I suppose I should be, if I were not very exacting; but let us conclude that I am satisfied, while I beg you to listen to me for one instant."

"Oh, please let us go to the others. Don't let us begin talking about disagreeable things again!"

He regarded her with flashing eyes, his handsome eyebrows contracting into a frown.

"Do you wish me to understand that *I* am disagreeable to you?"

"Certainly not, Mr. Clifford; papa's friends are never disagreeable to me."

"Denise!" he cried passionately, "tell me that you wish me to go away, that my presence annoys you, and I shall leave you forever and never trouble you again, so help me Heaven!"

All the color died out of her face; she looked at him with troubled eyes.

"But I shall not tell you to go away; I do not desire that you should—though perhaps," a little wistfully, "it would be better so."

He bent forward, an eager light in his eyes.

"Denise! I warn you I am not a man to be trifled with, and I will not leave you until you give me a proper explanation; you owe me that at least. If there is another whom you prefer to me, you are cruel not to tell me so; but if you are free, why will you not let me try to win you?"

"Because," she replied, with an evident effort to speak calmly—"because I know how proud and sensitive you are. Do you think I can ever forget all you said that day, long ago, when we were crossing the river at Beechville, about the poor girl whom you heard sing on the streets of London? It convinced me then how merciless you could be in your judgments, and it convinces me now that if you were made acquainted with *one* act of *mine* in the past, your love for me would be changed into contempt."

She spoke bravely, but she was very pale; her eyes were clear and proud, but dark with emotion.

His face flushed, his eyes flashed open with something like horror as he retreated a step; but as he met her glance the flush disappeared; he stretched out both hands and moved swiftly to her side.

"Tell me what it is that you mean, Denise! I will not believe that you *could* do anything unworthy. I could trust you unreservedly with what is dearer to me than life—my honor!"

"Perhaps, when you know *all*," she answered quietly, not touching his outstretched hands, "you will think I have done something very unworthy; but since I have said so much I will tell you all, and your verdict shall decide between us. You will please to remember, Mr. Clifford, that you have *forced* this confidence from me, and you will strive to respect it, even should you be disappointed in your estimate of me."

"I give you my word of honor that any confidence

with which you may favor me will be most sacred to me; but first let me say, if the recital will give you pain, spare yourself, since I have all trust in your goodness and truth. Forget that you were going to tell me anything. I desire to know nothing of your past, convinced that you could never lend yourself to anything for which a modest girl should blush."

She raised her head with a haughty gesture, her clear eyes meeting his unflinchingly.

"I wish you to understand *distinctly*, Mr. Clifford," she said proudly, "that I am not ashamed of the act to which I allude; nay, should a like necessity again occur, I do not hesitate to affirm that I should most inevitably repeat it. I cannot accept your very generous confidence in my goodness; for I *know* that just as surely as I would take advantage of such unreserved trust, so surely, after a time, you would begin to doubt me, and end by imagining something very dreadful. I could not live under misapprehension; so if you care to listen I will tell you, and I am sure that when you hear what I have to say you will confess that I am right in saying it would be better for you to go away and think no more about me."

"You might just as well tell me to raise my voice and command the sun to stand still. In both cases the effect would be much the same—the sun, unheeding my presumptuous command, would go serenely on his course, and I would go on loving you and thinking of you. But if you prefer to make me acquainted with this incident in your past, I shall feel honored by your confidence; yet let me assure you that nothing which you can tell me could have power to change my love for you. To me you will ever be the best, the truest, the dearest girl on earth!"

"Ah!" she breathed sadly, "you would not feel like that toward me if you knew that *I*, Denise D'Arcy, am the girl you so cruelly condemned—the girl you heard sing before the Albany that bitter February afternoon."

For a moment her words seemed to take his breath away. His face went deathly pale, then flushed a dusky red. The next instant he came a step nearer to her, a great tenderness shining in his eyes.

"Tell me all, Denise," he said gently.

She did not look at him. She was pale and trembling now, the pride which had hitherto sustained her all gone. Leaning for support against the bole of a tree, she told her story simply, unaffectedly, in low but clear tones.

"I dare scarcely hope that you will pardon me," he said, very humbly, very contritely. "I spoke heartlessly, inconsiderately. My words must have sounded brutal in your ears, as they did in my own when Miss D'Arcy so eloquently defended the unknown singer and administered such a well-merited rebuke on my insolence. From my soul, Denise, I implore your forgiveness."

"It is granted, Mr. Clifford," she answered quietly. "And now, if you please, we will return to the others."

"Stop a moment!" he pleaded hastily. "You said that when you had told me all my verdict should decide between us. Am I not right?"

"You are right," she faltered.

"Denise," he said gravely, tenderly, "let me assure you that that heroic act of yours has raised you in my estimation a hundredfold. I loved you before with all my heart; you are now, my fair cantatrice, more precious in my eyes than rubies and diamonds—a pearl above price."

Mr. Clifford did not start on his homeward journey next morning. After breakfast he had a long interview with Mr. D'Arcy, who had the satisfaction of learning that the dearest wish of his heart was about to be realized: Denise had promised to become the wife of Marmaduke Clifford, and her father gladly, proudly gave his consent.

Every one was pleased, Connor more especially, and so it was settled.

In a few days their guests would take their departure; after which it was decided that Denise would accompany her father and step-mother to New York, where in three months the marriage was to take place.

Kate's fears and anxieties were set at rest when Denise told her of the explanation she had had with her *fiancé*.

Lotta was to be bridesmaid, and Mrs. Felix Rooney, who was then in Italy, in a little congratulatory note promised to be present on the happy occasion.

Judging from her letters, Eva was happy and had no thought beyond the gayety of the present moment.

Denise often wondered how she found time to write the long letters which she so unfailingly sent her—letters filled with glowing accounts of the brilliant scenes in which she mingled and of the places which she visited.

It was the third morning after the picnic. Lotta was in the poultry-yard surrounded by a feathered flock cackling and cooing as they darted hither and thither excitedly after the grain which she was scattering about for them. Oscar was standing gravely by her side, a basket of snowy eggs held firmly in his teeth.

"Ah, Oscar, bad dog! what are you doing?" she cried, in sudden alarm, as he dropped the basket at her feet with a precipitancy that threatened the utter ruin of its contents, and barked sharply, to the evident terror of the fowls.

"Now, Oscar, you shall not come here another morning if you behave so badly." But Oscar had disappeared with another sharp, joyful bark.

"If you please, ma'am, there's a gentleman wants to

see you," Dan said, appearing at this juncture in evident excitement.

"A gentleman!" Lotta repeated, in some surprise.

"Yes, ma'am; one of the gentlemen from Butternut Farm and Mr. Teddy."

She was startled, but instantly recovered herself.

"Just see if Oscar has smashed those eggs," she said quietly; "if not, take them in at once to Mrs. Morgan."

Then she passed into the shrubbery and came face to face with Sir Arthur Cardlyon and Teddy, who was being joyfully welcomed by Oscar.

"Sir Arthur!" she cried almost breathlessly.

There was no embarrassment, only pleased surprise in her face as she extended both hands.

"This is very kind of you, Sir Arthur. I did not expect this pleasure."

"My young friend here has driven me over. I thought I should like to see your home," he replied, taking her hands in his with a pleased smile.

She greeted Teddy cordially, then led the way into the house, and gave her long tan gloves and hat to Malinda, who came to meet her, before passing into the cool, shady dining-room.

With an air of easy dignity she drew a chair into one of the open windows for Sir Arthur, who watched her movements with a low, regretful sigh; she looked so cool and graceful in her white gown, with a cluster of fragrant carnations at her throat.

They talked pleasantly for some time, and Teddy, feeling that he was *de trop*, availed himself of the first break in the conversation to make a hasty apology and join Oscar out-of-doors.

"Carlotta," the baronet said quickly as Teddy disappeared, "I desire you to tell me truly if you are happy here. Do not through a mistaken sense of duty and gratitude ruin all your future life, but tell me unreservedly, can I assist you in any way?"

She looked at him through blinding tears.

"Dear grandfather!" she said gently, "I cannot find words in which to thank you for the interest you take in me. If anything could add to my happiness it is this, but I would indeed be most ungrateful to the best, the kindest of uncles if I were not happy. There is one favor that I would ask of you: it is that when you are far away, when you have returned to those who have so long enjoyed your affection, you will try sometimes to spare a kind thought for the granddaughter who will always remember you in her distant home."

She sank upon her knees beside him, and rested her head on the arm of his chair to hide the tears that *would* flow.

"You are a noble girl, Carlotta," he said, touching her hair with a tender, caressing hand, "and—yes, I will confess I regret deeply that I have lost such a treasure. But remember what I have already said to you: if you should regret this decision, or if anything should occur—you understand—while I live my home shall ever be open to you, ever await your coming."

She was too much overcome to speak; but she kissed his slender hand, and the tears which she could not restrain fell upon it. Through all the coming years of her life, Lotta would remember this morning.

They talked long and earnestly. At the end of an hour, to Lotta's surprise Sir Arthur asked to see her uncle. She knew that just then he was engaged with his foreman, but she sent for him, delighted to have been asked.

She watched the meeting of the two men, a smile of

pleasure curving her proud lips. The baronet had laid aside his *hauteur* for the time being; for Lotta's sake he had determined to be amiable to the man who had been so kind to her. But despite his pride and preconceived prejudices he was favorably impressed, and was soon conversing unrestrainedly with Mr. von Rosenberg, to whom in the course of conversation he spoke of the offer which he had made his granddaughter and her rejection of it.

For an instant a suspicious moisture gathered in Mr. von Rosenberg's clear blue eyes as they turned upon Lotta.

"My Lottchen is good and true," he said with emotion. "She knows the poor old uncle has no one else to care for him in all the world; while you, Sir Arthur, have many."

He saw that this haughty old man was deeply disappointed; that notwithstanding his suave, courteous manner, Lotta's refusal of his offer had pained him exceedingly, and he looked at her proudly, knowing all she had relinquished for his sake.

Chapter XXVIII.

"Life is only bright when it proceedeth
 Toward a truer, deeper life above;
 Human love is sweetest when it leadeth
 To a more divine and perfect love."
　　　　　　　　　　　—A. PROCTER.

"Every noble life leaves the fibres of it interwoven forever in the work of the world."—RUSKIN.

LOTTA'S visit to New York terminated a few weeks after Denise's marriage; she knew that her uncle would feel lonely during her absence, and she was right. He was overjoyed when she wrote telling him she longed to return, and he gladly hastened to New York to bring her home.

Denise and her husband had gone to their handsome Virginia home.

Mr. and Mrs. Felix Rooney had returned to Europe, intending to winter in Rome.

To the delight of every one, Teddy was becoming quite strong and had decided upon entering the Church.

At first Mr. D'Arcy had opposed that wish, but seeing that his opposition was likely to affect Teddy's health and spirits he at length gave his sanction, and Teddy was made happy.

Kate and Connor had returned to the valley, and their lives had fallen back into their former grooves; but Connor had lost all interest in his pursuits, and all through the winter months he fluctuated between the desire to sell the farm and return to Europe or to remain.

He had striven to overcome Lotta's resolution, but she could not be convinced that she was not in some way accountable for Bertie Haviland's untimely death.

"What right have I to be happy?" she would reply to Connor's entreaties. "But for me, poor Bertie Haviland would not now be numbered among the dead! It is the only manner in which I can atone. Do not urge me, Connor."

How empty the world seemed to Connor as he passed from her presence and from the house!

At a turn of the road he came face to face with Mr. von Rosenberg.

"*Ach!* this is a pleasure," the latter cried heartily. "Been to see *mein Lottchen?*"

The hopeless expression on Connor's face arrested the words on his lips, and he looked at him with a glance of blank surprise for an instant.

"What is it, my young friend?" he inquired anxiously. "You look troubled. You are unhappy. What has happened?"

"You are right, Mr. von Rosenberg. I *am* unhappy," Connor responded honestly. "You know how I love Lotta. I have sought and obtained your permission to win her; but while admitting her love for me, she is deaf to all my pleadings. I cannot remain here. I am restless and miserable and shall sell out and leave the States."

"*Ach, nein,* that must not be, my young friend. I shall speak to my Lottchen. She shall not spoil her own life and yours because of a foolish feeling over Bertie Haviland's death."

While they were still talking Father Burke joined them, and Mr. von Rosenberg at once explained.

"You see," he burst out, "my Lottchen with her scruples on the matter of young Haviland's death is going to make herself and everybody else miserable."

"She is morbid on that subject," the good priest responded. "I have frequently striven to remove her scruples—scruples which would never have entered the mind of one less sensitive and refined. I believe her nerves have never recovered their healthy tone since the shock of the tragedy; but I promise to do all I can, as her spiritual director, to help you."

Lotta stood by the parlor window, gazing thoughtfully out and seeing nothing but the universal whiteness of the garden and the snow-covered landscape beyond, now bathed in the level sunshine of the afternoon.

While she stood thus,

> "Telling her memories over
> As you tell your beads,"

the jingle of sleigh-bells sounded on the clear, crisp air.

Speeding along the road came a sleigh, at sight of which a lovely blush overspread her face.

She had recognized Red Prince, Connor's favorite horse, and the muffled figure ensconced in the sleigh.

She watched until it passed through the open gateway and swept up to the door.

Then she went to meet Connor with quickened pulses, wondering at his coming.

He had thrown aside his mufflings and turned quickly at the sound of her light step.

"It is good of you to come!" she said, giving him her hand. "Is Squire Haviland better?"

"Yes, the squire is out of danger and will soon be able to return home."

"Ah, thank Heaven! that is good news!" she said, leading the way into the warm parlor and pushing forward a rocking-chair beside the glowing fire for her visitor. "Uncle has gone with the foreman to see Jacob Potter; the poor old man is laid up with a severe attack of rheumatism. How pleased uncle will be to hear that the squire is out of danger!"

Connor did not take the chair which she had placed for him, but stood looking down upon her.

She paused confused and turned aside.

"I have had another letter from grandfather," she said hastily, "such a kind letter. He wishes me to go to England next summer and spend a few months at Ludleigh Hall."

"And you will go?" he asked very quietly.

"Oh, no, I could not leave uncle; but it is very kind of Sir Arthur, you know, Connor."

"Lotta," he said, following her to the window, "there is something I want to say to you, a proposal I desire to make. I have come to you to-day—it is for the last time, remember—that you may decide my future. Listen to me patiently, Lotta dearest, and do not say you cannot do that. I have your uncle's sanction to speak to you, and it rests with you alone whether I remain here permanently or sell out and leave America forever."

"Oh, Connor!" she pleaded, with pale lips and startled eyes, "do not say that! What would Miss D'Arcy do if you should go away?"

"You think more of her happiness than of mine," he said bitterly. "But Duke and Denise are both most desirous that she should reside with them; and there is my father's home ever open to receive her, if she should prefer residing with him and Mrs. D'Arcy. I came here to speak to you on what most intimately concerns ourselves: why will you sacrifice the happiness of our lives to this foolish sentiment? If a man becomes a murderer, *you* are in no way responsible for that man's crime. We might just as reasonably take the crimes of all the world upon our shoulders, and go about doing penance for the rest of our lives. Heaven made you instrumental in bringing this young man into the fold of the Church; but that is no reason why you should offer yourself up as a sacrifice for the sin of another. You say you love me, Lotta; promise to become my wife, and I vow to build a church to Bertie Haviland's memory."

She stood gazing out on the white snow with a piteous look in the clear eyes, never once glancing at the dark, handsome face so eagerly bent toward her.

He saw the clasping and unclasping of the slender, white hands, the vain efforts she made to speak; and he waited patiently. At length she turned and laid her hand upon his arm.

"I cannot tell you, Connor, how grateful I am to you," she said gently, "but although Father Burke has striven to show me that I was not to blame—and, Heaven knows, I never gave either poor Bertie or his murderer encouragement—yet I cannot divest myself of the feeling that through me he lost his life. If I have been the cause of pain to you, Connor, forgive me, for though you are more to me than all the world I cannot do what you ask me, and I cannot leave my poor uncle; it would break his heart."

"I will never ask you to leave him, Lotta. Do not send me away with this answer if you really care for me."

"I cannot give you any other, Connor, indeed I cannot!"

"And thus ends the one dream of my life!" he said bitterly.

. . . . . .

The storms and snows of winter were past.

Connor and Kate were still at the valley, but there was a rumor that Butternut Farm was again for sale, and Lotta, dreading to hear the rumor confirmed, never alluded to it in Kate's presence.

The season had been very late, but now the work of nature and of man was being pushed forward with energy. It was scarcely a time at which to expect visitors, and Lotta was both surprised and pleased when, in the first week of June, she saw Squire Haviland approaching the house.

He had scarcely taken a seat when her uncle entered, and a meaning glance passed between the two men as they exchanged greetings.

Since the loss of his son the squire had aged visibly. He had become thin and bent, his pleasant, rugged face was deeply lined, and his bluff good-nature had given place to a subdued earnestness. Lotta watched him with a feeling of pain as he talked to her uncle.

After a time the conversation turned on Butternut Farm.

"I don't like to think of it passing into other hands," the squire said, and at the words Lotta suddenly paused in the act of pouring out a cup of tea, the light fading from her face.

"He's done a heap of good every way you take it," pursued the squire. "He's a credit to the county, and I'll be main sorry when he goes away. I'll never forget that I owe my life to Connor D'Arcy—not that the same life's worth much now, but then, you see, he came near losing his own life that day last February when he went down into the gully and fetched me out of the snowdrift. It was a dreadful day that. If I had taken the wife's advice I wouldn't have gone out that day; after my spell of illness it wasn't the thing to do, but the snow didn't commence till I was some distance from the house. It didn't promise to be much at first, and I thought I would get all right to Carter's before there was any danger. All of a sudden the snow came down so thick and blinding that everything became black before me. I turned my horse to go home again, but I must have got confused and lost my way. I remember the horse standing still. I tried to coax him on; he went a little way; then all at once he stumbled and threw me. I heard the muffled sound of a human voice shouting to me; I tried to shout back but could not. Then I felt myself falling down, down, down, rolling over in the soft snow, which gave way as I strove to clutch it. I knew no more until I woke up at Butternut Farm and saw that bright, pretty creature, Miss D'Arcy, sitting beside my bed, and everything looking so warm and cheerful around me.

"Since we lost our poor boy life is no longer of value to me; but I am not ungrateful, and I know that I owe young D'Arcy a debt I can never repay. If I had been their own father they could not have been more tender and kind to me; they nursed me back to life. I think I was more sorry than glad when I was well enough to go home and didn't need to stay at the valley any longer.

"When Miss D'Arcy would leave me for an hour Connor would come and sit beside me, and we used to talk about everything. I saw he was in trouble, and I kind of guessed what was wrong; and as I'm a plain man, my dear," turning to Lotta and taking her hand in his, "I put the question plainly to him and he honestly told me his trouble. You remember, my dear, that I promised poor Bertie you should be to me as my own daughter; that promise has brought me here to-day. It's good of you to think so much of my poor boy. It isn't every girl that would refuse young D'Arcy; he's a fine, handsome young fellow. Though I couldn't give him Bertie's place in my heart, I have come to like him better than I ever thought to like any man again. It's a pleasure to hear his voice, to see his fine, manly figure, to look in his honest, straightforward eyes. If he's a bit proud, you feel he is true to the core; that's the true grit for a man; every man has a right to value himself at just what he knows he's worth, and I reckon young D'Arcy's very properly proud of himself.

"Now, my dear, I want you to be happy. There is no use spoiling your life and his; it won't bring our Bertie back, and if all the preachers tell us is true, he's where he'll know all about your goodness now, and he'll be pleased to know that you'll be happy. I have a right to a say in this matter, and I'll never know peace till I see you young D'Arcy's wife. What do you say, friend von Rosenberg?"

The squire leaned back as he concluded, still holding Lotta's hand.

"I say you are right, squire. A few short years at most, and I will be called away and *mein Herzliebchen* be left all alone! She has refused wealth and splendor to stay with her old uncle, and I will not repay her by making her life miserable when I am gone. I shall die happier for the knowledge that I am leaving her the wife of a good man. Nay, thou must not speak, *mein Kind*, for *I* say, unless thy heart says against it, thou shalt in another month become the *verlobte*—betrothed—of Connor D'Arcy, with my blessing."

"But, uncle, I feel that I should not; indeed, indeed, I do not want to leave you, and surely you cannot desire to send me away!" she said with a faint smile.

"*Ach! gut*, no more, *mein Herz*. While I live we shall not be separated; but it must be as I say. Think it well over to-night; to-morrow I will go to see the young man."

"Your hand upon that, friend!" the squire cried, extending his hand, and Mr. von Rosenberg heartily responded.

"Now, my dear, that that is settled, I will take my cup of tea," the squire said, kindly patting Lotta's hand before releasing it.

As she turned to the table, Father Burke drove up to the door in his buggy.

"Good-evening, and God's blessing be here," the good priest said in his bright, cheery way. "I see I am just in time for a cup of my favorite beverage. Glad to see you able to go about again, squire. Don't disturb yourself, Miss von Rosenberg—I'll just take this chair."

He shook hands cordially with every one and took a chair near the squire, with whom he had become somewhat friendly of late.

The conversation turned on various topics of interest, and it was not until Lotta left the room to fetch some newspapers which she had just received from England that Father Burke was made acquainted with what had preceded his coming.

The prospect of Connor D'Arcy leaving the valley had for some time been a source of infinite regret to Father Burke, and his feelings of relief and satisfaction were intense when he learned that in all probability he would remain.

He was heartily glad; his influence had done much, and he felt that in some measure he had been instrumental in vanquishing Lotta's scruples.

When, an hour later, in company with Squire Haviland, he drove away from Fall Farm, the good priest was highly elated.

Chapter XXIX.

"Death ends all tales, but this he endeth not;
 They grew not gray within the valley fair
Of hollow Lacedæmon, but were brought
 To Rhadamanthus of the golden hair.

"Beyond the wide world's end; ah, never there
 Comes storm nor snow; all grief is left behind,
And men immortal, in enchanted air,
 Breathe the cool current of the Western Wind."
—LANG'S "*Helen of Troy.*"

MRS. FELIX ROONEY had returned from Europe to find herself at once acknowledged as society's queen. Her pathway was strewn with the roses of life; her beauty and wealth, her grace and "chic," her brilliant entertainments took the *élite* of New York by storm.

Her horses were the finest English thoroughbreds, her dress and jewels were pronounced perfect by the most severe critics; she was the admired of all, the envied of many.

Old Barney Rooney had fulfilled his part of the contract; and within thirty miles of the Empire City a noble residence was being erected.

The Old World as well as the New contributed its share of skilled labor to the erection of this lordly pile.

English and Italian decorators were specially engaged to beautify Mrs. Felix Rooney's suite of apartments.

Old Barney was proud of his daughter-in-law, and well content to live in the reflected glory of this brilliant planet which had suddenly burst upon the fashionable horizon. She was Felix's wife. She had the world at her feet. She was a D'Arcy, and far outshone Gerald D'Arcy's young wife: what more could his heart desire?

Ah, yes, there was something more, something which he longed for—something which all Barney's wealth could not purchase. There was a little Gerald D'Arcy at the D'Arcy mansion, but there was no little Rooney to hand down that *illigant* patronymic to posterity.

If he had not returned to the States a *gentleman*, Felix Rooney's travels in Europe had taken the sharp edge off his vulgarity and lessened his conceit.

His clothes, boots, and gloves were ultra fine, and the fashionable swagger which he had acquired gave *ton* to his drawl.

In his wife's presence there was about Felix Rooney an air of conscious inferiority which was painfully apparent to all.

And it is just possible that Mrs. Felix had succeeded in impressing her husband with a due sense of his unworthiness and of her great condescension in becoming his wife.

He followed her about like a spaniel, and rendered her a silent but none the less profound worship; for Mrs. Felix objected to any display of affection, merely tolerating his presence as a necessary adjunct to the matrimonial contract. She was willing to spend his wealth, to wear his jewels, to grace his home, to give him a social status; but there her recognized duties ended.

Felix Rooney was not a man to inspire love in the heart of a refined and cultured woman; but under ordinary circumstances he might have made a good-enough husband for any sensible young woman in the rank of life from which he sprang.

To do her justice, Eva had never deceived him.

She had told him in her straightforward way that she did not love him and never should; and that if she became his wife it would only be on certain conditions. Heartless she decidedly was, but not untruthful, and if he was disappointed in the result he had nobody but himself to blame.

Eva at least seemed to thoroughly enjoy every hour of her life, and drank deeply at the fountain of pleasure.

Seeing her thus fêted and worshipped, witnessing her social triumphs, Gerald D'Arcy never doubted but that Eva was happy in the choice she had made, and after a time came to regard her marriage as, on the whole, highly satisfactory. The preparations for her summer campaign were all completed, and Mrs. Felix was on the point of taking her departure for Newport, when she received a letter from Kate announcing Connor and Lotta's betrothal and the date fixed for their marriage.

The perusal of that letter changed all her plans.

She countermanded her orders for Newport, telegraphed to her Parisian *modiste* an order for a suitable dress to wear at her brother's wedding, and arranged to start West the following week with her father and Mrs. D'Arcy.

When all her arrangements had been made she intimated her intention of visiting her aunt and brother to her astonished husband, who, never having presumed to question her royal will, meekly responded that he would be ready to accompany her.

They were met at the country way-station by Connor and Marmaduke Clifford.

Mrs. Felix Rooney greeted both young men rapturously.

"It is so good to have two big brothers!" she cried, with her pretty rippling laugh. "Why, Connor, dear, you are handsomer than ever! Lotta should be a proud girl."

Connor flushed hotly.

"If Lotta had been a proud girl," he said, with an accent of displeasure, "she would have preferred returning to England and taking her proper place in society as the granddaughter of Sir Arthur Cardlyon to becoming *my* wife."

"Well, of course, that goes without saying; and if she had, she would have been presented at court and in all probability have married a lord. But it is just possible that his lordship would not be as handsome or as clever as our unpretending Connor D'Arcy."

Every one laughed but Connor.

"Don't be silly, Eva!" he said, a trifle impatiently, as they drove away from the station.

"Is Lottchen very much altered?" she asked presently. "I thought she made just the loveliest kind of bridesmaid at Denise's wedding."

"She could never be other than lovely and perfect," he rejoined briefly.

He could not even yet forgive her her mercenary marriage. That she, the daughter of a millionaire, with her youth and her beauty, should have voluntarily elected to become the wife of Felix Rooney had filled him with unspeakable amazement and disgust.

And while Eva expatiated on the picturesque beauty of the road, he made his team speed swiftly along under the mild suggestion of the whip.

"Oh, papa, what a quite too lovely place Connor has here!" Mrs. Felix cried ecstatically as the two-seated "democrat" wagon drew up in front of the house in the valley. "I had no idea it was one-half so—oh, here are Aunt Kate and Denise!"

"Allow me, my dear," Mr. Rooney said, coming eagerly to her assistance.

But she thrust his hand aside with a mocking little laugh, and springing lightly to the ground flung herself into Kate's extended arms.

"Oh, you dear, darling auntie!" showering warm kisses on Kate's glowing face. "How good it is to be with you again! and Denise—dear, precious Denise! It's just like old times when you used to pet and care for me and—and——" To the astonishment of all present, Mrs. Felix Rooney dropped her face on her sister's shoulder and burst into a passion of tears.

"Oh, my dearest!" her husband gasped in dismay, watching her helplessly.

For the space of a minute no one spoke.

Then Mrs. Felix raised her head, great tears shining like crystal drops on the long, curling lashes.

"Such an exhibition!" she said with a nervous laugh. "Oh, please pardon me! It was quite too absurd; but I couldn't help it, really, you know."

"My dear," Mrs. D'Arcy said in her soft tones, "why apologize to those who love you for an emotion at once beautiful and natural?"

She had long doubted the wisdom of her step-daughter's choice; and this little scene—this involuntary display of feeling—convinced her that the young wife had discovered, when too late, her fatal mistake.

Was she right? Who can tell?

"But it was so babyish," Eva protested with a pretty pout as she followed Denise.

"You must take me to see Lottchen after I have rested, Connor," she said, pausing at the top of the stairs. "I hope you have not forgotten to send an invitation to Mr. Brand? We must gather the clans, you know."

She laughed gayly, and passing on entered her room.

"You are a very lucky girl, Denise," she said, turning to her sister. "I think Duke is just splendid!"

"He is the noblest man on earth!" Denise declared warmly, with eloquent eyes.

"Oh, of course he is, my dear. It's always that way, isn't it? Every woman gets 'the noblest man on earth!'" She yawned and sank languidly onto a couch as she spoke. "I wish you would send my maid, Delphine, to me."

"I will bring you a cup of tea first, dear," Denise said, kissing her sister tenderly and hurrying from the room. Like her step-mother, Mrs. Clifford was convinced that Eva had made shipwreck of her life, and her heart ached for her beautiful young sister.

"I want you to take me over to Fall Farm to-day, Connor," Mrs. Felix Rooney said the following morning at breakfast. "I am positively dying to see darling Lottchen."

"I will drive you over after dinner," he answered, smiling into the beautiful face, and wondering if he had not been mistaken the previous evening in thinking this radiant creature was unhappy.

"Let me have that pleasure, Mrs. Rooney," said Marmaduke Clifford, "if you prefer going over at once, since Connor is so busy. I have made so many pilgrimages to Fall Farm with Denise that I am quite familiar with the road."

"Thanks, ever so much; but Connor would be going over in any case, you know, so I shall just wait for him."

The afternoon was glorious and the drive to Fall Farm

delightful. Eva was in the highest spirits—so bright, so vivacious, chatting and laughing with all the childish *abandon* of the days that were before she became Mrs. Felix Rooney, and Connor listened, marvelling at her pretty, quaint fancies.

Lotta saw them in the distance and came into the porch to meet them.

"*Ach! mein bestes Lottchen!*" Eva cried, flinging her arms around Lotta and kissing her warmly.

"I have come to tell you how pleased I am, and to stay with you to-day. It will be like old times, you know. But what is the matter, *mein Herz?* There are tears in your eyes and on your face. A bride should not weep, Lottchen."

"Ah, but they are happy tears, dear," Lotta answered, returning Mrs. Rooney's kiss and giving Connor her hand in welcome. "This," she said, taking a letter from the table as they entered the parlor, "has been the cause of my tears. It is from grandfather; and see, Connor, he inclosed this draft for a thousand pounds, to purchase my *trousseau!* Read the letter, Connor, it is so kind—so kind!"

Connor obediently complied, a pleased flush suffusing his face as he read.

"He is just the very nicest kind of a grandfather," commented Mrs. Felix approvingly, some three hours later.

Connor had gone with Mr. von Rosenberg to look at a new threshing-machine, and the two girls were left alone.

"That sum should buy you a handsome *trousseau*, Lottchen," pursued Mrs. Felix. "You must write at once to Madame Adolphe, Rue de la Paix, Paris, and inclose a photo of yourself with your order. She will know just what to send you. She has the most exquisite taste. Her creations are the most *recherché*, the—why do you laugh?" indignantly.

"Don't be vexed, dear," Lotta cried, still laughing. "But do you imagine I would send to Paris for a *trousseau?* What should I do with Madame Adolphe's exquisite creations out here? I am not going to marry a millionaire, but a farmer, and shall be very pleased with a *trousseau* that will not cost me one-fifth of a thousand pounds."

"You are quite too absurd, Lottchen!" Mrs. Felix retorted scornfully. "You will want to look nice on your bridal tour. You will be going to Europe, I presume? You cannot remain here always, wasting your grace and beauty upon this desert air. Sir Arthur Cardlyon's granddaughter must go into society."

"I shall be in the very best society—my husband's!" rejoined Lotta, with a lovely blush.

Mrs. Felix laughed a sweet, mocking laugh.

"What nonsense!" with a contemptuous shrug of her graceful shoulders. "I think you are going to be quite as ridiculous over your husband as Mrs. D'Arcy is over baby Gerald. It is such a bore. He might be the one baby in all the world, she is so particular about everything that concerns him."

Lotta raised her head with a haughty gesture, her beautiful hazel eyes flashing. At that instant she looked in very truth the young patrician—dainty, high-bred, a true Cardlyon in every feature of the proud, beautiful face.

"I consider it a grievous mistake," she said, in her sweet, refined tones, "when one is not rich to plunge into gayety at the very outset of one's married life. And *à propos* of Mrs. D'Arcy, she has a right to be proud of her baby; it is the *one* baby in all the world to *her*, you know, Mrs. Rooney."

"Oh, don't call me by that *horrid* name, Lottchen; I hate the very sound of it!"

"But no woman should hate the sound of her husband's name! What's in a name? Would not a rose by any other name smell quite as sweet?"

"A rose! Ah, yes, dear, when one is lucky enough to get a rose, but——"

A low, nervous "Hem!" broke in upon her words, and with an apologetic "Mrs. Rooney, my dear," Mr. Felix Rooney advanced into the room.

"You said you would return to the valley at five o'clock, so I came for you," he announced. "It is close upon five now, and if you are ready——" looking at his watch uneasily, for the cool, questioning glance of his wife's eyes was very disconcerting.

"I am sure," she said sweetly, "the exercise will do you good. You can return at *once*, and please say to Miss D'Arcy that I shall remain with Miss von Rosenberg to-night."

He stood twirling his hat between his faultlessly gloved hands, looking so humble and crestfallen that Lotta, feeling deeply pained on his account, glanced at Eva appealingly. But that lady, having turned her back upon her husband, seemed oblivious of his presence.

With sudden desperation he advanced a step.

"My dear Mrs. Rooney!" he ventured to expostulate. "Miss D'Arcy will be very much astonished by this change in your intentions; you know, you——"

Mrs. Felix turned upon him with a gesture of haughty surprise. "Did I not say you might *go?*" she inquired, with raised eyebrows. "Why do you still remain? Miss D'Arcy will not be astonished at anything *I* may do or say. If I should think of returning to-morrow—which is problematic—Mr. von Rosenberg will drive me over in the evening."

"Oh, don't trouble Mr. von Rosenberg. I shall come for you, my dear!" he said hastily.

"I should not like you to be disappointed, as you certainly would be should you come for me to-morrow, as it is just possible I shall remain where I am indefinitely, if Miss von Rosenberg will have me."

"There can be no 'ifs' on that point, Eva, between you and me," Lotta rejoined quickly, a faint rose-blush mantling her lovely face. "I shall always be pleased to have you; there is plenty of room, and should——"

"You are *so* good, Lottchen," Eva interrupted quickly, knowing quite well what Lotta was about to say, and determined that she should not utter the invitation which her husband was eagerly expecting, "so that settles it. Of course I shall remain. I think there is nothing more to say, Mr. Rooney," turning to her husband, "and I need not detain you. *Au revoir*."

His look of blank disappointment was good to see. He was silent an instant, glancing furtively at Lotta.

"You will require a change of dress," he said suddenly. "I will send Delphine with a trunk."

She uttered a low, musical laugh.

"If you like," she responded with a careless shrug of her shoulders and turned away.

That evening one of Connor's men assisted Delphine and a well-filled trunk into the wagonette and drove both to Fall Farm.

"You can ask some of the men to carry that trunk into one of the outhouses, Delphine," her mistress said serenely when her waiting-woman and trunk arrived. "I shall not want either it or you while I am here."

Connor was angry at Eva's treatment of her husband, and spoke to his aunt that evening on the subject.

"Why did she marry the man if she must publicly show her contempt of him?" he said hotly. "Father told me he used every argument at his command to dissuade her from this marriage, but she overruled all his objections and assured him over and over again that she could only be happy with Felix Rooney. Now she treats him with absolute rudeness."

"Eva is very much changed," Kate answered, in pained tones. "Poor child, she was dazzled by the thought of his great wealth, and in her ignorance made the most fatal mistake of her life—a mistake which, I fear, she is already beginning to discover. You must drive me over to Fall Farm to-morrow, and I shall speak to her."

But Kate's speaking to Mrs. Rooney had not the desired effect.

"You are the very dearest auntie in the world," she said gayly; "but your rhetoric and sympathy are entirely thrown away. If I did not occasionally snub the man and keep him in his place, he would become intolerable. His ideas are the ideas of Plutocracy and Plebeia, and he is apt to mistake underbred familiarity for well-bred *bonhomie*. Oh, I assure you, dear, I have never changed in my treatment of Mr. Felix Rooney since the first hour I became his wife. So please let us dismiss the man from our thoughts and return to Lottchen."

There was a look of disappointment on Kate's eloquent face which Lotta could not fail to see, but Mrs. Felix talked gayly while she sipped her tea.

"I presume, Lottchen," she remarked, putting down her cup and strolling to the window, "you have decided to accept Sir Arthur's invitation? It is only right that Connor and you should pay him a visit. You cannot possibly intend to shut yourselves up in the valley for the natural term of your lives, in that Darby and Joan fashion."

"I have not decided upon anything; Connor must do that. But while my uncle is spared to me I will remain near him. I promised the dear father that I should be as a good daughter to him, and I shall not break that promise."

"I think you are quite too absurd, Lottchen, effacing yourself in that way, and running the chance of displeasing Sir Arthur after all his kindness, and Lord and Lady Riversmede sending you those beautiful gifts," Mrs. Felix remarked, beginning to drum on the window-pane with her dainty fingers and hum a soft Italian air.

"They are very beautiful," Kate said, glancing admiringly at the open cases on a table beside them.

"This diamond bracelet, the earl's gift, I prefer to all her ladyship has sent me, because of the few kind words which accompanied it."

At that moment Mrs. Felix uttered an excited little shriek.

"I declare I think it is—yes, positively, it *is* Mr. Brand!" she cried, and, with all her old impulsiveness, rushed from the room.

Kate blushed vividly and bent her head over the bracelet. A minute later Mrs. Felix returned, leading in Frank Brand triumphantly, closely followed by Mr. von Rosenberg and Connor.

Frank shook hands warmly with Lotta and heartily congratulated her. Then he glanced toward Kate, and crossing to her side shook hands with her.

After that there was a good deal of pleasant talk and more tea-drinking.

"I declare," Kate said with a laugh as she glanced

out of the window, "Dan has put the horses to the wagonette and is bringing it to the gate."

"He thinks it is time you were going," said Mr. von Rosenberg, with a roar of laughter. "But that is our good Connor's fault. He told Dan to put the horses to in half an hour; now he seems to have forgotten. That is his way."

There was a general laugh at Connor's expense.

"I am going too, auntie," Mrs. Felix announced as Kate, having made her adieux, walked to the door.

Kate nodded and strolled down the path.

"I have a letter here from Father Donnatti which I should like you to see," said a voice she well knew.

She paused with a vivid blush.

"It is very short," he continued. "Will you read it now?"

With a sudden new shyness Kate took the letter which Frank Brand held toward her.

Her heart was beating wildly and her hand trembled as she drew the inclosure from its envelope.

He stood by her side watching her eagerly while she read it to the end.

"Is this *really* true?" she asked, looking up, tears standing in her blue eyes, her pretty face radiant with a great joy.

"Yes," he answered. "I fought against conviction and Father Donnatti until I was forced to cry *peccavi*. As I think you have read in the good Father's letter, he received me into the Church a fortnight since. Are you pleased?"

"Thank God! and God bless Father Donnatti," she responded fervently.

"Amen to that," he said with deep reverence. "And now, Kate, since Heaven has condescended to enlighten my darkened soul, I have come to ask you the question which you once promised to answer me. Will you be my wife, dearest?"

"Yes," she said with a happy blush, tears of joy standing in her eyes as she gave him her hand.

He raised it to his lips and kissed it tenderly.

"Happy at last!" he said as Connor and Eva issued from the house.

THE END.

www.ingramcontent.com/pod-product-compliance
Lightning Source LLC
Chambersburg PA
CBHW032044230426
43672CB00009B/1470